Conceptual Foundations of Language Science

No scientific work proceeds without conceptual foundations. In language science, our concepts about language determine our assumptions, direct our attention, and guide our hypotheses and our reasoning. Only with clarity about conceptual foundations can we pose coherent research questions, design critical experiments, and collect crucial data. This series publishes short and accessible books that explore well-defined topics in the conceptual foundations of language science. The series provides a venue for conceptual arguments and explorations that do not require the traditional book-length treatment, yet that demand more space than a typical journal article allows.

In this series:

1. Enfield, N. J. Natural causes of language.

2. Müller, Stefan. A lexicalist account of argument structure: Template-based phrasal LFG approaches and a lexical HPSG alternative

3. Schmidtke-Bode, Karsten, Natalia Levshina, Susanne Maria Michaelis & Ilja A. Seržant (eds.). Explanation in typology: Diachronic sources, functional motivations and the nature of the evidence

ISSN: 2363-877X

Explanation in typology

Diachronic sources, functional motivations and the nature of the evidence

Edited by

Karsten Schmidtke-Bode

Natalia Levshina

Susanne Maria Michaelis

Ilja A. Seržant

language
science
press

Schmidtke-Bode, Karsten, Natalia Levshina, Susanne Maria Michaelis & Ilja A. Seržant (eds.). 2019. *Explanation in typology: Diachronic sources, functional motivations and the nature of the evidence* (Conceptual Foundations of Language Science 3). Berlin: Language Science Press.

ISBN: 978-3-96110-147-4 (Digital)
        978-3-96110-148-1 (Hardcover)

ISSN: 2363-877X
DOI:10.5281/zenodo.2583788
Source code available from www.github.com/langsci/220
Collaborative reading: paperhive.org/documents/remote?type=langsci&id=220

Cover and concept of design: Ulrike Harbort
Typesetting: Karsten Schmidtke-Bode, Sebastian Nordhoff
Proofreading: Aleksandrs Berdičevskis, Alexandr Rosen, Alexis Pierrard, Amir Ghorbanpour, Andreea Calude, Barend Beekhuizen, Benjamin Saade, Eran Asoulin, Gereon Kaiping, Ivica Jeđud, Janina Rado, Jeroen van de Weijer, Lachlan Mackenzie, Luigi Talamo, Mykel Brinkerhoff, Richard Griscom, Stefan Hartmann, Steve Pepper, Susanne Vejdemo, Ulrike Demske, Vadim Kimmelman, Yvonne Treis
Fonts: Linux Libertine, Libertinus Math, Arimo, DejaVu Sans Mono, UMing
Typesetting software: XƎLATEX

Language Science Press
Unter den Linden 6
10099 Berlin, Germany
langsci-press.org

Storage and cataloguing done by FU Berlin

Freie Universität Berlin

Contents

Contents

Introduction

Karsten Schmidtke-Bode

Leipzig University and Friedrich Schiller University Jena

The present volume addresses a foundational issue in linguistic typology and language science more generally. It concerns the kinds of explanation that typologists provide for the cross-linguistic generalizations they uncover, i.e. for so-called universals of language. The universals at issue here are usually probabilistic statements about the distribution of specific structures, such as the classic Greenbergian generalizations about word order and morphological markedness patterns. Some examples are given in (1)–(4) below:

(1) With overwhelmingly greater than chance frequency, languages with normal SOV order are postpositional. (Greenberg 1963: 62)

(2) A language never has more gender categories in nonsingular numbers than in the singular. (Greenberg 1963: 75)

(3) If a language uses an overt inflection for the singular, then it also uses an overt inflection for the plural. (Croft 2003: 89, based on Greenberg 1966: 28)

(4) In their historical evolution, languages are more likely to maintain and develop non-ergative case-marking systems (treating S and A alike) than ergative case-marking systems (splitting S and A). (Bickel et al. 2015: 5)

As can be seen from these examples, cross-linguistic generalizations of this kind may be formulated in terms of preferred types in synchronic samples or in terms of higher transitional probabilities for these types in diachronic change (see also Greenberg 1978; Maslova 2000; Cysouw 2011; Bickel 2013 for discussion of the latter approach). But this is, strictly speaking, independent of the question we are primarily concerned with here, namely how to best account for such generalizations once they have been established.

Karsten Schmidtke-Bode. 2019. Introduction. In Karsten Schmidtke-Bode, Natalia Levshina, Susanne Maria Michaelis & Ilja A. Seržant (eds.), *Explanation in typology: Diachronic sources, functional motivations and the nature of the evidence*, iii–xii. Berlin: Language Science Press. DOI:10.5281/zenodo.2583802

The most widespread typological approach to explanation is grounded in functional properties of the preferred structural types: For example, typical correlations in the ordering of different types of phrases (e.g. object–verb and NP–postposition) have been argued to allow efficient online processing (e.g. Hawkins 1994; 2004). Markedness patterns in morphology (e.g. the distribution of zero expression in case, number or person systems) have been attributed to economy, i.e. the desire to leave the most frequent and hence most predictable constellations unexpressed, or rather to a competition between economy and the motivation to code all semantic distinctions explicitly (e.g. Haiman 1983; Comrie 1989; Aissen 2003; Croft 2003; Haspelmath 2008, among many others). The general idea behind this approach is thus that speech communities around the world are subject to the same kinds of cognitive and communicative pressures, and that the languages they speak tend to develop structures that respond to these pressures accordingly, or, as Bickel (2014: 118) puts it, "in such a way as to fit into the natural and social eco-system of speakers: that they are easy to process, that they map easily to patterns in nonlinguistic cognition, and that they match the social and communicative needs of speakers."

There is a clear parallel to evolutionary biology here, in that languages are said to *converge* on similar structural solutions under the same functional pressures, just like unrelated species tend to develop similar morphological shapes in order to be optimally adapted to the specific environment they co-inhabit (Deacon 1997; Caldwell 2008; Evans & Levinson 2009; Givón 2010). When applied to language, this line of explanation at least implicitly invokes what is known as "attractor states", i.e. patterns of structural organization that languages are drawn into in their course of development.[1] For this reason, one could also speak of a RESULT-ORIENTED approach to explanation.

There is, however, another way of looking at the same patterns, one that redirects attention from the functional properties to the diachronic origins of the linguistic structures in question. On this view, many universal tendencies of order and coding are seen as by-products, as it were, of recurrent processes of morphosyntactic change, notably grammaticalization, but without being adaptive in the above sense: There is no principled convergence on similar structural traits because these traits might be beneficial from the perspective of processing, iconicity or economical communicative behaviour. Instead, the current

---

[1]The term attractor state (or basin of attraction) is adopted from the theory of complex dynamic systems (e.g. Cooper 1999; Howe & Lewis 2005; Holland 2006), which has become increasingly popular as a way of viewing linguistic systems as well (see Beckner et al. 2009 and Port 2009 for general overviews, and Haig 2018 or Nichols 2018 for very recent applications to typological data).

synchronic distributions are argued to be long-term reflections of individual diachronic trajectories, in particular the diachronic sources from which the structures in question originate. Givón (1984) and Aristar (1991), for example, suggested that certain word-order correlations may simply be a consequence of a given ordering pair (e.g. Gen–N & Rel–N, or V–O & Aux–V) being directly related diachronically: Auxiliaries normally grammaticalize from main verbs that take other verbs as complements, and since these complements follow the verb in VO languages, they also follow the auxiliary in the resulting Aux–V construction; the mirror-image pattern holds for OV languages (see also Lehmann 1986: 12–13). If this line of reasoning extends to most other word-order pairs, there is no need to motivate the synchronic correlations in functional-adaptive terms, e.g. by saying that the correlations arise *in order to* facilitate efficient sentence processing.

In the domain of morphology, Garrett (1990) argued that patterns in case marking, specifically of differential ergative marking, are exhaustively explained by the properties of the source of the ergative marker: When ergative case arises from the reanalysis of instrumental case, the original characteristics of the latter, such as a restriction to inanimate referents, are directly bequeathed to the former. The result is a pattern in which animate A-arguments are left unmarked, but since this is a direct "persistence effect" (Hopper 1991) of the history of the ergative marker, there is again no need for an additional functional-adaptive explanation in terms of other principles, such as a drive for economical coding patterns. Rather than being result-oriented, then, this way of explaining universals can be characterized as SOURCE-ORIENTED.

Such source-oriented explanations thus move away from attractor states of grammatical organization and often emphasize the importance of "attractor trajectories" instead (Bybee & Beckner 2015: 185): In some domains of grammar, the patterns of reanalysis and ensuing grammaticalization are so strikingly similar across the world's languages that it is not surprising that they yield similar outcomes, such as strong correlations between V–O & Aux–V or V–O & P–NP ordering. In other cases, it is argued that many individual, and partly very different, diachronies are capable of producing a uniform result, but without any consistent functional force driving these trajectories. Cristofaro (2017), for instance, claims that this is the case for plural markers: An initial system without number marking can develop an overt plural morpheme from many different sources – usually by contextual reanalysis – and thus ultimately come to contrast a zero singular with an overt plural, but these developments are neither triggered nor further orchestrated by a need for economical coding: They do not happen to keep the (generally more frequent) singular unmarked and the (generally less frequent) plural overtly signalled.

In other words, whether the individual diachronic trajectories are highly similar or rather diverse, the premise of the source-oriented approach is that they can scale up to produce a predominant structural pattern in synchronic samples. Hence they obviate the need for highly general functional principles tying these patterns together.

While the source-oriented approach was still a more marginal position in previous volumes on explaining language universals (e.g. Hawkins 1988a; Good 2008), it has gained considerable ground over the last decade, notably in a series of articles by Cristofaro (e.g. Cristofaro 2012; 2014; 2017) but also in other publications (e.g. Anderson 2016; Creissels 2008; Gildea & Zúñiga 2016). Moreover, while the basic thrust of the two explanatory approaches is straightforward, clarification is needed on a number of – equally fundamental – details. After all, both approaches are functionalist in nature, as they rely on domain-general mechanisms (Bybee 2010) to explain the emergence of language structure and linguistic universals; and in both approaches, these mechanisms constrain how languages "evolve into the variation states to which implicational and distributional universals refer" (Hawkins 1988b: 18). But as Plank (2007: 51) notes, "what is supposed to be the essence and force of diachronic constraints would merit livelier discussion." It is the goal of the present book to offer precisely a discussion of this kind.

The volume begins with a programmatic paper by **Martin Haspelmath** on what it means to explain a universal in diachronic terms. He aims to clarify how diachrony is involved in result-oriented and source-oriented accounts, respectively, and thus lays out a general conceptual framework for the explanation of universals. At the same time, Haspelmath opens the floor for debating the strengths and weaknesses of the two explanatory accounts at issue here. His own position is that, in many cases, current source-oriented explanations are ill-equipped to truly explain the phenomena they intend to account for, and hence cannot replace result-oriented motivations. Haspelmath's arguments for this position, as well as his terminological proposals, provide a frame of reference to which all other contributions respond in one way or another.

The lead article is followed by two endorsements of source-oriented explanations, articulated by **Sonia Cristofaro** and **Jeremy Collins**, respectively. They both describe the approach in widely accessible terms, allowing also readers outside of linguistic typology to appreciate the general argument as well as the specific examples discussed. The phenomena themselves involve domains that are particularly well-known for being explained in functional-adaptive terms, namely differential argument marking, number marking and word-order correlations, and these are all argued to be best captured by persistence effects from their respective diachronic origins.

We then proceed to papers that allow for progressively more room for functional-adaptive motivations and, importantly, for methodological discussions on how to obtain evidence for such pressures. Accordingly, all of these papers adduce novel empirical data and discuss them in light of the present debate.

Matthew Dryer's paper is an immediate follow-up on Collins's discussion of word-order correlations. On the one hand, Dryer argues that the various correlates of adposition–noun ordering (e.g. O–V and NP–P, and Gen–N and NP–P) are, indeed, best accounted for in source-oriented terms. In particular, only this approach proves capable of explaining the occurrence (and the individual semantic types) of both prepositions and postpositions in SVO languages. On the other hand, however, Dryer contends that there are some significant correlations for which a source-based account either fails to offer an explanation or else makes the opposite prediction of the patterns we find synchronically. Dryer concludes, therefore, that neither a purely source-based nor a purely result-based explanation is sufficient to deal with word-order correlations.

In a similar fashion to Dryer's paper, **Holger Diessel**'s article demonstrates that different aspects of the same grammatical domain – in this case adverbial clause combinations – are amenable to different types of explanation. Diessel focuses specifically on the structure and development of preposed adverbial clauses and argues that some of their typological characteristics, notably the properties of their subordinating morphemes, receive a satisfactory explanation in terms of the respective source construction(s), thereby supplanting earlier processing-based explanations. On the other hand, he proposes that the position of adverbial constructions (in general) is clearly subject to a number of functional-adaptive pressures, and that these may already have affected the diachronic sources from which the current preposed adverbial clauses have grammaticalized.

Karsten Schmidtke-Bode offers a review of John Hawkins's (2004; 2014) research programme of "processing typology", examining the plausibility of Hawkins's functional-adaptive ideas in diachronic perspective. On a theoretical level, it is argued that a predilection for efficient information processing is operative mostly at the diffusion stage of language change, regardless of the source from which the respective constructions originate. On a methodological level, the paper proposes that the cross-linguistic predictions of Hawkins's programme can be tested more rigorously than hitherto by combining static and dynamic statistical models of large typological data sets; this is demonstrated in a case study on the distribution of article morphemes in VO- and OV-languages, respectively.

An important methodological point is also made by **Ilja A. Seržant**, who claims that certain functional-adaptive pressures may not actually surface in standard typological analysis because they are weak forces, clearly at work but also easily overridden by other, language-specific factors. Because of their weak nature, they may not be directly visible anymore in a synchronic type, but they can be detected in qualitative data from transition phases. Based on diachronic data from Russian, Seržant shows how the development of differential object marking was crucially influenced by considerations of ambiguity avoidance (and hence a classic functional-adaptive motivation), over and above the constraints inherited from the source construction. In the absence of such longitudinal data, transition phases can be identified on the basis of synchronic variability, and Seržant shows that a wide variety of languages currently exhibit variation in differential object marking that mirrors the diachronic findings from Russian, and that is not predictable from the source meaning of the marker in question.

Susanne Maria Michaelis adds another source of data to the debate at hand. She argues that creole languages provide a unique window onto the relationship between synchronic grammatical patterns and their diachronic trajectories, as the latter are often relatively recent and also accelerated when compared to normal rates of grammatical change. The developments are, consequently, more directly accessible and less opaque than in many other cases. By inspecting creole data on possessive forms in attributive and referential function (e.g. *your* versus *yours*), Michaelis finds evidence for the development of the same kinds of coding asymmetries that this domain shows in non-contact languages around the world. She proposes that the data are indicative of result-oriented forces that drive diverse diachronic pathways towards the same synchronic outcome. This stance contrasts most explicitly with Cristofaro's, who interprets such situations in exactly the opposite way (i.e. as providing evidence *against* a unifying functional explanation).

Natalia Levshina, finally, adopts an entirely different methodological approach to illuminate the present discussion: In her paper, she showcases the paradigm of artificial language learning, which can be employed to inspect whether users of such newly acquired languages develop performance biases that are in keeping with hypothesized functional principles, such as an increasingly efficient distribution of morphological marking. Her case study clearly demonstrates such biases and discusses where they may ultimately come from, i.e. how they fit into the new conceptual framework of constraints offered by Haspelmath's position paper.

The volume is rounded off by a brief **epilogue** in which **Karsten Schmidtke-Bode** and **Eitan Grossman** summarize and further contextualize the arguments put forward by the contributors.

Overall, the purpose of the present book is to provide a state-of-the-art overview of the general tension between source- and result-oriented explanations in linguistic typology, and specifically of the kinds of arguments and data sources that are (or can be) brought to bear on the issue. It should be made clear from the outset that the two types of explanation are framed as antagonistic here even though in most cases, an element of both will be needed in order to fully account for a given grammatical domain. As we emphasize in the epilogue, the diachronic source of a grammatical construction certainly constrains its further development, but the major issue at stake here is the extent to which result-oriented, functional-adaptive motivations enter these developments as well. At the end of the day, universals of language structure will thus differ in the *degree* to which they are shaped by such adaptive pressures.

Acknowledgements

The present volume originated in the context of the project *Form-frequency correspondences in grammar* at Leipzig University. The support of the European Research Council (ERC Advanced Grant 670985, Grammatical Universals) is gratefully acknowledged. An oral precursor to this volume was a workshop on the topic at the 49th Annual Conference of the Societas Linguistica Europaea in Naples in 2016, co-organized by the editors of this book. We would like to thank the participants and the audience of that workshop for insightful contributions and discussion. We would also like to thank Eitan Grossman and Mark Dingemanse for extensive feedback on all papers in the present volume. Finally, we are grateful to Jingting Ye for assistance in bibliographical research, to Sebastian Nordhoff and his team at Language Science Press as well as to the participants of Language Science Press's community proofreading.

References

Aissen, Judith. 2003. Differential object marking: Iconicity vs. economy. *Natural Language and Linguistic Theory* 21(3). 435–483. DOI:10.1023/A:1024109008573

Anderson, Stephen R. 2016. Synchronic versus diachronic explanation and the nature of the Language Faculty. *Annual Review of Linguistics* 2(1). 11–31. DOI:10.1146/annurev-linguistics-011415-040735

Aristar, Anthony R. 1991. On diachronic sources and synchronic pattern: An investigation into the origin of linguistic universals. *Language* 67(1). 1–33.

Beckner, Clay, Richard Blythe, Joan L. Bybee, Morten H. Christiansen, William Croft, Nick C. Ellis, John Holland, Jinyun Ke, Diane Larsen-Freeman & Tom Schoenemann. 2009. Language is a complex adaptive system: Position paper. *Language Learning* 59(s1). 1–26. DOI:10.1111/j.1467-9922.2009.00533.x

Bickel, Balthasar. 2013. Distributional biases in language families. In Balthasar Bickel, Lenore A. Genoble, David A. Peterson & Alan Timberlake (eds.), *Language typology and historical contingency*, 415–444. Amsterdam, Philadelphia: John Benjamins. DOI:10.5167/uzh-86870

Bickel, Balthasar. 2014. Linguistic diversity and universals. In Nick J. Enfield, Paul Kockelman & Jack Sidnell (eds.), *The Cambridge handbook of linguistic anthropology*, 101–124. Cambridge: Cambridge University Press. DOI:10.5167/uzh-98910

Bickel, Balthasar, Alena Witzlack-Makarevich, Kamal K. Choudhary, Matthias Schlesewsky & Ina Bornkessel-Schlesewsky. 2015. The neurophysiology of language processing shapes the evolution of grammar: Evidence from case marking. *PLoS ONE* 10(8). e0132819. DOI:10.1371/journal.pone.0132819

Bybee, Joan L. 2010. *Language, usage and cognition.* Cambridge: Cambridge University Press. DOI:10.1017/CBO9780511750526.011

Bybee, Joan L. & Clay Beckner. 2015. Emergence at the cross-linguistic level: Attractor dynamics in language change. In Brian MacWhinney & William O'Grady (eds.), *The handbook of language emergence*, 183–200. Oxford: Blackwell. DOI:10.1002/9781118346136.ch8

Caldwell, Christine A. 2008. Convergent cultural evolution may explain linguistic universals. *Behavioral and Brain Sciences* 31(5). 515–516. DOI:10.1017/S0140525X08005050

Comrie, Bernard. 1989. *Language universals and linguistic typology: Syntax and morphology.* 2nd edn. Chicago: University of Chicago Press.

Cooper, David L. 1999. *Linguistic attractors: The cognitive dynamics of language acquisition and change.* Amsterdam, Philadelphia: John Benjamins. DOI:10.1075/hcp.2

Creissels, Denis. 2008. Direct and indirect explanations of typological regularities: The case of alignment variations. *Folia Linguistica* 42(1). 1–38. DOI:10.1515/FLIN.2008.1

Cristofaro, Sonia. 2012. Cognitive explanations, distributional evidence, and diachrony. *Studies in Language* 36(3). 645–670. DOI:10.1075/sl.36.3.07cri

Cristofaro, Sonia. 2014. Competing motivation models and diachrony: What evidence for what motivations? In Brian MacWhinney, Andrej L. Malchukov & Edith A. Moravcsik (eds.), *Competing motivations in grammar and us-*

age, 282–298. Oxford: Oxford University Press. DOI:10.1093/acprof:oso/9780198709848.001.0001

Cristofaro, Sonia. 2017. Implicational universals and dependencies. In Nick J. En-field (ed.), *Dependencies in language: On the causal ontology of linguistic systems*, 9–22. Berlin: Language Science Press. DOI:10.5281/zenodo.573777

Croft, William. 2003. *Typology and universals*. 2nd edn. Cambridge: Cambridge University Press. DOI:10.1017/CBO9780511840579

Cysouw, Michael. 2011. Understanding transition probabilities. *Linguistic Typology* 15(2). 415–431. DOI:10.1515/lity.2011.028

Deacon, Terrence. 1997. *The symbolic species: The co-evolution of language and the brain*. New York: W. W. Norton & Company. DOI:10.1136/bmj.319.7211.715

Evans, Nicholas & Stephen C. Levinson. 2009. The myth of language universals: Language diversity and its importance for cognitive science. *Behavioral and Brain Sciences* 32(5). 429–448. DOI:10.1017/S0140525X0999094X

Garrett, Andrew. 1990. The origin of NP split ergativity. *Language* 66(2). 261–296. DOI:10.2307/414887

Gildea, Spike & Fernando Zúñiga. 2016. Referential hierarchies: A new look at some historical and typological patterns. *Linguistics* 54(3). 483–529. DOI:10.1515/ling-2016-0007

Givón, Talmy. 1984. *Syntax: A functional-typological introduction. Vol. I*. Amsterdam, Philadelphia: John Benjamins. DOI:10.1075/z.17

Givón, Talmy. 2010. The adaptive approach to grammar. In Bernd Heine & Heiko Narrog (eds.), *The Oxford handbook of linguistic analysis*, 27–49. Oxford: Oxford University Press. DOI:10.1093/oxfordhb/9780199544004.013.0002

Good, Jeff (ed.). 2008. *Linguistic universals and language change*. Oxford: Oxford University Press. DOI:10.1093/acprof:oso/9780199298495.001.0001

Greenberg, Joseph H. 1963. Some universals of grammar with particular reference to the order of meaningful elements. In Joseph H. Greenberg (ed.), *Universals of language*, 58–90. Cambridge, MA: MIT Press.

Greenberg, Joseph H. 1966. *Language universals, with special reference to feature hierarchies*. The Hague: Mouton. DOI:10.1515/9783110899771

Greenberg, Joseph H. 1978. Diachrony, synchrony and language universals. In Joseph H. Greenberg, Charles A. Ferguson & Edith A. Moravcsik (eds.), *Universals of human language I: Method and theory*, 61–92. Stanford: Stanford University Press.

Haig, Geoffrey. 2018. The grammaticalization of object pronouns: Why differential object indexing is an attractor state. *Linguistics* 56(4). 781–818. DOI:10.1515/ling-2018-0011

Haiman, John. 1983. Iconic and economic motivation. *Language* 59(4). 781–819. DOI:10.2307/413373

Haspelmath, Martin. 2008. Creating economical morphosyntactic patterns in language change. In Jeff Good (ed.), *Language universals and language change*, 185–214. Oxford: Oxford University Press. DOI:10.1093/acprof:oso/9780199298495.003.0008

Hawkins, John A. (ed.). 1988a. *Explaining language universals.* Oxford: Blackwell.

Hawkins, John A. 1988b. Explaining language universals. In John A. Hawkins (ed.), *Explaining language universals*, 3–28. Oxford: Blackwell.

Hawkins, John A. 1994. *A performance theory of order and constituency.* Cambridge: Cambridge University Press. DOI:10.1017/CBO9780511554285

Hawkins, John A. 2004. *Efficiency and complexity in grammars.* Oxford: Oxford University Press. DOI:10.1093/acprof:oso/9780199252695.001.0001

Hawkins, John A. 2014. *Cross-linguistic variation and efficiency.* Oxford: Oxford University Press. DOI:10.1093/acprof:oso/9780199664993.001.0001

Holland, John H. 2006. Studying complex adaptive systems. *Journal of Systemic Science and Complexity* 19. 1–8. DOI:10.1007/s11424-006-0001-z

Hopper, Paul J. 1991. On some principles of grammaticization. In Elizabeth C. Traugott & Bernd Heine (eds.), *Approaches to grammaticalization. Vol. I: Focus on theoretical and methodological issues*, 17–35. Amsterdam, Philadelphia: John Benjamins. DOI:10.1075/tsl.19.1.04hop

Howe, Mark L. & Marc D. Lewis. 2005. The importance of dynamic systems approaches for understanding development. *Developmental Review* 25(3). 247–251. DOI:10.1016/j.dr.2005.09.002

Lehmann, Christian. 1986. Grammaticalization and linguistic typology. *General Linguistics* 3. 3–22.

Maslova, Elena. 2000. A dynamic approach to the verification of distributional universals. *Linguistic Typology* 4(3). 307–333. DOI:10.1515/lity.2000.4.3.307

Nichols, Johanna. 2018. Non-linguistic conditions for causativization as a linguistic attractor. *Frontiers in Psychology* 8. 2356. DOI:10.3389/fpsyg.2017.02356

Plank, Frans. 2007. Extent and limits of linguistic diversity as the remit of typology – but through constraints on what is diversity limited? *Linguistic Typology* 11(1). 43–68. DOI:10.1515/LINGTY.2007.005

Port, Robert. 2009. Dynamics of language. In Robert A. Meyers (ed.), *Encyclopedia of complexity and systems science*, 2310–2323. New York: Springer. DOI:10.1007/978-0-387-30440-3_143

Chapter 1

Can cross-linguistic regularities be explained by constraints on change?

Martin Haspelmath

MPI-SHH Jena & Leipzig University

This paper addresses a recent trend in the study of language variation and universals, namely to attribute cross-linguistic patterns to diachrony, rather than to other causal factors. This is an interesting suggestion, and I try to make the basic concepts clearer, by distinguishing clearly between language-particular regularities, universal tendencies, and mere recurrent patterns, as well as three kinds of causal factors (preferences, constraints, restrictions). I make four claims: (i) Explanations may involve diachrony in different ways; (ii) for causal explanations of universal tendencies, one needs to invoke mutational constraints (change constraints); (iii) in addition to mutational constraints, we need functional-adaptive constraints as well, as is clear from cases of multi-convergence; and (iv) successful functional-adaptive explanations do not depend on understanding the precise pathways of change.

1 Language universals: Constraints on cross-linguistic distributions as explananda

Since Greenberg (1963), it has been widely recognized that comparison of languages with world-wide scope can give us not only taxonomies (as in earlier typology, e.g. von Schlegel 1808; Schleicher 1850: 5–10; Sapir 1921), but intriguing limits on cross-linguistic distributions: Especially when one looks at several parameters simultaneously, not all logically possible types are attested, or some types are far more common and others far less common than would be expected by chance. We would like to know why – or in other words, we are looking for causal explanations.

Martin Haspelmath. 2019. Can cross-linguistic regularities be explained by constraints on change? In Karsten Schmidtke-Bode, Natalia Levshina, Susanne Maria Michaelis & Ilja A. Seržant (eds.), *Explanation in typology: Diachronic sources, functional motivations and the nature of the evidence*, 1–23. Berlin: Language Science Press. DOI:10.5281/zenodo.2583804

Martin Haspelmath

Since at least Chomsky (1981), many generative grammarians have also been interested in cross-linguistic regularities, and have often interpreted them as following from innate principles of Universal Grammar (UG) and their parametric variation. Others have tended to prefer functional explanations of universals (e.g. Comrie 1989; Stassen 1985; Dixon 1994; Dik 1997; Hawkins 2014), but these authors have likewise appealed primarily to general principles of language and sometimes have even adopted the term "universal grammar" (Keenan & Comrie 1977; Foley & Van Valin 1984; Stassen 1985).

In contrast to these two dominant approaches of the 1970s–1990s, there is an alternative view, according to which the explanation for universals of language structure comes from diachrony. The first well-known author in this tradition is Greenberg (1969), who stated that "[s]ynchronic regularities are merely the consequence of [diachronic] forces" (1969: 186). A straightforward example of the explanatory role of diachrony is the generalization that in languages with prepositions, the possessor generally follows the possessed nonpossessive construction, while in languages with postpositions, it generally precedes it (Greenberg's (1963) Universal 2; Dryer 1992). This can be explained on the basis of the diachronic regularity that new adpositions generally arise from possessed nouns in processes of grammaticalization (Lehmann 2015[1982]: §3.4.1; Bybee 1988: 353–354; Collins 2019; Dryer 2019 [both in this volume]). For example, English *because (of)* comes from *by + cause (of)*. Since the order of the elements remains stable in grammaticalization, we have an explanation for the fact that the possessed noun and the adposition tend to occur in the same position in languages.

The view that the explanation of language universals comes (at least sometimes) from diachrony has apparently been gaining ground over the last decade and a half. The early papers by Greenberg (1969; 1978) and Bybee (1988) represented minority views (though Givón 1979 and Lehmann 2015[1982] discussed diachronic change extensively and contributed to giving it a prominent place in functional-typological linguistics). Prominent papers in this vein in more recent years are Aristar (1991), Anderson (2005; 2008; 2016), Cristofaro (2012; 2013; 2014), Creissels (2008), Gildea & Zúñiga (2016), and in phonology, Blevins (2004) is a book-length study that adopts a similar approach (see also Blevins 2006). The following are a few key quotations from some of these papers (and from some others):

(1)   a.   "The question for typology is perhaps not what kinds of system are possible, but what kinds of change are possible." (Timberlake 2003: 195)

b. "recurrent synchronic sound patterns are a direct reflection of their diachronic origins, and, more specifically, ... regular phonetically based sound change is the common source of recurrent sound patterns" (Blevins 2006: 119–120)

c. "statistical universals are not really synchronic in nature, but are rather the result of underlying diachronic mechanisms that cause languages to change in preferred or 'natural' ways" (Bickel et al. 2015: 29)

d. "there are no (or at least very few) substantive universals of language, and the regularities arise from common paths of diachronic change having their basis in factors outside of the defining properties of the set of cognitively accessible grammars" (Anderson 2016: 11)

This paper has two major goals: First, I would like to contribute to conceptual clarification, sorting out what kinds of claims have been made and what terms have been used for which kinds of phenomena (§2).

Second, I argue that there are two ways in which diachrony and universals may interact: Some cross-linguistic generalizations are due to change constraints, as envisaged by the authors in (1), but others are due to functional-adaptive constraints. More specifically, I want to make four points:

- The notion of "diachronic explanation" is too vague, because explanations may involve diachrony in rather different ways (§3).

- Universal tendencies cannot be explained by common pathways of change, only by change constraints, or what I call mutational constraints (§4).

- Multi-convergence clearly shows that functional-adaptive constraints are needed in order to explain at least some cross-linguistic regularities (§5).

- Functional-adaptive explanations do not depend on understanding the pathways of change, though knowing about the pathways illuminates the explanations (§6).

Before arguing for these four points, I will discuss some technical terms in the next section, because there is often confusion between terms for language-particular regularities (§2.1), cross-linguistic regularities (§2.2), and causal factors (§2.3).

2 Regularities and causal factors: Concepts and technical terms

General terms such as *restriction, constraint, preference, tendency, bias*, and *motivation* have been used in diverse and sometimes confusing ways by linguists. This section clarifies how these terms are used in the present paper, noting along the way what other meanings some of them have been given and what other terms have been used for (roughly) the same concepts. I distinguish between terms for regularities and terms for causal factors, and within the terms for regularities, I distinguish between language-particular and cross-linguistic regularities.

2.1 Language-particular regularities

Regularities within a particular language can concern language use or the conventional language system. Regularities of language use are increasingly studied by corpus linguistics, and they are often thought to be at the root of system regularities, especially in what is often called a "usage-based" view (Bybee 2010). However, regularities of use and system regularities are conceptually different, and linguists normally distinguish clearly between *parole* (language use) and *langue* (language system). In what follows, I focus on the systems of linguistic conventions.

For regularities within language systems, linguists normally use the general terms *rule* and *construction* (or *schema*). In addition, descriptive linguists use many other well-established class (or category) terms like *clause, noun phrase, suffix, dative case*, or terms for relations between constructions such as *alternation* or *derivation*. All of these relate to systems of particular languages.

The term *constraint* is sometimes applied to language-particular regularities, e.g. in constraint-based formalisms such as HPSG, and optimality theory also uses constraints for language-particular regularities. However, I will use this term exclusively for causal factors, as explained in §2.3 below.

Language-particular regularities can also be seen as "explanations", at least in the weak sense that they answer why-questions about lower-level regularities ("Why is there a Dative case on the object of this sentence? Because the verb's valency requires a Dative."). Statements of rules or constructions may thus be called "descriptive explanations" if one wishes. In this paper, however, I focus on causal explanations that help us explain the conventional systems of languages themselves.

2.2 Cross-linguistic regularities: Recurrent patterns and universal tendencies

Cross-linguistic regularities are typically generalizations over language-partic-ular regularities,[1] and I will distinguish two kinds of regularities here. On the one hand, similar phenomena may be found in different parts of the world, e.g. ejective consonants, or high vowel epenthesis, or optative mood forms, or func-tive markers (Creissels 2014). These are called RECURRENT PATTERNS. On the other hand, some regularities are so strong that we call them UNIVERSALS, because they occur with much greater than chance frequency. I also often use the term UNI-VERSAL TENDENCIES, because there is no claim that there are no exceptions.[2]

Recurrent patterns are not accidental similarities, in the sense that there must be something in the human condition that makes it possible for very similar linguistic categories to appear independently in languages that have no historical connection. However, the discovery of a recurrent pattern does not imply a claim about further languages.

By contrast, the discovery of a universal implies a claim about all other lan-guages: If a universal holds (i.e. is found with much greater than chance fre-quency in a reasonably representative sample), it is claimed that it also holds in any other representative sample. Thus, claims of universal tendencies can be tested by examining data from the world's languages, while claims of recurrent patterns can only be strengthened by additional further observations, but neither confirmed nor disproven by additional data.

Universal tendencies need to be distinguished, in particular, from family-spe-cific or region-specific trends, so they need to be based on a world-wide sample. A well-known example is the finding that in all major world regions, languages with OV order tend to have postpositions, and languages with VO order tend to have prepositions (Greenberg 1963: Universal 2; Dryer 1992: 83), even though many languages are exceptions. Another universal tendency is the limitation of nominal suppletion to the most frequent nouns (Vafaeian 2013), even though many languages do not have nominal suppletion at all. We may even identify universal tendencies within patterns that are quite rare, e.g. universals of infixa-tion (Yu 2007), because universal tendencies can be implicational ("If a language has infixation, then...").

---

[1] However, comparative corpus linguistics studies comparable corpora of language use, so there is no necessary connection between cross-linguistic comparison and the study of systems (as opposed to use).

[2] Another term for a cross-linguistic distribution is Bickel's (2013) family bias, which means 'preponderance within a family'. Note that this use of *bias* is quite different from the more common use as in *cognitive bias* (e.g. Tversky & Kahneman 1974); a term like *family tendency* would probably be more transparent.

Recurrent patterns, by contrast, are not associated with any kind of global claim, so they could be called *frequent patterns*, or *sporadic patterns*, depending on one's subjective assessment of their frequency. They are no doubt important for a complete account of human language, but they will be left aside in what follows, as it is not clear what causal factors might illuminate them.

2.3 Causal factors: Preferences, constraints, restrictions

In addition to documenting language-particular systems and cross-linguistic distributions, we also want to know what might explain the distributions in causal terms. The explanatory devices are called *causal factors*, or *(system-external) motivations*, or *constraints*. Especially the latter term is short and relatively clear, so I will use it as the default term for a causal factor. (Two other terms that are used commonly as well, especially outside core linguistics, are *force* and *pressure*. It seems that all these terms are basically synonymous.)

If a constraint is very strong, it can also be called *restriction*, and if it is weaker, it can be called *preference*.[3] This seems to be in line with much current usage in linguistics. There is thus no objective difference between restrictions, constraints and preferences, and we could use one of the three terms for all types of constraints. (This situation is similar to the cases of sporadic and frequent patterns, which are subjective sub-cases of recurrent patterns.)

Depending on the way in which they affect cross-linguistic distributions, here I distinguish four types of constraints (or restrictions, or preferences), which can be briefly characterized as in (2).

(2) a. *functional-adaptive constraints*: what facilitates communication (including processing) for speakers and hearers

　　 b. *representational constraints*: what is innately preferred or necessary in the cognitive representation of language

　　 c. *mutational constraints*: what is preferred or necessary in language change (= change constraints)

　　 d. *acquisitional constraints*: what is preferred or necessary in acquisition by children

---

[3] Another term for system-external causal factors is *bias*, which is used in particular by psychologists for cognitive preferences. Typical biases seem to be quite weak, so that even detecting them is an important part of research. By contrast, linguists' constraints are often very strong, and controversy concerns primarily the nature (functional-adaptive, representational, mutational) and the interaction of the constraints.

FUNCTIONAL-ADAPTIVE CONSTRAINTS are the kinds of factors that have been invoked by functionalists to explain cross-linguistic distributions (e.g. Tomlin 1986; Malchukov 2008; Hawkins 2014; among many others). For example, phonological inventories favour five-vowel systems because these make the best use of the acoustic space (De Boer 2001), and case systems favour overt ergatives for low-prominence nominals and overt accusatives for high-prominence nominals because of the association between roles and prominence status (Dixon 1994). These constraints are called *functional-adaptive* rather than merely *functional* to emphasize their role in explaining systems, not usage (the functioning of language). Functional linguists often focus on understanding the functioning of language in usage, but here my interest is in explaining how systems come to have properties that facilitate communication.[4] Good (2008) uses the term "external explanation" in roughly this sense (cf. also Newmeyer 1998: §3.4), but all four types of constraints are external in that they are not part of the system. ("System-internal explanation" is just another word for general regularities of language-particular systems, cf. §2.1 above; I do not think that the notion of causality is relevant for such statements, so all causal explanatory factors are external.)

REPRESENTATIONAL CONSTRAINTS are the kinds of factors that have been invoked by generativists to explain grammatical universals, as noted in §1. In the Principles and Parameters framework (Chomsky 1981), they were called the principles of Universal Grammar. For example, the principles of X-bar theory or binding theory have been regarded as representational constraints, as well as universal features and hierarchies of functional categories such as determiner (e.g. Cinque 1999). The general idea is that "the unattested patterns do not arise as they cannot be generated in a manner consistent with Universal Grammar" (Smith et al. 2018). Representational constraints are usually regarded as very strong, i.e. as restrictions (and thus Universal Grammar is said to be *restrictive*; cf. also Haspelmath 2014).[5] However, there is no intrinsic reason why representational constraints could not be weaker preferences, e.g. why there could not be a weak innate preference to put elements into a "determiner" category (though this possibility is almost never considered by linguists). In Good's (2008) survey, representational constraints are treated under the label of "structural explana-

---

[4] Another term for functional-adaptive constraint is "naturalness parameter" (Dressler et al. 1987), and functional-adaptive changes have been called "natural changes".

[5] Cognitive linguists have also sometimes invoked representational constraints to explain universals, though these are not referred to as UG. An example might be the idea in Croft (1991) that all event types are modeled on the basic force-dynamic agent-patient event type. This is not very strong, i.e. it is a preference, but apparently a preference having to do with cognitive representations, not with communicative or processing preferences.

tions", but this term (like "system-internal explanations") is better reserved for general statements of regularities of language-particular systems.

MUTATIONAL CONSTRAINTS (or change constraints) are constraints on possible diachronic transitions or possible diachronic sources, which can have an effect on synchronic distributions. For example, if nasal vowels only ever arise from VN sequences, this explains that all languages with nasal vowels also have nasal consonants, and that nasal vowels are rarer than oral vowels in the lexicon (Greenberg 1978). Likewise, if infixes only ever arise by metathesis from adfixes (= prefixes or suffixes), this explains that they only occur in peripheral position (Plank 2007: 51). And if adpositions only arise from nouns in possessor-noun constructions, this explains that their position correlates with the position of possessed nounspossessive construction, as noted in §1. The notion of mutational constraints is not new (Plank 2007: §2 calls them "diachronic laws"), but I introduce a new term here in order to make clear that the causal factor is located within the process of change, rather than diachronic change merely realizing a pattern that is driven by functional-adaptive constraints (see §3 below). One could also frame the contrast between mutational constraints and functional-adaptive constraints in terms of *source-oriented* vs. *result-oriented* factors (Cristofaro 2017),[6] or one could say that mutational constraints locate the causal factors within the *mechanisms* of change (Bybee 2006). These are just alternative ways of saying that cross-linguistic distributions are due to mutational constraints.

Finally, ACQUISITIONAL CONSTRAINTS are factors that impact the acquisition of language and that have an effect on cross-linguistic distributions. Such constraints are briefly discussed by Anderson (2016), but they do not seem to play a big role in linguistics (but cf. Levshina 2019 [this volume] for discussion). Generative linguists who are concerned with learnability issues generally assume that what can be represented can also be learned, so that there is no distinction between representational constraints and what can be learned. This type of constraint is mentioned here only in passing, for the sake of completeness. It will play no role in what follows.

3 Two ways in which causal explanations involve diachrony

The peculiar term *mutational constraint* that I adopt here may raise questions: Is it necessary to use a new term for something that is very straightforward?

---

[6]Informally, instead of talking about "result-oriented factors", one could also say that functional-adaptive constraints are "pull forces" that attract the variable development into a certain preferred state.

The reason I am using this term here is that the possible alternatives "diachronic constraint" or "diachronic explanation" are not fully clear. First of all, diachronic explanations may simply be explanations of diachronic changes, but here we are concerned with causal factors leading to universals. Second, "diachronic" and "historical" are often used interchangeably (cf. Good's (2008) term "historical explanation" for what I call mutational explanations), and when we speak about historical explanations, we often mean contemporary idiosyncrasies that are better understood if one knows their origins (e.g. the vowel alternation in *foot/feet* finds a historical explanation in the earlier productive pattern of vowel fronting conditioned by a high vowel in the following syllable). But all of this is irrelevant in the present context, where we are concerned with possible and impossible pathways (and sources) of change.

Most importantly, the term *mutational constraint* is necessary because there are two ways in which causal explanations involve diachrony: synchronic distributions may be diachronically DETERMINED, or they may come about by the diachronic REALIZATION of preferred outcomes. The term *mutational constraint* highlights the fact that change is seen as a causal factor here, not merely the way in which the cross-linguistic distributions arise. By contrast, when universal tendencies are explained by functional-adaptive constraints, diachronic change merely serves to realize the adaptation. It plays an important role, indeed a crucial role, because functional adaptation is impossible without change. In this sense, functional-adaptive explanations are also diachronic (cf. Haspelmath 1999a). But functional-adaptive change is not the cause of the adaptation – the cause is the facilitation of communication for speaker and hearer. Mutational constraints are situations where the causal factor resides in the change itself.

Two types of mutational constraints may be distinguished: Source constraints and directionality constraints. Most of the diachronic regularities discussed by Cristofaro (2017) concern constraints on possible sources. The best-known directionality constraint is the irreversibility of grammaticalization (Haspelmath 1999b, 2004).[7]

Another reason for avoiding the terms "diachronic constraint" or "diachronic explanation" is that they invite a contrast with "synchronic constraint" and "synchronic explanation". But these terms are themselves very problematic, because they seem to conceive of explanation in noncausal terms. The term "synchrony"

---

[7]Mutational constraints are themselves in need of explanation, of course. I say nothing about this in the current paper, because it is already long and complicated enough. Their explanation could itself be "functional" in some sense (to be made more precise), but it cannot be functional-adaptive, because the latter type of explanation (as I understand it here) by definition applies only to language systems, not to changes.

has a clear application with reference to an abstract, idealized language system (de Saussure's *langue*), but in §2.1 I noted that language-particular system regularities should be described in terms of constructions or rules, and that causal constraints cannot play any role in them.[8]

Instead of "mutational constraint", one could use "constraint on change" (as in the title of this paper), but the new term "mutational" is more salient (it can be found more easily in automatic text searches), and since it is more specific, it can be used in new combinations like "mutational explanation" (an explanation in terms of a mutational constraint) or "mutational approach".

4 Universals are not explained by recurrent pathways of change, only by constraints on change

It has long been known that there are recurrent kinds of changes in phonology (lenition of consonants between vowels, diphthongization of long vowels, assimilation, etc.), and over the last few decades, recurrent changes in morphosyntax have become prominent as well, especially changes falling under the broad category of grammaticalization (Lehmann 2015[1982]; Heine et al. 1991; Bybee et al. 1994; and much related work).

Bybee (2006) highlights recurrent or common pathways of change in the tense-aspect domain (perfectives coming from anteriors and ultimately from completive, resultative or movement constructions; imperfectives coming from progressives and ultimately from locational or reduplicative constructions; and futures coming from volitional or movement constructions), and makes the claim that "the true universals of language are the mechanisms of change that propel the constant creation and recreation of grammar" (Bybee 2006: 179–180).

But she does not distinguish clearly between recurrent pathways of change and constraints on possible changes. There is no doubt that the tense-aspect changes that she discusses are widespread and significant developments, but nobody knows how widespread they are, compared to other possible changes. There are many perfective, imperfective and future markers about whose sources we know little, or markers whose sources do not fit into any of Bybee's categories. It is true that the recurrence of the changes makes it virtually certain that the

---

[8]Of course, in practice linguists often use the terms "synchronic explanation" and "synchronic constraint", but what they mean is either (i) very general language-particular statements ("descriptive explanations", §2.1), or (ii) representational constraints. The latter are biological limitations, which can hardly be labeled felicitously with the Saussurean term *synchronic*.

similarities are not accidental, but we do not know enough about tense-aspect developments to assert with confidence that no other sources are possible or likely, nor even that these sources are clearly predominant over other possibilities.

In one passage Bybee asserts that "the diachronic paths present much stronger cross-linguistic patterns than any comparison based solely on synchronic grammars" (2006: 180; see also Bybee 2008: 169). But her evidence is not sufficient to show this, at least for tense and aspect, where the pathways of change are highly diverse, and few people would venture a claim that certain kinds of change are impossible or highly unlikely.

In order to explain universal tendencies, one needs to appeal to something that is stronger than "recurrent (or common) pathways of change", namely mutational constraints, of the type mentioned earlier. Such constraints allow causal explanations of synchronic cross-linguistic distributions, just like functional-adaptive constraints. In phonological change, also discussed by Bybee, some common pathways may indeed qualify as mutational constraints: It could well be that changes involving [h] are highly uniform (especially [s]/[x] > [h] > Ø), so that we are dealing with a mutational constraint, not just a recurrent pathway.[9] Since such mutational constraints entail certain synchronic distributions, they qualify as true explanations, and if a synchronic distribution can be explained by a change constraint, it is not "accidental" (as Collins 2019 [this volume] calls the universal that adposition order correlates with verb–object order).[10]

At this point it is reasonable to ask how one can distinguish in practice between recurrent pathways and mutational constraints. The way to distinguish between synchronic cross-linguistic regularities and recurrent patterns is by gathering representative world-wide data samples (§2.2), and in principle, one would have to do the diachronic counterpart in order to establish a mutational constraint. As Collins (2019 [this volume]: 54) puts it, "we need large databases of attested grammaticalisation pathways". This is not very practical, however, as there are few solidly attested cases of grammaticalization, mostly from European (and a few Asian) languages, and most of what we think we know about

---

[9]It is true, of course, that there are some really interesting constraints on morphosyntactic change, notably the constraint that grammaticalization cannot be reversed (Haspelmath 1999b). However, such mutational constraints need not give rise to synchronic universal tendencies. Grammaticalization as such does not result in any universal tendencies, and Bybee (2006: §8) is apparently right that the lenition of [s] or [x] via [h] to Ø does not give rise to any synchronic universals either.

[10]It could be that Collins thinks that only representational or functional-adaptive constraints can explain synchronic universals, or it could be that he does not think that the sources of adpositions are sufficiently constrained. See the next paragraph for more on that possibility.

general change patterns is based on indirect inferences and cannot be subjected to statistical testing the way this is possible with synchronic patterns. Thus, in practice, linguists rely on their general experience when making judgments, or they cite a range of examples to persuade their colleagues. This method is much less rigorous than the study of synchronic regularities, but it seems to be uncontroversial to assert that in general, both types of diachronic regularities exist: mutational constraints (where a particular outcome has no other possible source), and recurrent changes. This is all I want to argue for in this paper, and I make no strong claims about particular instances (e.g. whether adpositions are constrained to arise only from possessed nouns and transitive verbs, or whether these are merely recurrent sources).

5 Multi-convergence can only be explained by functional-adaptive constraints

Since mutational constraints are one possible source of synchronic universals, it could be that in fact all synchronic universals are due to mutational constraints of one kind or another, and that functional-adaptive and representational constraints are not needed. This is a fairly radical position, but Cristofaro (2017) comes close to adopting it.

Perhaps the strongest reason to believe that we also need functional-adaptive explanation is that there are many cases of multi-convergence, i.e. situations in which a uniform result comes about through diverse pathways of change that yield a very similar result. For example, I note in Haspelmath (2017) that inalienable adpossessive constructions tend to have shorter coding or zero, whereas alienable adpossessive constructions have overt or longer coding, and I also observe that these patterns can come about in different ways. The inalienable pattern may be shorter because of special shortening, or it may be shorter because only the alienable pattern got a special new marker. Kiparsky (2008: 37) makes a very similar argument against Garrett's (1990) explanation of split ergativity in mutational terms, noting that "[Garrett's] historical account is insufficiently general [...] because the phenomenon to be explained has several historical sources".

Interestingly, two of the advocates of mutational explanations of universal tendencies observe the heterogeneity of the pathways themselves. Anderson (2016) is concerned with case-marking patterns in perfective and imperfective aspects across languages, and Cristofaro (2017) is concerned with the coding asymmetry of zero singulars and overt plurals:

As it happens, common sources for a new perfective, on the one hand, and for a new imperfective, on the other, converge on similar patterns of split ergativity, although they are quite unrelated to each other. (Anderson 2016: 23; cf. also Anderson 1977)

Different instances of the same configuration can also be a result of very different processes. For example, phonological erosion, meaning transfer from a quantifier to an accompanying element, and the grammaticalization of distributives into plural markers can all give rise to a configuration with zero marking for singular and overt marking for plural, yet they do not obviously have anything in common. (Cristofaro 2017: 18–19)

Anderson and Cristofaro are thus aware of the multi-convergence patterns, but for some reason they do not draw the conclusion that we need an additional causal factor to explain the convergence – and as far as I can see, this factor can only be a functional-adaptive constraint.[11]

The convergence of diverse processes on a uniform result could conceivably be accidental, but in this case it could not explain a universal tendency, because a universal tendency is by definition non-accidental. A universal tendency still holds if more and more languages are looked at, whereas accidental similarities of the results of diverse processes would not be repeated if more phenomena were considered. On the analogy of biological usage, where "convergent evolution" refers to the independent development of similar traits for adaptive reasons, one should probably avoid the term "convergence" if one thinks that the similarities are accidental and will not be confirmed by a larger sample. Thus, Anderson and Cristofaro should think of their observations in terms of coincidental similarity rather than convergence.

6 Functional-adaptive explanations need not specify pathways of change

One point of criticism of functional-adaptive explanations is that they do not say how the change comes about. Especially Bybee and Cristofaro have argued that for a functional explanation of cross-linguistic regularities to be accepted, it

---

[11]In principle, it could also be a representational constraint (i.e. Universal Grammar), but since the patterns involve implicational universals, this would be difficult to argue for. In general, implicational universals cannot be easily explained by representational constraints.

must be shown how the functional motivation plays a role in the way in which the resulting patterns comes about.

I agree that the functional motivation must play a role in the way in which the pattern comes about, but I do not agree that the manner in which it influences the change must be identified for a successful explanation. Below are two relevant quotations.

> [I]n language universals, causal factors are linguistic changes that create particular synchronic states, and the existence of massive cross-language similarity in synchronic states implies powerful parallels in linguistic change. ... the validity of a principle as explanatory can only be maintained if it can be shown that the same principle that generalizes over the data also plays a role in the establishment of the conventions described by the generalization. (Bybee 1988: 352)

> These [functional] explanations ... have mainly been proposed based on the synchronic distribution of the relevant grammatical phenomena, not the actual diachronic processes that give rise to this distribution in individual languages. In what follows, it will be argued that many such processes do not provide evidence for the postulated dependencies between grammatical phenomena, and suggest alternative ways to look at implicational universals in general. (Cristofaro 2017: 10)

The problem with Bybee's claim is that the changes are seen as causal factors themselves: Bybee does not seem to envisage the possibility of a "pull force" that increases the probability of change toward a particular kind of outcome, without determining the way in which the change comes about. Moreover, she formulates the requirement that one should be able to *demonstrate* that the functional-adaptive principle plays a role in the change, but this requirement is too strong. In general, we do not know much about language change and how and why it happens. The primary evidence for functional-adaptive explanations is the fit between the causal factor and the observed outcome. If there is a good fit, e.g. if languages overwhelmingly prefer the kinds of word orders that allow easy parsing (Hawkins 2014), or if they tend to show economical coding of grammatical categories (Haspelmath 2008), the best explanation is in functional-adaptive terms, as long as there is a way for languages to acquire these properties. The latter requirement is always met, as there are no synchronic states which cannot have arisen from other states. Thus, we may not know how exactly the zero singulars and overt plurals in Hebrew (e.g. *sus* 'horse', *sus-im* 'horses') may have come about, as they are found in much the same way in Proto-Semitic, but we know various ways in which plurals can arise (Cristofaro 2013: §4), so there is no problem in assuming that the functional motivation of economical coding of the singular played a role in the development of the contrast.

Cristofaro is right that when we look at the changes that give rise to apparently functionally motivated distributions, we do not (necessarily) find evidence that the changes were driven by the need to obey the functional constraints, but finding such evidence is not necessary for a successful explanation. The evidence for the functional motivation does not come from the manner in which the change happened, but from the fit between the motivation and the observed outcomes. If there is a universal tendency, and it can be explained by a universal motivating factor, then that explanation should be accepted unless a better explanation becomes available.

Explanations of regularities in the world-wide distribution of cultural traits often appeal to functional-adaptive factors in adjacent fields as well. For example, anthropologists sometimes explain religion by prosociality, or monogamy by group-beneficial effects (e.g. Paciotti et al. 2011; Henrich et al. 2012). The issue here is whether better explanations are available, not whether there is a way for religion or marriage to develop. We know little about how religion and marriage first arose or generally arise in societies, and it is very difficult to study the diachronic developments. But we can try to correlate structural traits of human societies with other traits and draw inferences about possible causal factors. There is no perceived need in this literature to show that the mechanisms by which religion or monogamy arise must be of a particular type.[12] Basically, when the result is preferred, any kind of change can give rise to the result, and we do not need to understand the nature of the change, let alone show that the change was motivated by the result.

Another striking example from linguistics is the shortness of frequent words, which is surely adaptive. But there are quite diverse paths to shortness. According to Zipf (1935), shorter words are shorter because they underwent clipping processes (e.g. *laboratory > lab*), and according to Bybee (2007: 12), short words are short because "high-frequency words undergo reductive changes at a faster rate than low-frequency words [...] the major mechanism is gradual phonetic reduction". But actually in most cases, rarer words are longer because they are (originally) complex elements, consisting of multiple morphs, e.g. *horse* vs. *hippopotamus, car* vs. *cabriolet, church* vs. *cathedral*. Drastic shortening of longer

---

[12] The same is true for adaptive explanations in evolutionary biology: The fact that wings are adaptive can be inferred from the way wings are used by animals, and we do not expect that wings arise in uniform ways (wings of birds, bats and insects have diverse origins and arose by diverse paths of change, whose nature is not relevant to the adaptive explanation).

words seems to occur primarily in the modern age with its large number of technical and bureaucratic innovations, but even here, clipping is only one of many possibilities; for example, Ronneberger-Sibold (2014) discusses a number of fairly diverse "shortening techniques" in German. What unites all of these processes is only one feature: the outcomes of the changes, which are functionally adapted.

When Cristofaro (2014: 297) writes that "any model of the principles that lead to the use of particular constructions [...] should take into account the diachronic development of these constructions, rather than just their synchronic distribution", I certainly agree, because I think that the diachronic developments can illuminate the functional adaptation, and a close study of whatever we can learn about diachrony can tell us whether any mutational constraints might play a role. But when there is strong evidence for a universal tendency and there is a good functional-adaptive explanation available, the diachronic evidence is not strictly speaking necessary.

7 A cost scale of constraints

What are we to do when there are several possible explanations, using different kinds of causal factors? For example, what do we do when word-order correlations can be explained either by functional adaptation (processing efficiency, Hawkins 2014) or by mutational constraints? Or when case-marking splits can be explained either by Universal Grammar (Kiparsky 2008: §2.3) or by efficiency of coding?

The answer is that there is a COST SCALE of constraints:

(3)   less costly ⟵————————————————————⟶ more costly

       mutational > functional-adaptive > representational constraints

The "cheapest" type of explanation is the mutational mode, because language change can be observed, and if we find that certain changes simply do not occur (for whatever reason), we do not need to make more far-reaching claims. Thus, Bybee (2010: 111) discusses the Greenbergian word order correlations and notes that "grammaticalization gives us the correct orders for free" – a formulation that reflects the assessment that mutational constraints do not involve any additional "cost".[13]

---

[13]Cf. also the similar argumentation in Kiparsky (2008: 33), in connection with a different phenomenon (involving reflexives): "That is really all that needs to be said [...] The historical explanation covers the data perfectly." I completely agree with Bybee and Kiparsky in this respect.

The next type of explanation on the scale appeals to functional-adaptive constraints. These are more costly because we cannot observe their effects directly and have to rely heavily on inference. But they are less costly than representational constraints, because they are far more general, applying also in other domains of cognitive processing and communication, often also in nonhuman animals. Again, this is not really controversial: In his chapter on Universal Grammar, Jackendoff (2002: 79) says that "we should be conservative in how much linguistic structure we ascribe to an innate UG. We should welcome explanations of linguistic universals on more general cognitive grounds."

It is only when we observe a cross-linguistic regularity that cannot be explained either by mutational constraints or by functional-adaptive constraints that we need to appeal to representational constraints. These involve the most specific (and thus most costly) mechanism, which should only be invoked as a last resort.

8 Conclusion

In this paper I have argued that cross-linguistic regularities may be explained either by mutational constraints or by functional-adaptive constraints (or perhaps by representational constraints, as in generative grammar) (§2). Both kinds of explanations involve diachrony, but in different ways: Mutational constraints are constraints on possible sources or pathways of change, while functional-adaptive constraints influence the results of changes (§3). In order to explain a universal tendency, we need to appeal to mutational constraints; merely noting a frequent pathway of change is not enough (§4). We can be sure that a cross-linguistic regularity is due to a functional-adaptive rather than a mutational constraint if there are diverse pathways of change which converge on a single result (§5). The functional-adaptive constraint must influence language change in such a way that change in a particular direction becomes more likely, but this need not be visible in the change itself (§6). But when we have good reasons to think that there is a mutational constraint, it takes precedence over functional-adaptive and representational explanations (§7).

Thus, the answer to the question in the title of this paper ("Can cross-linguistic regularities be explained by constraints on change?") is: Yes, some regularities can apparently be explained in this way, but clearly not all of them. There remains an important role for functional-adaptive constraints in explaining language universals.

Martin Haspelmath

Acknowledgement

The support of the European Research Council (ERC Advanced Grant 670985, Grammatical Universals) is gratefully acknowledged.

References

Anderson, Stephen R. 1977. On mechanisms by which languages become ergative. In Charles N. Li (ed.), *Mechanisms of syntactic change*, 317–332. Austin: University of Texas Press.

Anderson, Stephen R. 2005. Morphological universals and diachrony. In Geert Booij & Jaap van Marle (eds.), *Yearbook of Morphology 2004* (Yearbook of Morphology), 1–17. Dordrecht: Springer. DOI:10.1007/1-4020-2900-4_1

Anderson, Stephen R. 2008. The logical structure of linguistic theory. *Language* 84(4). 795–814. DOI:10.1353/lan.0.0075

Anderson, Stephen R. 2016. Synchronic versus diachronic explanation and the nature of the Language Faculty. *Annual Review of Linguistics* 2(1). 11–31. DOI:10.1146/annurev-linguistics-011415-040735

Aristar, Anthony R. 1991. On diachronic sources and synchronic pattern: An investigation into the origin of linguistic universals. *Language* 67(1). 1–33.

Bickel, Balthasar. 2013. Distributional biases in language families. In Balthasar Bickel, Lenore A. Genoble, David A. Peterson & Alan Timberlake (eds.), *Language typology and historical contingency*, 415–444. Amsterdam, Philadelphia: John Benjamins. DOI:10.5167/uzh-86870

Bickel, Balthasar, Alena Witzlack-Makarevich, Kamal K. Choudhary, Matthias Schlesewsky & Ina Bornkessel-Schlesewsky. 2015. The neurophysiology of language processing shapes the evolution of grammar: Evidence from case marking. *PLoS ONE* 10(8). e0132819. DOI:10.1371/journal.pone.0132819

Blevins, Juliette. 2004. *Evolutionary phonology: The emergence of sound patterns.* Cambridge: Cambridge University Press. DOI:10.1017/CBO9780511486357

Blevins, Juliette. 2006. A theoretical synopsis of Evolutionary Phonology. *Theoretical Linguistics* 32(2). 117–166. DOI:10.1515/TL.2006.009

Bybee, Joan L. 1988. The diachronic dimension in explanation. In John A. Hawkins (ed.), *Explaining language universals*, 350–379. Oxford: Blackwell.

Bybee, Joan L. 2006. Language change and universals. In Ricardo Mairal & Juana Gil (eds.), *Linguistic universals*, 179–194. Cambridge: Cambridge University Press. DOI:10.1017/CBO9780511618215.009

Bybee, Joan L. 2007. Introduction. In Joan L. Bybee (ed.), *Frequency of use and the organization of language*, 5–22. Oxford: Oxford University Press. DOI:10.1093/acprof:oso/9780195301571.001.0001

Bybee, Joan L. 2008. Formal universals as emergent phenomena: The origins of structure preservation. In Jeff Good (ed.), *Linguistic universals and language change*, 108–121. Oxford: Oxford University Press. DOI:10.1093/acprof:oso/9780199298495.003.0005

Bybee, Joan L. 2010. *Language, usage and cognition.* Cambridge: Cambridge University Press. DOI:10.1017/CBO9780511750526.011

Bybee, Joan L., Revere D. Perkins & William Pagliuca. 1994. *The evolution of grammar: Tense, aspect and modality in the languages of the world.* Chicago: University of Chicago Press.

Chomsky, Noam A. 1981. *Lectures on government and binding.* Dordrecht: Foris.

Cinque, Guglielmo. 1999. *Adverbs and functional heads: A cross-linguistic approach.* New York, Oxford: Oxford University Press.

Collins, Jeremy. 2019. Some language universals are historical accidents. In Karsten Schmidtke-Bode, Natalia Levshina, Susanne Maria Michaelis & Ilja A. Seržant (eds.), *Explanation in typology: Diachronic sources, functional motivations and the nature of the evidence*, 47–61. Berlin: Language Science Press. DOI:10.5281/zenodo.2583808

Comrie, Bernard. 1989. *Language universals and linguistic typology: Syntax and morphology.* 2nd edn. Chicago: University of Chicago Press.

Creissels, Denis. 2008. Direct and indirect explanations of typological regularities: The case of alignment variations. *Folia Linguistica* 42(1). 1–38. DOI:10.1515/FLIN.2008.1

Creissels, Denis. 2014. Functive phrases in typological and diachronic perspective. *Studies in Language* 38(3). 605–647. DOI:10.1075/sl.38.3.07cre

Cristofaro, Sonia. 2012. Cognitive explanations, distributional evidence, and diachrony. *Studies in Language* 36(3). 645–670. DOI:10.1075/sl.36.3.07cri

Cristofaro, Sonia. 2013. The referential hierarchy: Reviewing the evidence in diachronic perspective. In Dik Bakker & Martin Haspelmath (eds.), *Languages across boundaries: Studies in memory of Anna Siewierska*, 69–93. Berlin: De Gruyter Mouton. DOI:10.1515/9783110331127.69

Cristofaro, Sonia. 2014. Competing motivation models and diachrony: What evidence for what motivations? In Brian MacWhinney, Andrej L. Malchukov & Edith A. Moravcsik (eds.), *Competing motivations in grammar and usage*, 282–298. Oxford: Oxford University Press. DOI:10.1093/acprof:oso/9780198709848.001.0001

Cristofaro, Sonia. 2017. Implicational universals and dependencies. In Nick J. Enfield (ed.), *Dependencies in language: On the causal ontology of linguistic systems*, 9–22. Berlin: Language Science Press. DOI:10.5281/zenodo.573777

Croft, William. 1991. *Syntactic categories and grammatical relations: The cognitive organization of information*. Chicago: University of Chicago Press.

De Boer, Bart. 2001. *The origins of vowel systems*. Oxford: Oxford University Press.

Dik, Simon C. 1997. *The theory of functional grammar. Part 1: The structure of the clause*. Kees Hengeveld (ed.). 2nd edn. Berlin, New York: Mouton de Gruyter.

Dixon, R. M. W. 1994. *Ergativity*. Cambridge: Cambridge University Press. DOI:10.1017/CBO9780511611896

Dressler, Wolfgang U., Willi Mayerthaler, Oswalt Panagl & Wolfgang U. Wurzel. 1987. *Leitmotifs in natural morphology*. Amsterdam, Philadelphia: John Benjamins. DOI:10.1075/slcs.10

Dryer, Matthew S. 1992. The Greenbergian word order correlations. *Language* 68(1). 81–138. DOI:10.1353/lan.1992.0028

Dryer, Matthew S. 2019. Grammaticalization accounts of word order correlations. In Karsten Schmidtke-Bode, Natalia Levshina, Susanne Maria Michaelis & Ilja A. Seržant (eds.), *Explanation in typology: Diachronic sources, functional motivations and the nature of the evidence*, 63–95. Berlin: Language Science Press. DOI:10.5281/zenodo.2583810

Foley, William A. & Robert D. Jr. Van Valin. 1984. *Functional syntax and universal grammar*. Cambridge: Cambridge University Press.

Garrett, Andrew. 1990. The origin of NP split ergativity. *Language* 66(2). 261–296. DOI:10.2307/414887

Gildea, Spike & Fernando Zúñiga. 2016. Referential hierarchies: A new look at some historical and typological patterns. *Linguistics* 54(3). 483–529. DOI:10.1515/ling-2016-0007

Givón, Talmy. 1979. *On understanding grammar*. New York: Academic Press. DOI:10.1075/z.213

Good, Jeff. 2008. Introduction. In Jeff Good (ed.), *Linguistic universals and language change*, 1–19. Oxford: Oxford University Press. DOI:10.1093/acprof:oso/9780199298495.003.0001

Greenberg, Joseph H. 1963. Some universals of grammar with particular reference to the order of meaningful elements. In Joseph H. Greenberg (ed.), *Universals of language*, 58–90. Cambridge, MA: MIT Press.

Greenberg, Joseph H. 1969. Some methods of dynamic comparison in linguistics. In Jan Puhvel (ed.), *Substance and structure of language*, 147–203. Berkeley: University of California Press.

Greenberg, Joseph H. 1978. Diachrony, synchrony and language universals. In Joseph H. Greenberg, Charles A. Ferguson & Edith A. Moravcsik (eds.), *Universals of human language I: Method and theory*, 61–92. Stanford: Stanford University Press.

Haspelmath, Martin. 1999a. Optimality and diachronic adaptation. *Zeitschrift für Sprachwissenschaft* 18(2). 180–205. DOI:10.1515/zfsw.1999.18.2.180

Haspelmath, Martin. 1999b. Why is grammaticalization irreversible? *Linguistics* 37(6). 1043–1068. DOI:10.1515/ling.37.6.1043

Haspelmath, Martin. 2004. On directionality in language change with particular reference to grammaticalization. In Olga Fischer, Muriel Norde & Harry Perridon (eds.), *Up and down the cline: The nature of grammaticalization*, 17–44. Amsterdam, Philadelphia: John Benjamins. DOI:10.1075/tsl.59.03has

Haspelmath, Martin. 2008. Frequency vs. iconicity in explaining grammatical asymmetries. *Cognitive Linguistics* 19(1). 1–33. DOI:10.1515/COG.2008.001

Haspelmath, Martin. 2014. Comparative syntax. In Andrew Carnie, Yosuke Sato & Dan Siddiqi (eds.), *The Routledge handbook of syntax*, 490–508. London: Routledge. DOI:10.4324/9781315796604.ch24

Haspelmath, Martin. 2017. Explaining alienability contrasts in adpossessive constructions: Predictability vs. iconicity. *Zeitschrift für Sprachwissenschaft* 36(2). DOI:10.1515/zfs-2017-0009

Hawkins, John A. 2014. *Cross-linguistic variation and efficiency*. Oxford: Oxford University Press. DOI:10.1093/acprof:oso/9780199664993.001.0001

Heine, Bernd, Ulrike Claudi & Friederike Hünnemeyer. 1991. *Grammaticalization: A conceptual framework*. Chicago: University of Chicago Press.

Henrich, Joseph, Robert Boyd & Peter J. Richerson. 2012. The puzzle of monogamous marriage. *Phil. Trans. R. Soc. B* 367(1589). 657–669. DOI:10.1098/rstb.2011.0290

Jackendoff, Ray S. 2002. *Foundations of language*. Oxford: Oxford University Press. DOI:10.1093/acprof:oso/9780198270126.001.0001

Keenan, Edward L. & Bernard Comrie. 1977. Noun phrase accessibility and universal grammar. *Linguistic Inquiry* 8(1). 63–99.

Kiparsky, Paul. 2008. Universals constrain change; change results in typological generalizations. In Jeff Good (ed.), *Linguistic universals and language change*, 23–53. Oxford: Oxford University Press. DOI:10.1093/acprof:oso/9780199298495.003.0002

Lehmann, Christian. 2015[1982]. *Thoughts on grammaticalization*. 3rd edn. Berlin: Language Science Press. DOI:10.17169/langsci.b88.99

Levshina, Natalia. 2019. Linguistic Frankenstein, or How to test universal constraints without real languages. In Karsten Schmidtke-Bode, Natalia Levshina, Susanne Maria Michaelis & Ilja A. Seržant (eds.), *Explanation in typology: Diachronic sources, functional motivations and the nature of the evidence*, 203–221. Berlin: Language Science Press. DOI:10.5281/zenodo.2583820

Malchukov, Andrej L. 2008. Animacy and asymmetries in differential case marking. *Lingua* 118(2). 203–221. DOI:10.1016/j.lingua.2007.02.005

Newmeyer, Frederick J. 1998. *Language form and language function*. Cambridge, MA: MIT Press.

Paciotti, Brian, Tim Waring, Mark Lubell, Billy Baum, Richard McElreath, Ed Edsten, Charles Efferson & Peter J. Richerson. 2011. Are religious individuals more generous, trusting, and cooperative? An experimental test of the effect of religion on prosociality. In Lionel Obadia & Donald C. Wood (eds.), *The economics of religion: Anthropological approaches*, 267–305. Bardford: Emerald Group Publishing Limited. DOI:10.1108/S0190-1281(2011)0000031014

Plank, Frans. 2007. Extent and limits of linguistic diversity as the remit of typology – but through constraints on what is diversity limited? *Linguistic Typology* 11(1). 43–68. DOI:10.1515/LINGTY.2007.005

Ronneberger-Sibold, Elke. 2014. Tuning morphosemantic transparency by shortening. In Franz Rainer, Francesco Gardani, Hans Christian Luschützky & Wolfgang U. Dressler (eds.), *Morphology and meaning: Selected papers from the 15th International Morphology Meeting, Vienna, February 2012*, 275–287. Amsterdam, Philadelphia: John Benjamins. DOI:10.1075/cilt.327.19ron

Sapir, Edward. 1921. *Language: An introduction to the study of speech*. New York: Harcourt Brace.

Schleicher, August. 1850. *Die Sprachen Europas in systematischer Uebersicht*. Bonn: H. B. König. DOI:10.1075/acil.4

Smith, Peter W., Beata Moskal, Ting Xu, Jungmin Kang & Jonathan Bobaljik. 2018. Case and number suppletion in pronouns. *Natural Language & Linguistic Theory, First Online*. DOI:10.1007/s11049-018-9425-0

Stassen, Leon. 1985. *Comparison and universal grammar*. Oxford, New York: Blackwell.

Timberlake, Alan. 2003. Review of "G. C. Corbett: Number (2000)" and of "G. Senft (ed.): Systems of nominal classification (2000)". *Journal of Linguistics* 29. 189–195. DOI:10.1017/S002222670225197X

Tomlin, Russell S. 1986. *Basic word order: Functional principles*. London: Croom Helm. DOI:10.4324/9781315857466

Tversky, Amos & Daniel Kahneman. 1974. Judgment under uncertainty: Heuristics and biases. *Science* 185. 1124–1131.   DOI:10.1126/science.185.4157.1124

Vafaeian, Ghazaleh. 2013. Typology of nominal and adjectival suppletion. *Sprachtypologie und Universalienforschung* 66(2). 112–140.   DOI:10.1524/stuf.2013.0007

von Schlegel, Friedrich. 1808. *Ueber die Sprache und Weisheit der Indier: Ein Beitrag zur Begründung der Alterthumskunde.* Heidelberg: Mohr und Zimmer. DOI:10.1017/CBO9781107049444

Yu, Alan C. L. 2007. *A natural history of infixation.* Oxford: Oxford University Press.   DOI:10.1093/acprof:oso/9780199279388.001.0001

Zipf, George K. 1935. *The psycho-biology of language: An introduction to dynamic philology.* Cambridge, MA: MIT Press.

Chapter 2

Taking diachronic evidence seriously: Result-oriented vs. source-oriented explanations of typological universals

Sonia Cristofaro

University of Pavia

Classical explanations of typological universals are result-oriented, in that particular grammatical configurations are assumed to arise because of principles of optimization of grammatical structure that favor those configurations as opposed to others. These explanations, however, are based on the synchronic properties of individual configurations, not the actual diachronic processes that give rise to these configurations cross-linguistically. The paper argues that the available evidence about these processes challenges result-oriented explanations of typological universals in two major ways. First, individual grammatical configurations arise because of principles pertaining to the properties of particular source constructions and developmental mechanisms, rather than properties of the configuration in itself. Second, individual configurations arise through several distinct diachronic processes, which do not obviously reflect some general principle. These facts point to a new research agenda for typology, one focusing on what source constructions and developmental mechanisms play a role in the shaping of individual cross-linguistic patterns, rather than the synchronic properties of the pattern in itself.

1 Introduction

In the functional-typological approach that originated from the work of Joseph Greenberg, language universals (henceforth, typological universals) are skewed cross-linguistic distributional patterns whereby languages recurrently display certain grammatical configurations as opposed to others. Explanations for these

Sonia Cristofaro. 2019. Taking diachronic evidence seriously: Result-oriented vs. source-oriented explanations of typological universals. In Karsten Schmidtke-Bode, Natalia Levshina, Susanne Maria Michaelis & Ilja A. Seržant (eds.), *Explanation in typology: Diachronic sources, functional motivations and the nature of the evidence*, 25–46. Berlin: Language Science Press.
DOI:10.5281/zenodo.2583806

patterns are usually result-oriented, in the sense that at least some of the relevant configurations are assumed to arise because of some postulated principle of grammatical structure, which favors those particular configurations and disfavors other logically possible ones.

For example, a number of word order correlations have been explained by assuming that speakers will recurrently select particular word orders as opposed to others because these orders lead to syntactic structures that are easier to process (Hawkins 2004, among others). Another case in point is provided by explanations of the use of explicit marking for different grammatical meanings, for example the use of overt marking for different number values, or that of dedicated case marking for different NP types occurring in particular argument roles. Crosslinguistically, explicit marking may be restricted to less frequent meanings, for example plural rather than singular, animate rather than inanimate P arguments, or inanimate rather than animate A arguments, but is usually not restricted to more frequent meanings.[1] This has been assumed to reflect a principle of economy whereby speakers will tend to use explicit marking only when they really need to do so. Explicit marking can be restricted to less frequent meanings because more frequent ones are easier to identify, and hence less in need to be disambiguated (Greenberg 1966; Corbett 2000; Croft 2003; Haspelmath 2006; 2008).

These explanations are based on the synchronic properties of the relevant distributional patterns, not the actual diachronic processes that shape these distributions from one language to another. For example, assumptions about the role of processing ease in determining particular word order correlations are based on the synchronic syntactic configurations produced by particular word orders, not the actual diachronic origins of these orders from one language to another. Similarly, the idea that the use of explicit marking reflects economy is based on the synchronic cross-linguistic distribution of particular constructions across different contexts (e.g. zero vs. overt marking across singular and plural, dedicated case marking across animate and inanimate A and P arguments), not the actual diachronic processes that give rise to this distribution in individual languages.

This paper discusses various types of diachronic evidence about the cross-linguistic origins of two phenomena that have been described in terms of typological universals, the distribution of accusative vs. ergative case marking alignment across different NP types and that of zero vs. overt marking across singular and plural.

---

[1]Following a standard practice in typology (see, for example, Comrie 1989 or Dixon 1994), the labels A, P and S are used throughout the paper to refer to the two arguments of transitive verbs and the only argument of intransitive verbs.

This evidence, it will be argued, challenges classical, result-oriented explanations of typological universals in two major ways. First, recurrent grammatical configurations cross-linguistically do not appear to arise because of principles that favor those particular configurations in themselves. This challenges
the idea that these principles play a role in the emergence of the distributional
patterns described by the relevant universals. Second, individual configurations
arise through several distinct diachronic processes, which do not obviously reflect some general principle. This challenges the idea that explanations for particular distributional patterns can be read off from the synchronic properties of
the relevant grammatical configurations, because these properties can originate
differently in different cases. These facts call for a source-oriented approach to
typological universals, one in which the patterns described by individual universals are accounted for in terms of the actual diachronic processes that give rise
to the pattern, rather than the synchronic properties of the pattern in itself.

2 The animacy/referential hierarchy: Some possible origins of alignment splits in case marking

One of the most famous typological universals is the animacy/referential hierarchy in (1):

(1) 1st person pronouns > 2nd person pronouns > 3rd person pronouns >
     human > animate > inanimate (Croft 2003: 130, among others)

Among other phenomena, this hierarchy captures some recurrent splits in the
distribution of accusative and ergative case marking alignment across different
NP types. Accusative alignment can be restricted to a left end portion of the hierarchy (e.g. pronouns, human and animate nouns), but is usually not restricted to
a right end portion of the hierarchy (e.g. inanimate nouns, nouns as opposed to
pronouns). Conversely, ergative alignment is sometimes restricted to a right end
portion of the hierarchy (e.g. inanimate nouns, nouns as opposed to pronouns,
nouns and 3rd person pronouns), but is usually not restricted to a left end portion of the hierarchy (1st/2nd person pronouns, pronouns as opposed to nouns,
pronouns and animate nouns).

A classical result-oriented explanation for this distribution invokes the economy principle mentioned in Section 1. Speakers tend to use dedicated case marking only when it is really needed, that is, when some grammatical role is more
in need of disambiguation. The NPs towards the right end of the hierarchy (inanimates, nouns as opposed to pronouns) are more likely to occur as P arguments,

hence, when they do, the P role is relatively easy to identify, and hence less in need of disambiguation. Dedicated case marking for P arguments, leading to accusative alignment, may then be limited to the NPs towards the left end of the hierarchy (pronouns, animate nouns). By contrast, these NPs are more likely to occur as A arguments, hence, when they do, the A role is less in need of disambiguation. Dedicated case marking for A arguments, leading to ergative alignment, may then be limited to the NPs towards the right end of the hierarchy (Silverstein 1976; Dixon 1979; 1994; Comrie 1981; DeLancey 1981; Song 2001; Croft 2003).

This explanation, however, is not supported by the available diachronic evidence about the origins of the relevant grammatical configurations across languages. In many cases where accusative or ergative alignment is restricted to particular NP types, the relevant alignment pattern is a result of the development of an accusative or ergative marker through the reinterpretation of a pre-existing element with similar distributional restrictions. In some cases, for example, accusative markers restricted to pronominal, animate or definite direct objects are structurally identical to topic markers. This is illustrated in (2) for Kanuri.

(2) Kanuri (Nilo-Saharan; Cyffer 1998: 52)

   a. Músa shí-**ga**   cúro.
       Musa 3SG-ACC saw

       'Musa saw him.'

   b. wú-**ga**
       1SG-as.for

       'as for me'

In such cases, the accusative marker plausibly originates from the topic marker in contexts where the latter refers to a P argument and is reinterpreted as a marker for this argument ('As for X' > 'X ACC': see, for example, Rohlfs 1984 and Pensado 1995 for Romance languages, and König 2008 for several African languages). Topics are usually pronominal, animate and definite, so topic markers are mainly used in the same contexts as the resulting accusative markers.

Ergative markers not applying to first and second person pronouns have been shown to originate from various types of source elements not applying to these pronouns either. Sometimes, for example, the ergative marker is derived from an indexical element, such as a demonstrative or a third person pronoun, as illustrated in (3) for Bagandji. McGregor (2006; 2008) argues that in such cases the indexical element is originally used to emphasize the referent of the A argument, as this referent is a new or unexpected agent. This strategy does not apply to first and second person pronouns because the referents of these pronouns are typically expected agents.

(3) Bagandji (Australian: Hercus 1982: 63)
     Yaḍu-ḍuru   gāndi-d-uru-ana.
     wind-DEM/ERG carry-FUT-3SG.SBJ-3SG.OBJ
     'This wind will carry it along / The wind will carry it along.'

In other cases, the ergative marker is derived from a marker used to encode instruments in transitive sentences with no overt third person arguments. In these sentences, the instrument can be reinterpreted as an agent, thus evolving into the A argument of the sentence. As a result, the marker originally used for the instrument becomes an ergative marker. This process has been reconstructed by Mithun (2005) for Hanis Coos, illustrated in (4). Instruments are typically inanimate, so the relevant markers do not usually occur with first and second person pronouns.

(4) Hanis Coos (Coosan; Mithun 2005: 84)
     K'wɨn-t   x̣=mɨl:aqətš.
     shoot-TR OBL/ERG=arrow
     'An arrow shot (him).' (from '(He) shot at him with an arrow.')

Restrictions in the distribution of particular alignment patterns across different NP types can also be a result of phonological processes targeting a subset of these NPs. In English, for example, accusative alignment became restricted to pronouns as a result of nouns losing the relevant inflectional distinctions due to sound change, as illustrated in Table 1.

Table 1: Pronominal and nominal declension in late Middle English (Blake 2001: 177–179)

	1st person	'name'
NOM	*ik*	*name*
ACC	*mē*	*name* (from *naman*)

In Louisiana Creole, A, S and P arguments were originally undifferentiated for both nouns and pronouns. Pronominal A and S forms, however, underwent phonological reduction, plausibly due to their high discourse frequency. As a result, as can be seen from Table 2, pronouns developed distinct forms for A and S arguments on the one hand and P arguments on the other, while nominal A, S, and P arguments remained undifferentiated. This led to an accusative case marking alignment pattern restricted to pronouns (Haspelmath & APiCS Consortium 2013).

Table 2: Pronominal declension in Louisiana Creole (Haspelmath & APiCS Consortium 2013)

		Subject	Object
Louisiana Creole	1SG	*mo*	*mwa*
	2SG	*to*	*twa*

These various processes do not appear to be triggered by the fact that, in the resulting grammatical configurations, dedicated case marking is restricted to roles more in need of disambiguation. In some cases, a pre-existing element is reinterpreted as a marker for a co-occurring argument. Topic markers are reinterpreted as markers for a co-occurring P argument, and demonstratives and third person pronouns are reinterpreted as markers for a co-occurring A argument. This is a metonymization process triggered by the contextual co-occurrence of the relevant elements. In other cases, a pre-existing element evolves into a case marker as a result of the reanalysis of the argument structure of the construction. Such processes are plausibly due to meaning similarities between the source construction and the resulting construction, for example, instruments can be reinterpreted as agents because of their role in the action being described, particularly in the absence of an overtly expressed agent. In yet other cases, an existing alignment pattern becomes restricted to particular NP types because other NPs, due to their phonological properties, lose their inflectional distinctions as a result of regular sound change. Finally, particular NPs may develop distinct forms for some argument roles as a result of the original forms undergoing phonological reduction due to their discourse frequency.

Restrictions in the distribution of accusative and ergative alignment, as determined by individual processes, directly follow from restrictions in the distribution of various source constructions, or in the domain of application of particular developmental mechanisms (such as particular phonological processes). These restrictions too, then, cannot actually be taken as evidence for principles that favor the resulting grammatical configurations independently of particular source constructions and developmental mechanisms. This is further supported by the fact that, when the source constructions or the developmental mechanisms involved are not subject to particular distributional restrictions, the distribution of accusative or ergative alignment does not display those restrictions either.

For example, accusative markers sometimes originate from 'take' verbs in constructions of the type 'Take X and Verb (X)', where the 'take' verb is reanalyzed as a marker for its former P argument (Lord 1993; Chappell 2013, among several others). The P arguments of 'take' verbs can be pronominal, nominal, animate or inanimate (e.g. 'take him, it, the child, the sword'), and the resulting accusative markers apply to all of these argument types. This is illustrated for Twi in (5), where the accusative marker *de*, derived from a 'take' verb, applies to both animate and inanimate P arguments.

(5)   Twi (Niger-Congo; Lord 1993: 66, 79)

a. Wǫ-**de**   no yeẹ   ǫsafohéne.
   they-ACC him make captain

   'They made him captain.'

b. O- **de** afoa   ce boha-m.
   he-ACC sword put scabbard-inside

   'He put the sword into the scabbard.'

Accusative and ergative markers can also develop from the reanalysis of possessor or oblique markers used on the notional A or P arguments of various types of source constructions, for example, 'X is occupied with the Verbing **of** Y > 'X is Verbing Y ACC', 'To X it will be the Verbing of Y' > 'X **ERG** will Verb Y', 'Y is X's Verbed thing', 'Y is Verbed **by** X' > 'X **ERG** Verbed Y'. These processes have been described for a wide variety of languages (see, for example, Harris & Campbell 1995; Bubenik 1998; Gildea 1998; Creissels 2008). In such cases too, the relevant A and P arguments can be nominal, pronominal, animate or inanimate NPs (e.g. 'The Verbing of you, of it, of the house'; 'You are Verbed, the house is Verbed'). The markers used for these arguments, then, will be used with all of these NPs, and the resulting accusative or ergative markers are used with all of these NPs too. This is illustrated in (6) and (7), where accusative and ergative markers derived in this way are used, respectively, with nominal inanimate and pronominal animate arguments.

(6) Wayana (Carib; Gildea 1998: 201)
i-pakoro-**n** iri pək wai.
1-house-ACC make occupied.with 1.be

'I'm (occupied with) making my house.' (originally 'I am occupied with
my house's making.')

(7) Cariña (Carib; Gildea 1998: 169)
A-eena-ri̵ i-'**wa**-ma.
2-have-NMLZ 1-ERG-3.be

'I will have you.' (from a nominalized construction 'To me it will be your
having.')

On a similar note, loss of inflectional distinctions through sound change, leading to the loss of particular alignment patterns, targets specific forms because of
their phonological properties. This process, then, can affect different NP types
cross-linguistically, provided that the relevant forms have specific phonological
properties. This leads to different distributional restrictions for particular alignment patterns. In English, as detailed earlier, the process affected nouns as opposed to pronouns, leading to accusative alignment becoming restricted to pronouns. In Nganasan, however, a combination of sound change and analogical
levelling led to a loss of inflectional distinctions for pronouns, but not for nouns
(Filimonova 2005: 94–98). As a result, as can be seen from (8), accusative alignment became restricted to nouns, even though this configuration should be disfavored in terms of economy, because nominal P arguments are less in need of
disambiguation than pronominal ones.

(8) Nganasan (Uralic; Filimonova 2005: 94)

    a. **Mənə** nanuntə mintəl'i-ʔə-ŋ.
       1SG 2SG.LOC-INSTR take-INDEF-2SG

       'You have taken me with you.' (pronominals originally had dedicated
       accusative forms, e.g. *mənə-m* '1SG-ACC')

    b. ŋülœʒə tundi̵-**m** tandarku-čü.
       wolf fox-ACC chase-3SG.A

       'The wolf is chasing the fox.'

If there were principles that favor or disfavor particular distributional restrictions for accusative and ergative aligment because of properties of the resulting

grammatical configurations, we would not expect the development of these restrictions to be tied to specific source constructions and developmental mechanisms.

Finally, individual distributional restrictions develop through several distinct processes, which are rather different in nature and provide independent motivations for the restriction. In some cases, particular restrictions arise as accusative and ergative case markers develop through processes of context-driven reinterpretation of various types of source elements, which, for different reasons, are restricted in the same way. In other cases, the restrictions reflect the domain of application of different phonological processes. To the extent that different diachronic processes provide different motivations for particular distributional restrictions, explanations for these restrictions cannot be read off from the restrictions in themselves, because these can originate differently in different cases.

3 Some possible origins of zero vs. overt marking for singular and plural

Another well-known typological universal pertains to the use of zero vs. overt marking for singular and plural. Languages can use overt marking for plural and zero marking for singular, but usually not the other way round. A classical, result-oriented explanation for this pattern, as mentioned in Section 1, is in terms of economy. Speakers tend to use overt marking only for meanings that are more in need of disambiguation, and plural is more in need of disambiguation than singular due to its lower discourse frequency. As a result, overt marking can be limited to plural, whereas it will not be limited to singular (Greenberg 1966; Croft 2003; Haspelmath 2008). This explanation, however, is not supported by a number of diachronic processes that lead languages to have zero marked singulars and overtly marked plurals.

Often, in languages which make no distinction between singular and plural, an overt plural marker evolves through the reinterpretation of pre-existing expressions, whereas singulars retain zero marking. Sometimes, some expression takes on a plural meaning originally associated with a co-occurring expression. For example, in partitive constructions involving plural quantifiers ('many **of** them' > 'they PL'), the partitive marker can take on the meaning of plurality associated with the quantifier as the latter is lost. This process took place in Bengali, as illustrated in (9).

(9)   Bengali (Indo-Aryan; Chatterji 1926: 735–736)

    a. āmhā-**rā** såbå
       we-GEN all
       'all of us' (14th century)

    b. chēlē-**rā**
       child-GEN
       'children' (15th century)

In other cases, plurality becomes the central meaning of expressions inherently or contextually associated with this notion but originally used to encode other meanings, for example, distributive expressions ('house here and there') or expressions of multitude ('all', 'people'). This is illustrated in (10) and (11).

(10)   Southern Paiute (Uto-Aztecan; Sapir 1930–1931: 258)
    qa'nɪ / **qaŋqa'nɪ**
    house / house.DISTR
    'house, houses'

(11)   Maithili (Indo-Aryan: Yadav 1997: 69)
    jən   **səb**
    laborer all
    'laborers'

Another process that leads languages to have zero marking for singular and overt marking for plural is the elimination of an overt singular marker through regular sound change in a situation where both singular and plural are originally overtly marked. This was, for example, the case in English, where singular and plural were both originally overtly marked in most cases. The current configuration with zero marked singulars and -s marked plurals resulted from a series of sound changes that led to the elimination of all inflectional endings except genitive singular -s and plural -es (Mossé 1949).

These various processes do not appear to be triggered by the higher need to disambiguate plural as opposed to singular. In some cases, an overt plural marker arises as a result of a metonymization process whereby plural meaning is transfered from a quantifier to some other component of a complex expression. This is plausibly due to the co-occurrence of the two. In other cases, some expressions evolves into a plural marker because it is contextually or inherently associated with the notion of plurality, and this notion becomes the central meaning of the expression as some other meaning component is bleached. In yet other cases, a pre-existing overt singular marker is eliminated due to regular sound changes driven by the phonological properties of the marker.

The end result of the various processes, the use of overt marking for plural rather than singular, is directly motivated in terms of the properties of particular source constructions and developmental mechanisms. In many cases, an overt marker is used for plural because the source construction is one associated with the notion of plurality. Alternatively, sound changes leading to the elimination of an overt marker target singular rather than plural markers due to the phonological properties of the former. The fact that overt marking is restricted to plural, then, cannot be taken as evidence for principles that favor this particular configuration independently of particular source constructions and developmental mechanisms. As in the case of accusative and ergative case marking alignment, this point is further supported by the fact that other source constructions and developmental mechanisms give rise to different configurations, that is, overt marking for both singular and plural, or just for singular.

A case in point is provided by Kxoe, illustrated in Table 3 below. This language has gender markers derived from third person pronouns (Heine 1982). As the pronouns have overt singular and plural forms, the resulting gender markers also encode singular and plural, so that the language has overt marking not only for plural, but also for singular.

Table 3: Gender/number markers and third person pronouns in Kxoe (Khoisan; Heine 1982: 211)

		SG	PL	
Nouns	M	|ő̃a-**mà**	|ő̃a-||**uʻa**	'boy'
	F	|ő̃a-**hὲ**	|ő̃a-**djì**	'girl
	C	|ő̃a-(**'à**), |ő̃a-**djì**	ő̃a-**nà**	'child'
Pronouns	M	xà-**á**, á-**mà**, i-**mà**	xà-||**u̜á**, á-||**u̜á**, í-||**u̜á**	'he'
	F	xà-**hὲ**, á-**hὲ**, i–**hὲ**	xà-**djí**, á-**djí**, í-**djí**	'she'
	C	(xa-**'à**)	xà-**nà**, á-**nà**, í-**nà**	'it'

Also, as described above, partitive case markers can evolve into plural markers by taking on the plural meaning associated with a co-occurring plural quantifier. In expressions where the quantifier is singular ('one of them'), however, this same process can lead to the development of singular markers, sometimes leading to a configuration where only singular is overtly marked. This was the case in Imonda, which has zero marked plurals, but developed an overt non-plural (singular and dual) marker from a source case marker used in partitive constructions (Seiler 1985: 38–39).

(12) Imonda (Border; Seiler 1985: 194, 219)

    a. Agõ-**ianèi**-m   ainam fa-i-kõhõ.
        women-NONPL-GL quickly CLF-LNK-go
        'He grabbed the woman.'

    b. mag-m ad-**ianèi**-m
        one-GL boy-SRC-GL
        'to one of the boys'

Similar observations apply to loss of number markers through sound change. This process can affect either singular or plural markers depending on the phonological properties of the marker. From one language to another, then, the process may lead either to zero marked singulars and overtly marked plurals, as detailed above for English, or to the opposite configuration. In the Indo-Aryan language Sinhala, for example, some inanimate nouns have overtly marked singulars and zero marked plurals (e.g. *pot-a/pot* 'book-SG/book.PL'). This was a result of sound changes leading to the loss of the plural ending of a specific inflectional class in the ancestor language (Nitz & Nordhoff 2010: 250–256). Similarly, in Nchanti, a Beboid language, nouns in classes 3/4 have overt marking in the singular and zero marking in the plural, e.g. *kʷə́ŋ/kə́ŋ* 'firewood.SG/firewood.PL, *kʷē̄ē̄/kē̄ē̄* 'moon.SG/moon.PL'. Originally, both singular and plural were marked overtly through the two prefixes **u-* and **i-* respectively. As these were eliminated, the singular prefix led to the labialization of the initial consonant of the stem, while the plural prefix left no trace (Hombert 1980).

Finally, just like distributional restrictions for accusative and ergative case marking alignment, the fact that a language uses zero marking for singular and overt marking for plural can be a result of a variety of diachronic processes, which lead to this particular configuration for different reasons. In many cases, both singular and plural are originally zero marked (i.e., the language makes no distinction between the two), but zero marking becomes restricted to singular because different expressions, for different reasons, evolve into plural markers. In other cases, both singular and plural are originally overtly marked, and sound change leads to the loss of singular markers due to their phonological properties. Explanations for why overt marking is restricted to plural, then, cannot be read off from this configuration in itself, because it can originate differently in different cases.

4 Rare grammatical configurations and result-oriented explanations

Result-oriented explanations of typological universals are crucially based on the fact that certain logically possible grammatical configurations are significantly rarer than others in the world's languages. This is usually accounted for by postulating principles that both disfavor those configurations and favor some of the other configurations. For example, the rarity of configurations where singular is overtly marked and plural is zero marked is assumed to be due to the fact that these configurations are disfavored by economy, and hence will usually not occur in the world's languages. This same principle is assumed to also favor the opposite configuration, zero marking for singular and overt marking for plural, thus providing a motivation for the occurrence of this configuration.

Haspelmath (2019 [this volume]) uses this line of reasoning to claim that result-oriented explanations should be invoked even in cases where the development of some grammatical configuration is accounted for by the properties of particular source constructions or developmental mechanisms, rather than synchronic properties of the configuration in itself. Haspelmath concedes that, in such cases, there is no direct evidence that the occurrence of the configuration is motivated by principles pertaining to its synchronic properties (functional-adaptive principles, in his terminology). He argues, however, that this hypothesis is supported by two types of indirect evidence: the fact that other logically possible configurations are significantly rarer, and what he calls multi-convergence, the fact that different diachronic processes all lead to that particular configuration. According to Haspelmath, these facts can only be accounted for by assuming that the occurrence of the configuration is ultimately motivated by principles that favor that configuration independently of the diachronic processes that give rise to it. Haspelmath draws a parallel with the notion of adaptiveness in evolutionary biology (and other domains): The development of particular traits is independent of the fact that those traits are adaptive to the environment, in the sense of conferring an evolutionary advantage to the organisms carrying them, but adaptiveness provides the ultimate explanation for their spread and survival in a population.

There is, however, a logical fallacy in the idea that, if some principle motivates the non-occurrence of some configuration (and hence its rarity), then the occurrence of some other configuration is motivated by the same principle. The fact that some principle A provides the motivation for some phenomenon X can be framed as a logical implication, X → A (because X will always involve A, unless other motivations for X are also postulated). This implication means, however, that the absence of A will lead to phenomena different than X, that is, ~A → ~X, not that phenomena different from X are also motivated by A. This would be a distinct logical implication, ~X → A, with a different truth table. For example, if the non-occurrence of configurations where singular is overtly marked and plural is zero marked (X) is assumed to be due to economy (A), this means that principles other than economy (~A) will lead to the occurrence of other configurations (~X), not that the latter phenomenon is also due to economy. This undermines the general logic of result-oriented explanations, including Haspelmath's argument: From the fact that some principle provides a motivation for the non-occurrence of some configuration, we cannot conclude that it also provides a motivation for the occurrence of other configurations.

As for the multi-convergence argument, this ignores the fact that different diachronic processes can all lead to the same synchronic output for different reasons, as detailed in Sections 2 and 3. If the same synchronic output is motivated differently in different cases, multi-convergence cannot be taken as evidence for principles that favor that output independently of the individual processes that give rise to it. Instead, to the extent that the various processes recurrently take place in different languages, the cross-linguistic distribution of the output will be a combined result of the effects of each process.

From a logical point of view, source-oriented explanations do not rule out that the cross-linguistic distribution of particular grammatical configurations may ultimately also be determined by properties pertaining to the synchronic properties of the configuration, as assumed by Haspelmath. For example, these factors could play a role in the transmission of the configuration from one speaker to another, or its retention across different generations of speakers. This would be the equivalent of the notion of adaptive evolution through natural selection in evolutionary biology: particular genetic traits do not develop because they they confer an evolutionary advantage to the organisms carrying them, but this provides the ultimate explanation for their distribution in a population.[2]

---

[2] A referee suggests that this is similar to Lass's (1990) use of the notion of exaptation: particular grammatical traits may lose their original function, but they are retained in the language because they are deployed for novel functions. This, however, is meant to account for why particular traits survive in a language despite losing their original function, not why they are selected over others, as is the case with result-oriented explanations of typological universals and explanations of biological evolution in terms of adaptiveness through natural selection.

In evolutionary biology, however, there is direct evidence for adaptiveness, in that particular genetic traits make it demonstrably more likely for the organisms carrying them to survive and pass them on to their descendants. For languages, on the other hand, there is generally no evidence that the fact that some grammatical configuration conforms to the principles postulated in result-oriented explanations, for example economy, makes it more likely for that configuration to spread and survive in a speech community. In fact, there is a long tradition of linguistic thought in which the propagation of individual constructions within a speech community is entirely determined by social factors independent of particular inherent properties of the construction (see, for example, McMahon 1994 and Croft 2000 for reviews of the relevant issues and literature).

In principle, there is another sense in which particular grammatical configurations could be adaptive. While individual configurations directly reflect the properties of particular source constructions or developmental mechanisms, it could be the case that the specific diachronic processes that give rise to the configuration are ultimately favored by principles pertaining to its synchronic properties. For example, different processes of context-driven reinterpretation leading to overt marking for less frequent types of argument roles could be favored by the need to give overt expression to these roles. Similarly, different processes leading to zero marking for singulars (zero marking becoming restricted to singular due to the development of an overt plural marker, phonological erosion of an existing overt singular marker) could be favored by the lower need to give overt expression to singular as opposed to plural.

These assumptions, however, are not part of any standard account of the relevant processes in studies of language change (see Bybee et al. 1994: 298–300 and Slobin 2002: 381 for an explicit rejection of this view in regard to grammaticalization, as well as Cristofaro 2017 for more discussion). In fact, diachrony provides specific evidence against the idea that particular grammatical configurations develop both because of properties of particular source constructions or developmental mechanisms and because of principles that favor the configuration in itself. As detailed in Sections 2 and 3, different source constructions and developmental mechanisms give rise to different grammatical configurations, even when this goes against some postulated principle that favors some of these configurations as opposed to the others. This is not what one would expect if there were principles favoring particular grammatical configurations independently of the specific source constructions or developmental mechanisms that give rise to them.

All this means that, to the extent that a principled source-oriented explanation is available for the occurrence of particular grammatical configurations, explanations in terms of the synchronic properties of the configuration are redundant, because we do not have either direct or indirect evidence for these explanations (see Blevins 2004 for similar arguments in phonology, and Newmeyer 2002; 2004 for an application of this line of reasoning to optimality-theoretic models of typological universals). Of course, one still needs to account for the fact that certain logically possible grammatical configurations are significantly rarer than others. This phenomenon, however, is logically independent of the possible motivations for the occurrence of the more frequent configurations, as detailed above. To the extent that individual grammatical configurations arise due to properties of particular source constructions or developmental mechanisms, any differences in the frequency of particular configurations will reflect differences in the frequency of the source constructions or developmental mechanisms that give rise to those configurations. The higher frequency of particular configurations will then be a result of the higher frequency of the source constructions and developmental mechanisms that give rise to them, while the rarity of other configurations will be due to the rarity of possible source constructions or developmental mechanisms for those configurations (see Harris 2008 for an earlier formulation of this point in regard to tripartite case marking alignment). Frequency differences in the occurrence of particular source constructions or developmental mechanisms need to be accounted for, but they need not be related to any properties of the resulting configurations, so they should be investigated independently.

5 Concluding remarks

Source-oriented explanations of typological universals are in line with classical views of language change held within grammaticalization studies and historical linguistics in general. These views are manifested, for example, in accounts of the development of tense, aspect and mood systems, or alignment patterns (Bybee et al. 1994; Harris & Campbell 1995; Gildea 1998; Traugott & Dasher 2002, among others). In these accounts, grammatical change is usually not related to synchronic properties of the resulting constructions, for example the fact that the use of these constructions complies with some postulated principle of optimization of grammatical structure. Rather, grammatical change is usually a result of the properties of particular source constructions and the contexts in which they are used. In particular, new grammatical constructions recurrently emerge through processes of context-induced reinterpretation of pre-existing ones, and their distribution originally reflects the distribution of the source constructions.

In source-oriented explanations, the patterns captured by typological universals originate from several distinct diachronic processes, which involve different source constructions and developmental mechanisms. These processes recurrently take place in different languages, and are plausibly motivated by the same factors from one language to another. Individual patterns, however, are a combined result of the cross-linguistic frequencies of the various processes, rather than a result of some overarching principle independent of these processes.

While this scenario is more complex and less homogeneous than those assumed in result-oriented explanations, it is consistent with what is known about the actual origins of the relevant grammatical configurations in individual languages, and it makes it possible to address several facts not accounted for in these explanations.

For example, the patterns captured by typological universals usually have exceptions. This is in contrast with the assumption that these patterns reflect principles of optimization of grammatical structure that are valid for all languages, because in this case one has to account for why these principles are violated in some languages. Also, individual principles invoked in result-oriented explanations are often in contrast with some of the grammatical configurations captured by individual universals. For example, the idea that zero marking of more frequent meanings is motivated by economy is in contrast with the fact that these meanings are overtly marked in many languages.

These facts have sometimes been dealt with in terms of competing motivations models, but a general problem with this approach is that it may lead to a proliferation of explanatory principles for which no independent evidence is available (Newmeyer 1998: 145–153, Cristofaro 2014, among others). If the patterns captured by typological universals reflect the properties of different source constructions and developmental mechanisms, however, then it is natural that they should have exceptions, because not all languages will have the same source constructions, nor will particular developmental mechanisms be activated in all languages. Principles pertaining to the synchronic properties of the pattern will fail to account for all of the relevant grammatical configurations because the pattern is not actually motivated by those principles.

Over the past decades, several linguists have emphasized the need for source-oriented explanations of typological universals (Bybee 1988; 2006; 2008; Aristar 1991; Gildea 1998; Cristofaro 2013; 2014; 2017; Anderson 2016). This view, however, has not really made its way into the actual typological practice, despite the close

Sonia Cristofaro

integration between typology and studies of language change (a fully fledged research approach along these lines is, on the other hand, the Evolutionary Phonology framework developed in Blevins 2004). While diachronic evidence about the origins of the patterns captured by individual universals is much scantier and less systematic than the synchronic evidence about these patterns, it poses specific foundational problems for existing result-oriented explanations of these universals. These problems point to a new research agenda for typology, one focusing on what source constructions and developmental mechanisms play a role in the shaping of individual cross-linguistic patterns, as well as why certain source constructions or developmental mechanisms are rarer than others.

Abbreviations

The paper conforms to the Leipzig Glossing Rules. Additional abbreviations include:

C	common	NONPL	non-plural
GL	goal	SRC	source
LNK	linker		

References

Anderson, Stephen R. 2016. Synchronic versus diachronic explanation and the nature of the Language Faculty. *Annual Review of Linguistics* 2(1). 11–31. DOI:10.1146/annurev-linguistics-011415-040735

Aristar, Anthony R. 1991. On diachronic sources and synchronic pattern: An investigation into the origin of linguistic universals. *Language* 67(1). 1–33.

Blake, Barry J. 2001. *Case*. 2nd edn. Cambridge: Cambridge University Press. DOI:10.1017/CBO9781139164894

Blevins, Juliette. 2004. *Evolutionary phonology: The emergence of sound patterns*. Cambridge: Cambridge University Press. DOI:10.1017/CBO9780511486357

Bubenik, Vit. 1998. *A historical syntax of late middle Indo-Aryan (Apabrahṃśa)*. Amsterdam, Philadalphia: John Benjamins. DOI:10.1075/cilt.165

Bybee, Joan L. 1988. The diachronic dimension in explanation. In John A. Hawkins (ed.), *Explaining language universals*, 350–379. Oxford: Blackwell.

Bybee, Joan L. 2006. Language change and universals. In Ricardo Mairal & Juana Gil (eds.), *Linguistic universals*, 179–194. Cambridge: Cambridge University Press. DOI:10.1017/CBO9780511618215.009

Bybee, Joan L. 2008. Formal universals as emergent phenomena: The origins of structure preservation. In Jeff Good (ed.), *Linguistic universals and language change*, 108–121. Oxford: Oxford University Press. DOI:10.1093/acprof:oso/9780199298495.003.0005

Bybee, Joan L., Revere D. Perkins & William Pagliuca. 1994. *The evolution of grammar: Tense, aspect and modality in the languages of the world.* Chicago: University of Chicago Press.

Chappell, Hilary. 2013. Pan-Sinitic object markers: Morphology and syntax. In Guangshun Cao, Hilary Chappell, Redouane Djamouri & Thekla Wiebusch (eds.), *Breaking down the barriers: Interdisciplinary studies in Chinese linguistics and beyond*, 785–816. Taipei: Academia Sinica.

Chatterji, Suniti Kumar. 1926. *The origin and development of the Bengali language.* Calcutta: Calcutta University Press.

Comrie, Bernard. 1981. *Language universals and linguistic typology: Syntax and morphology.* Chicago: University of Chicago Press.

Comrie, Bernard. 1989. *Language universals and linguistic typology.* 2nd edn. Oxford: Basil Blackwell.

Corbett, Greville C. 2000. *Number.* Cambridge: Cambridge University Press. DOI:10.1017/CBO9781139164344

Creissels, Denis. 2008. Direct and indirect explanations of typological regularities: The case of alignment variations. *Folia Linguistica* 42(1). 1–38. DOI:10.1515/FLIN.2008.1

Cristofaro, Sonia. 2013. The referential hierarchy: Reviewing the evidence in diachronic perspective. In Dik Bakker & Martin Haspelmath (eds.), *Languages across boundaries: Studies in the memory of Anna Siewierska*, 69–93. Berlin & New York: Mouton de Gruyter. DOI:10.1515/9783110331127.69

Cristofaro, Sonia. 2014. Competing motivations and diachrony: What evidence for what motivations? In Brian MacWhinney, Andrej Malchukov & Edith Moravcsik (eds.), *Competing motivations in grammar and usage*, 282–298. Oxford: Oxford University Press.

Cristofaro, Sonia. 2017. Implicational universals and dependencies between grammatical phenomena. In N. J. Enfield (ed.), *Dependencies in language: On the causal ontology of linguistic systems*, 9–24. Berlin: Language Science Press. DOI:10.5281/zenodo.573777

Croft, William. 2000. *Explaining language change: An evolutionary approach.* Harlow, Essex: Longman.

Croft, William. 2003. *Typology and universals.* 2nd edn. Cambridge: Cambridge University Press. DOI:10.1017/CBO9780511840579

Cyffer, Norbert. 1998. *A sketch of Kanuri*. Köln: Rüdiger Köppe.

DeLancey, Scott. 1981. An interpretation of split ergativity and related patterns. *Language* 57(3). 626–657. DOI:10.2307/414343

Dixon, R. M. W. 1979. Ergativity. *Language* 55(1). 59–138. DOI:10.2307/412519

Dixon, R. M. W. 1994. *Ergativity*. Cambridge: Cambridge University Press. DOI:10.1017/CBO9780511611896

Filimonova, Elena. 2005. The noun phrase hierarchy and relational marking: Problems and counterevidence. *Linguistic Typology* 9(1). 77–113. DOI:10.1515/lity.2005.9.1.77

Gildea, Spike. 1998. *On reconstructing grammar: Comparative Cariban morphosyntax*. Oxford: Oxford University Press.

Greenberg, Joseph H. 1966. *Language universals, with special reference to feature hierarchies*. The Hague: Mouton. DOI:10.1515/9783110899771

Harris, Alice C. 2008. On the explanation of typologically unusual structures. In Jeff Good (ed.), *Linguistic universals and language change*, 59–76. Oxford: Oxford University Press. DOI:10.1093/acprof:oso/9780199298495.003.0003

Harris, Alice C. & Lyle Campbell. 1995. *Historical syntax in cross-linguistic perspective*. Cambridge: Cambridge University Press. DOI:10.1017/CBO9780511620553

Haspelmath, Martin. 2006. Against markedness (and what to replace it with). *Journal of Linguistics* 42. 25–70. DOI:10.1017/S0022226705003683

Haspelmath, Martin. 2008. Creating economical morphosyntactic patterns in language change. In Jeff Good (ed.), *Linguistic universals and language change*, 185–214. Oxford: Oxford University Press. DOI:10.1093/acprof:oso/9780199298495.003.0008

Haspelmath, Martin. 2019. Can cross-linguistic regularities be explained by constraints on change? In Karsten Schmidtke-Bode, Natalia Levshina, Susanne Maria Michaelis & Ilja A. Seržant (eds.), *Explanation in typology: Diachronic sources, functional motivations and the nature of the evidence*, 1–23. Berlin: Language Science Press. DOI:10.5281/zenodo.2583804

Haspelmath, Martin & APiCS Consortium. 2013. Alignment of case marking of personal pronouns. In Susanne Maria Michaelis, Philippe Maurer, Martin Haspelmath & Magnus Huber (eds.), *The atlas of pidgin and creole language structures*, 232–235. Oxford: Oxford University Press.

Hawkins, John A. 2004. *Efficiency and complexity in grammars*. Oxford: Oxford University Press. DOI:10.1093/acprof:oso/9780199252695.001.0001

Heine, Bernd. 1982. African noun class systems. In Hansjakob Seiler & Christian Lehmann (eds.), *Apprehension: Das sprachliche Erfassen von Gegenständen, Teil I: Bereich und Ordnung der Phänomene*, 189–216. Tübingen: Narr.

Hercus, Luise A. 1982. *The Bagandji language* (Pacific Linguistics. Series B-67). Canberra: The Australian National University. DOI:10.15144/PL-B67

Hombert, Jean-Marie. 1980. Noun classes of the Beboid languages. *Southern California Occasional Papers in Linguistics* 8. 83–98.

König, Christa. 2008. *Case in Africa*. Oxford: Oxford University Press.

Lass, Roger. 1990. How to do things with junk: Exaptation in language evolution. *Journal of Linguistics* 26(1). 79–102. DOI:10.1017/S0022226700014432

Lord, Carol. 1993. *Historical change in serial verb constructions*. Amsterdam, Philadelphia: John Benjamins Publishing. DOI:10.1075/tsl.26

McGregor, William B. 2006. Focal and optional ergative marking in Warrwa (Kimberley, Western Australia). *Lingua* 116(4). 393–423. DOI:10.1016/j.lingua.2005.02.002

McGregor, William B. 2008. Indexicals as sources of case markers in Australian languages. In Folke Josephson & Ingmar Söhrman (eds.), *Interdependence of diachronic and synchronic analyses*, 299–321. Amsterdam, Philadelphia: John Benjamins. DOI:10.1075/slcs.103.15mcg

McMahon, April A. M. S. 1994. *Understanding language change*. Cambridge: Cambridge University Press. DOI:10.1017/CBO9781139166591

Mithun, Marianne. 2005. Ergativity and language contact on the Oregon Coast: Alsea, Siuslaw and Coos. *Berkeley Linguistics Society* 26(2). 77–95. DOI:10.3765/bls.v26i2.1172

Mossé, Fernand. 1949. *Manuel de l'anglais du moyen âge des origines au XIVme siècle. Moyen-anglais. Tome premier: Grammaire et textes*. Paris: Aubier.

Newmeyer, Frederick J. 1998. *Language form and language function*. Cambridge, MA: MIT Press.

Newmeyer, Frederick J. 2002. Optimality and functionality: A critique of functionally-based optimality-theoretic syntax. *Natural Language & Linguistic Theory* 20(1). 43–80.

Newmeyer, Frederick J. 2004. Typological evidence and universal grammar. *Studies in Language* 28(3). 527–548. DOI:10.1075/bct.7.03new

Nitz, Eike & Sebastian Nordhoff. 2010. Subtractive plural morphology in Sinhala. In Jan Wohlgemuth & Michael Cysouw (eds.), *Rara & Rarissima: Collecting and interpreting unusual characteristics of human languages*, 247–66. Berlin, New York: Mouton de Gruyter. DOI:10.1515/9783110228557.247

Pensado, Carmen. 1995. La creatión del complemento directo prepositional y la flexión de los pronombres personales en las lenguas románicas. In Carmen Pensado (ed.), *El complemento directo preposicional*, 179–233. Madrid: Visor Libros.

Rohlfs, Gerhard. 1984. *Von Rom zur Romania: Aspekte und Probleme romanischer Sprachgeschichte*. Tübingen: Narr.

Sapir, Edward. 1930–1931. *The Southern Paiute language*. Boston: American Academy of Arts & Sciences.

Seiler, Walter. 1985. *Imonda, a Papuan language* (Pacific Linguistics. Series B-93). Canberra: The Australian National University. DOI:10.15144/PL-B93

Silverstein, Michael. 1976. Hierarchy of features and ergativity. In R. M. W. Dixon (ed.), *Grammatical categories in Australian languages*, 112–171. Canberra: Australian Institute of Aboriginal Studies.

Slobin, Dan I. 2002. Language evolution, acquisition and diachrony: Probing the parallels. In Talmy Givón & Betram F. Malle (eds.), *The evolution of language out of pre-language*, 375–392. Amsterdam, Philadelphia: John Benjamins. DOI:10.1075/tsl.53.20slo

Song, Jae Jung. 2001. *Linguistic typology: Morphology and syntax*. Harlow: Longman.

Traugott, Elizabeth Closs & Richard B. Dasher. 2002. *Regularity in semantic change*. Cambridge: Cambridge University Press. DOI:10.1017/CBO9780511486500

Yadav, Ramawatar. 1997. *A reference grammar of Maithili*. New Delhi: Munshiram Manoharlal.

Chapter 3

Some language universals are historical accidents

Jeremy Collins

Radboud University Nijmegen

In this short paper, I elaborate on previous work by Givón (1971) and Aristar (1991) to argue that a substantial part of the well-known word-order correlations is best explained by grammaticalisation processes. Functional-adaptive accounts in terms of processing or learning constraints are currently weakly substantiated, and they suffer from the fact that they do not adequately control for language-internal inheritance patterns. More generally, historical relatedness between different types of phrases constitutes an important confound in typological research, one that needs to be taken seriously before word-order correlations are motivated by anything other than the diachronic patterns that link the word order pairs in question.

1 Introduction

There are surprisingly few properties that all languages share. Almost every attempt at articulating a genuine language universal tends to have at least one exception, as documented in Evans & Levinson (2009). However, there are nontrivial properties that are found in if not literally all languages, enough of them and across multiple language families and independent areas of the world, that they demand an explanation.

An example is the fact that languages have predictable word orders. If a language has the verb before the object, it tends to have prepositions rather than postpositions, as in English; if the verb is after the object, it is a good bet that the language will have postpositions rather than prepositions (Greenberg 1963). The ordering of different elements such as a possessed noun and its possessor, or a noun and elaborate modifiers (complex adjective phrases, relative clauses), are to some extent free to vary among languages, but again tend to fall into correlating

Jeremy Collins. 2019. Some language universals are historical accidents. In Karsten Schmidtke-Bode, Natalia Levshina, Susanne Maria Michaelis & Ilja A. Seržant (eds.), *Explanation in typology: Diachronic sources, functional motivations and the nature of the evidence*, 47–61. Berlin: Language Science Press. DOI:10.5281/zenodo.2583808 types (Dryer 1992; 2011). Why should knowing the word order of one category in a language help predict the orderings of other categories? One prominent view holds that these patterns reflect an innate harmonic ordering principle of Universal Grammar, which is ultimately argued to solve the logical problem of language acquisition (Pinker 1994; Baker 2001; Roberts 2007). This would amount to what Haspelmath (2019 [this volume]) calls a "representational constraint" on the shape of grammars. Another possible explanation is that word-order correlations have evolved in the service of efficient language processing (e.g. Hawkins 1994; Kirby & Hurford 1997), i.e. for functional-adaptive reasons. We find this view in the functional-typological literature (e.g. Dryer 1992; Evans & Levinson 2009) as well as in computer simulations in the literature on language evolution (Van Everbroeck 1999).

However, I would argue that many of these patterns are not evidence of our psychological preferences, but are accidental consequences of language history. More specifically, they are accidental in the sense that they arise as a by-product of grammaticalisation processes. These processes do not seem to have word-order correlations as a goal, nor is there good evidence for a "pull force" in that direction. Accordingly, grammaticalisation is an *alternative* to functional motivations here, and an understanding of this historical dimension is thus crucial to explaining word-order correlations. In this short paper, I first elaborate this claim (§2) based on an earlier publication (Collins 2012), before I outline its consequences for typological theory and practice (§3). In doing so, I am extending a line of argumentation by Givón (1971) and Aristar (1991), but I relate the discussion specifically to the concerns of the present volume, and to Haspelmath's position paper in particular.

2 Word-order correlations as a result of grammaticalisation

Grammaticalisation is the process by which new grammatical categories can be formed from other (often lexical) categories. For example, Mandarin Chinese has a class of words which might be called prepositions from a cross-linguistic point of view but which clearly have their historical roots in verbs. An example is 從 *cóng*, which in modern Mandarin is a preposition meaning 'from' but which in classical Chinese was a verb meaning 'to follow'. It has lost its ability to be used as a full verb, requiring another verb such as 'come' in the sentence, just as English requires a verb in the sentence *I come from London*. Other Chinese prepositions such as 跟 *gēn* 'with' also have a verbal origin, and many preposition-like words such as 給 *gěi* 'for' and 在 *zài* 'in/at' even retain verbal meanings ('give' and 'to be present') and verbal syntax (such as being able to be used as the sole verb in the sentence and to take aspect marking). These patterns of inheritance directly explain why the two types of constituents (i.e. PP and VP) have the same word order: Prepositions and verbs were once the same category, and they simply have not changed their word orders since then. Since the verb precedes its NP object in classical and modern Chinese, its prepositional offspring in modern Chinese also precedes its NP complement. Interestingly, Chinese also has postpositions, such as *li* 'in', and these, too, are simply continuations of their lexical sources (cf. also Dryer 2019 [this volume]). Thus *li* is etymologically 'interior' or 'village', hence *fangzi li* 'in the house' might be glossed more literally as 'the house's inside'. Again, the ordering of the younger construction as noun (*fangzi*)–postposition (*li*) reflects the order of the older construction with genitive (*fangzi*)–noun (*li*). Very similar remarks apply to Niger-Congo languages like Dagaare in Ghana, which also shows typologically mixed adpositional phrases (Bodomo 1997).

More generally, the pattern of adpositions inheriting the ordering of the noun or verb they derive from is replicated in different language families: We find it in many Oceanic languages (Lynch et al. 2002: 51), where adpositions are transparently nouns and reflect whatever ordering of genitive–noun the language has (hence it can be either prepositional, as in Hawaiian, or postpositional, as in Motu); we also see it in Indo-European languages (e.g. English *across* < 13 ct. Anglo-French *an cros* 'on cross' (Bordet & Jamet 2010: 16)), in Japanese (e.g. *kara* 'from' < 'way', *si* restrictive particle < 'do' (Frellesvig 2010: 132–135)), in Australian languages in which adpositions are morphologically still nouns (Dixon 2002), in Tibetan and Burmese (DeLancey 1997), and so on. Heine & Kuteva (2007: 62) even remark that "we are not aware of any language that has not undergone such a process".

Grammaticalisation can also often explain the ordering of verb and object correlating with genitive and noun ordering (Dryer 2011). Certain types of verb phrase derive historically from noun phrases made up of a nominalised verb and its patient argument in a possessive construction. An example is Ewe:

(1) Ewe (Atlantic-Congo, Gbe; Claudi 1994: 220)
      Me-le   é-kpɔ   dzí.
      1SG.-be.at 3SG.POSS/OBJ-see surface/on

      'I am seeing him.' (lit. 'I am on his seeing.').

Ewe is normally SVO but employs the genitive–noun ordering here ('his seeing'), creating a construction which is SOV. Nominalisations of this kind are used cross-linguistically for expressing aspect (such as the continuous aspect in Ewe), for subordinate clauses (expressing 'I was surprised that he saw me' as 'I was surprised at his seeing of me' in Javanese, cf. Ogloblin 2005: 618) and for voice marking (in Austronesian languages, cf. Himmelmann 2005: 174). These verb phrases can become the most frequently used and unmarked verb phrases in the languages, thus the basic verb–object order of a language can evolve from a genitive–noun construction, even if the nominal origins of the verb form are no longer transparent.

This development of (main-clause) verb phrases from nominalised verbs with a possessor object is again attested in very different language families, although it is more complicated to reconstruct. A typical example is the evolution of VOS ordering in Proto-Austronesian, which has been inherited by over a thousand Austronesian languages or evolved further into SVO or VSO (Adelaar 2005: 7). It is now generally accepted that verb phrases in Austronesian languages evolved from nominalising verbs, with a sentence such as 'The children are looking for the house' deriving from a Proto-Austronesian construction of the type 'The children are the searchers of the house'. Starosta et al. (1982) as well as Kaufman (2009) present several pieces of evidence in favour of this diachronic hypothesis: For example, the voice markers on verbs derive from nominalising morphemes, cognates of which still exist in Tagalog and other languages, such as the locative voice marker *an* which is also used for deriving place names (*aklat-an* 'library' < *aklat* 'book'). Moreover, the direct object of the verb is marked with the genitive marker *ng* or put into the genitive case if a pronoun. Both nominalisation and the use of equational sentences of the form AB 'A is B' are extremely common in conservative Austronesian languages and presumably were in Proto-Austronesian, allowing this frequently used construction to become a standard form of predication. Thus the verb–object ordering in Austronesian languages derives simply from the noun–genitive ordering of Proto-Austronesian, which is still retained in these languages. At a stroke this word-order correlation is accounted for in roughly a sixth of the world's languages.

As Sasse (2009: 167) notes in a comment on Kaufman (2009), the situation in Austronesian is "not as 'exotic' as it seemed to be at first sight, especially not for a Semiticist or an Afroasiaticist". He notes that the Cushitic languages also replaced their finite verb forms with participles and are used with dative marking on the agent, in effect saying 'I have heard it' as 'To me was hearing' (Sasse 2009: 174); and that the dative pronouns eventually grammaticalised further to finite verbal morphology. This change also took place in the Iranian and Indo-Aryan languages, stretching over a large linguistic area.

Sasse also notes independent developments of agents marked with genitive case in Mayan and Inuit languages, and Gildea (1997) made a similar reconstruction for the Cariban language family, of which the famous OVS language Hixkaryana is an example: It has genitive marking on the object, effectively expressing 'the enemy will destroy the city' as 'it will be the city's destruction by the enemy' (Gildea 1997: 153), explaining among other things why the subject is placed last, and why it has ergative marking. One can add to this list many languages in Asia, as described in Yap et al. (2011), such as Tibeto-Burman languages that often use nominalised forms in main clauses (e.g. 'goat-killing exists' for 'he is killing a goat', cf. DeLancey 2011: 349), and even Japanese, in which argument markers such as *ga* were originally genitive markers (Shinzato 2011: 461). Examples of Niger-Congo languages such as Ewe were given earlier and are discussed by Claudi (1994), while Heine describes how many Nilo-Saharan and Chadic languages render desiderative sentences in the following way:

(2) Angas (Afro-Asiatic, Chadic; Heine 2009: 31)
     Musa rot   dyip   kə-shwe.
     Musa want harvest POSS-corn

     'Musa wants to harvest corn.' (lit. 'Musa wants the harvesting of the corn.')

The historical data thus show that these processes of grammatical change are not limited to individual languages or families but can instead be found much more widely, and independently of one another. They lead us to predict, then, that ultimately all correlations between the ordering of elements in verb phrases (V–NP), adpositional phrases (P–NP) and possessive noun phrases (GEN–NP) are due to direct historical connections between pairs of phrases (cf. also Croft 2003: 77–78 for more discussion of such pairs). In the next section, I consider the implications of this assumption for both explanation and methodology in linguistic typology.

3 Consequences for typology

As historical evidence for the grammaticalisation account is accumulating, one may ask whether this makes alternative, functional-adaptive explanations invalid. Recall from above that on non-nativist approaches, word-order correlations are often argued to make sentences easier or more efficient to parse in real time, as compared to sentences with mixed head–dependent ordering patterns (e.g. Hawkins 2004). Is it possible that these factors play a role alongside grammaticalisation, such that, for example, processing demands filter out certain difficult-to-process constructions, as Kirby & Hurford (1997) suggest (cf. also Christiansen 2000)? Put somewhat differently, could it not be the case that grammaticalisation happens to produce orderings that are easy (or easier) to parse?

There is currently not much evidence to substantiate this view. From a theoretical perspective, there is no indication that the processes involved in grammaticalisation are instigated by considerations of efficient parsing or learning. They happen through pragmatic inference in specific communicative contexts (Hopper & Traugott 2003: Ch. 4), through widespread metaphorical mappings (cf. Deutscher 2005: Ch. 4) and by means of chunking of repeated sequences (Bybee 2002). Through these mechanisms, a new construction begins to emerge that gradually emancipates from its original lexical source. Since it is gradual, this process often creates a chain of intermediate cases, such as denominal adpositions in Tibetan, some of which still require genitive marking (e.g. *mdun* 'front') while others have shed this marking (e.g. *nang* 'inside'; cf. DeLancey 1997: 58–59). In other words, grammaticalisation has its origin in common non-linguistic processes (cf. also Bybee 2010: 6–8) and has predictable consequences, such as the gradual and sometimes only partial elimination of the morphology associated with the source. Importantly, a hallmark of grammaticalisation is syntagmatic "freezing" (Croft 2000: 159; cf. also Lehmann 2015[1982]: 168), so that the order of the elements in the new construction mirrors the order of elements in the source. The result is a "correlation" between the syntagmatic structure of the old and the new construction, but one that effectively rests on inertia rather than overarching processing principles that work towards a correlation.

From a methodological perspective, processing and learning accounts are an example of a broader trend of the "ad hoc search for functions that match the universals to be explained", as Kirby (1999: 13) puts it. Attempts in the evolutionary literature to simulate processing or learning with computers in order to derive Greenberg's word order universals (e.g. Van Everbroeck 1999; Kirby & Christiansen 2003), have a particularly "just-so" flavour: All that computer simulations can do is show that processing or learning preferences of individuals can cause these correlations to emerge over time, all other historical factors being equal, not that they are actually responsible. What we would thus need is independent historical evidence that processing concerns do, in fact, guide historical change. There are some attempts to show this, for example, in earlier English (e.g. Fischer 1992; Clark et al. 2008), when the language appeared to converge on the word-order correlations after a period of freer word order. This could indeed be evidence for word-order correlations emerging at least in part out of processing considerations; but there are other possibilities in this case which need to be investigated further, such as it being related to the rise of analytic verb forms and periphrastic *do*, to the loss of inflections or as a result of contact from French (cf. also Fischer & van der Wurff 2006: 187–188 for some of the controversies). The historical role of processing is unclear even in this case, and there is no conclusive cross-linguistic evidence for it either.

One possibility for establishing such causal relations cross-linguistically would be to look for cases of correlated evolution, i.e. situations in which a change in one word order can be shown to be followed by a change in another word order in the history of a language, or in its descendants. For example, if a language has verb–object order and prepositions but then changes to having object–verb order and postpositions, then this suggests that the two word orders are functionally linked (if this event takes place after any grammaticalisation linking these verbs and postpositions). The only solid statistical test of this so far has been a widely discussed study by Dunn et al. (2011). Dunn and colleagues examined the ways in which four language families have developed (Bantu, Austronesian, Indo-European and Uto-Aztecan) and tested models of word order change using a Bayesian phylogenetic method for analysing correlated evolution. They found that some word orders do indeed change together: For example, the order of verb and object seems to change simultaneously with the order of adposition and noun in Indo-European. A model in which these two word orders are dependent is preferred over a model in which they are independent with a Bayes factor of above 5, a conventional threshold for significance. This seems to vindicate the idea that adpositions and verb-object order are functionally linked in Indo-European, and the pattern also holds up in Austronesian. It does not show up in the smaller and younger families Uto-Aztecan and Bantu, although that may be because of the low statistical power of this test when applied to small language families (cf. Croft et al. 2011). But a more important drawback is that there is no control for language contact. What could be happening is that some Indo-European languages in India have different word orders because of the languages that they are near, such as Dravidian languages, which also have object-verb order and postpositions. A similar point could be made about the Austronesian languages that undergo word order change, which are found in a single group of Western Oceanic languages on the coast of New Guinea, which is otherwise dominated by languages with object–verb order and postpositions.

In the context of the present discussion, an important result of Dunn et al.'s (2011) paper is that word orders are very stable, staying the same over tens of thousands of years of evolutionary time (i.e. the total amount of time over multiple branches of the families). In this light, it is also instructive to note that some typologically "mixed" or non-correlating languages show the same inert behaviour: Despite the fact that grammaticalisation has produced a mixture of prepositions and postpositions (e.g. in Chinese or Dagaare), the resulting systems have also survived for many generations, or even thousands of years, without showing any inclination to change. This, too, is a problem for processing-based theories, which sometimes explicitly predict that such inconsistencies should die out (e.g. Kirby & Hurford 1997).

In the absence of convincing evidence for functional-adaptive motivations, I suggest that we accept that different types of syntactic constituents share their ordering patterns because they are historically related to each other, i.e. because they are linked by common ancestry. This also has important methodological consequences for typology. The kind of historical relatedness we observe here qualifies as a subtle, language-internal variant of Galton's problem (cf. Cysouw 2011 for an introduction), and it is thus actually a *confound* in typological samples. Just as other, more widely known, types of historical relatedness, such as a genealogical or areal interaction between two data points in a sample, need to be controlled for before one can test for a typological correlation, so does the language-internal historical relatedness between the grammatical patterns that make up that correlation. Put differently, languages in which possessor arguments are known to have developed from former object arguments and have simply adopted their order from this source, do not constitute an independent data point in support of the alleged word-order correlation. For typological practice, this entails that we need large databases of attested grammaticalisation pathways, and that we need to examine more carefully the actual markers and their (likely) etymologies before we set out to test a functional-adaptive hypothesis. In principle, it would then be possible to inspect whether certain grammaticalisation pathways tend to be taken only in certain types of languages; for example, do postpositions only develop from nouns in a genitive construction ('table's head' > 'table on') if the language also places the verb after the object? It is easy enough to find exceptions to that, such as Dagaare (Atlantic-Congo), which has taken this route to postpositions despite being a VO language (Bodomo 1997). But in a large database, we might still find interesting structural constraints, as well as geographical patterns, that could potentially speak for or against functional-adaptive motivations in addition to grammaticalisation.

For now, the major point is that the historical non-independence of data points can create correlations that are not causal. Such spurious correlations are well-known from non-linguistic research (cf., e.g., the spurious correlation between chocolate consumption and Nobel Prize winners; cf. also Roberts & Winters 2013 for further discussion), and my claim in this paper is that this is a serious methodological pitfall in the domain of word-order correlations. Given the naturalness of grammaticalisation, and the above observation that word orders tend to be preserved and long retained after grammaticalisation, invoking functional-adaptive motivations to explain the correlations in question is not only redundant, but actually wrong-headed. It is as if one wanted to claim that there was a deeper ecological reason why chimpanzees and humans share 98.8% or so of their DNA, rather than just the primary historical reason, which is that they have a common ancestor.

Having said this, it should be pointed out that I am neither arguing against functional-adaptive explanations in general, nor am I denying the relevance of processing to understanding word order patterns as such, including some combinations of word order that tend to be preferred over others. For example, the fact that VO languages strongly tend to have postnominal relative clauses is plausibly related to processing constraints (Hawkins 2004). Similarly, correlations between numeral–noun and adjective–noun ordering do not have a clear explanation in terms of grammaticalisation, but they do seem to be functionally linked and hence show interesting dependencies in experiments in artificial language learning (e.g. Culbertson et al. 2012; cf. also Dryer 2019 [this volume]). But with more and more diachronic evidence coming to light, historical links between many grammatical categories (VPs, auxiliaries, genitives, adpositions) can no longer be dismissed as marginal and as "lack[ing] generality" (Hawkins 1983: 131). Our default assumption, then, should be that the core word-order correlations are first and foremost an accidental by-product of grammaticalisation.

Haspelmath (2019 [this volume]) actually acknowledges this type of explanation, at least for the ordering patterns of adpositional phrases, and labels it a "mutational constraint" – a situation in which historical sources and grammaticalisation pathways directly determine the synchronic outcomes and hence make functional-adaptive explanations superfluous. On the other hand, he rejects "common pathways" as too weak to have explanatory power in typology. But how common is "common", and when do we begin to speak of a mutational constraint? It is perfectly possible that common pathways (such as those documented in Heine & Kuteva 2002; 2007), while not exhausting the possible sources and routes, are still frequent enough to produce a principled synchronic result. Therefore, I disagree with Haspelmath (p. 15) that we need not be able to understand the diachronic patterns behind a universal tendency if there is a good functional-adaptive motivation available for it. In the case of word-order correlations, and possibly other domains of grammar, it is the other way around: We first need to understand the diachronic links between different types of phrases and then control for them when we attempt to establish whether there are universal correlations beyond historical dependencies at all. It may turn out that the real question is why it should ever be the case that the order of grammaticalised categories, such as adpositions, genitives or auxiliaries does *not* correlate with that of their source constructions.

4 Conclusion

Word-order correlations are often invoked as evidence for universals of language acquisition or language processing. In this paper, I have argued that, before we can do so, it is important to understand the historical background of these patterns, which standard interpretations do not take into account. Given the naturalness and the non-teleological nature of grammaticalisation processes, it should be our default assumption that the order of grammaticalised categories retains the order of their respective source constructions. From this perspective, word-order correlations are far from mysterious and, in many cases, do not require functional-adaptive motivations (such as specific processing principles) or innate constraints (such as a head-ordering parameter). Instead, the correlations arise during the creation of new constructions by extending old constructions. The grammaticalisation processes involved are well-understood and ubiquitous (cf. Bybee 2015). And although we will never be able to have a full picture of the possible routes that lead to adpositions, auxiliaries, genitives, etc., the ones we know of seem common enough to produce the correlations in question. At the very least, they constitute language-internal dependencies, in Galton's spirit, that need to be controlled for in any typological investigation of word-order correlations, in addition to areal dependencies that hold across languages. If they are not, one runs the risk of erroneously inferring causation from correlation, as the word-order correlations would appear so strong that they require a deeper explanation, when in fact they are largely dependencies built into the sample.

Acknowledgements

I would like to thank the editors of the present volume, and Karsten Schmidtke-Bode in particular, for detailed discussion and extensive editorial help in compiling this paper, which is based largely on an earlier publication (Collins 2012) and a more recent blog post (Collins 2016).

References

Adelaar, Alexander. 2005. The Austronesian languages of Asia and Madagascar: A historical perspective. In Alexander Adelaar & Nikolaus P. Himmelmann (eds.), *The Austronesian languages of Asia and Madagascar*, 1–42. London, New York: Routledge. DOI:10.4324/9780203821121

Aristar, Anthony R. 1991. On diachronic sources and synchronic pattern: An investigation into the origin of linguistic universals. *Language* 67(1). 1–33.

Baker, Mark C. 2001. *The atoms of language: The mind's hidden rules of grammar.* Oxford: Oxford University Press.

Bodomo, Adams. 1997. *The structure of Dagaare.* Stanford: CSLI publications.

Bordet, Lucile & Denis Jamet. 2010. Are English prepositions grammatical or lexical morphemes? *Cercles: Occasional Papers.* 1–26.

Bybee, Joan L. 2002. Sequentiality as the basis of constituent structure. *Typological Studies in Language* 53. 109–134. DOI:10.1075/tsl.53.07byb

Bybee, Joan L. 2010. *Language, usage and cognition.* Cambridge: Cambridge University Press. DOI:10.1017/CBO9780511750526.011

Bybee, Joan L. 2015. *Language change.* Cambridge: Cambridge University Press. DOI:10.1017/CBO9781139096768

Christiansen, Morten H. 2000. Using artificial language learning to study language evolution: Exploring the emergence of word order universals. In Jean-Louis Dessalles & Laleh Ghadakpour (eds.), *The evolution of language: 3rd international conference*, 45–48. Paris: École Nationale Supérieure des Télécommunications.

Clark, Brady, Matthew Goldrick & Kenneth Konopka. 2008. Language change as a source of word order correlations. In Regine Eckardt, Gerhard Jäger & Tonjes Veenstra (eds.), *Variation, selection, development: Probing the evolutionary model of language change*, 75–102. Berlin, New York: Mouton de Gruyter. DOI:10.1515/9783110205398.2.75

Claudi, Ulrike. 1994. Word order change as category change: The Mande case. In William Pagliuca (ed.), *Perspectives on grammaticalization*, 191–231. Amsterdam, Philadelphia: John Benjamins. DOI:10.1075/cilt.109.04cla

Collins, Jeremy. 2012. The evolution of the Greenbergian word order correlations. In Thomas C. Scott-Phillips, Mónica Tamariz, Erica A. Cartmill & James R. Hurford (eds.), *The evolution of language: 9th international conference*, 72–79. Singapore: World Scientific. DOI:10.1142/9789814401500_0010

Collins, Jeremy. 2016. Some language universals are historical accidents. In. http://humans-who-read-grammars.blogspot.co.uk/2016/08/some-language-universals-are-historical.html, accessed 2016-8-28. Blogpost at Humans Who Read Grammars.

Croft, William. 2000. *Explaining language change: An evolutionary approach*. London: Harlow. DOI:10.1075/jhp.6.1.09rau

Croft, William. 2003. *Typology and universals*. 2nd edn. Cambridge: Cambridge University Press. DOI:10.1017/CBO9780511840579

Croft, William, Tanmoy Bhattacharya, Dave Kleinschmidt, D. Eric Smith & T. Florian Jaeger. 2011. Greenbergian universals, diachrony, and statistical analyses. *Linguistic Typology* 15(2). 433–453. DOI:10.1515/lity.2011.029

Culbertson, Jennifer, Paul Smolensky & Géraldine Legendre. 2012. Learning biases predict a word order universal. *Cognition* 122(3). 306–329. DOI:10.1016/j.cognition.2011.10.017

Cysouw, Michael. 2011. Understanding transition probabilities. *Linguistic Typology* 15(2). 415–431. DOI:10.1515/lity.2011.028

DeLancey, Scott. 1997. Grammaticalization and the gradience of categories: Relator nouns and postpositions in Tibetan and Burmese. In Joan L. Bybee, John Haiman & Sandra A. Thompson (eds.), *Essays on language function and language type*, 51–69. Amsterdam, Philadelphia: John Benjamins. DOI:10.1075/z.82.07del

DeLancey, Scott. 2011. Finite structures from clausal nominalization in Tibeto-Burman. In Foong Ha Yap, Karen Grunow-Hårsta & Janick Wrona (eds.), *Nominalization in Asian languages: Diachronic and typological perspectives, Vol. 1*, 343–360. Amsterdam, Philadelphia: John Benjamins. DOI:10.1075/tsl.96.12del

Deutscher, Guy. 2005. *The unfolding of language*. London: Random House.

Dixon, R. M. W. 2002. *Australian languages: Their nature and development*. Cambridge: Cambridge University Press. DOI:10.1017/CBO9780511486869

Dryer, Matthew S. 1992. The Greenbergian word order correlations. *Language* 68(1). 81–138. DOI:10.1353/lan.1992.0028

Dryer, Matthew S. 2011. The evidence for word order correlations. *Linguistic Typology* 15(2). 335–380. DOI:10.1515/lity.2011.024

Dryer, Matthew S. 2019. Grammaticalization accounts of word order correlations. In Karsten Schmidtke-Bode, Natalia Levshina, Susanne Maria Michaelis & Ilja A. Seržant (eds.), *Explanation in typology: Diachronic sources, functional motivations and the nature of the evidence*, 63–95. Berlin: Language Science Press. DOI:10.5281/zenodo.2583810

Dunn, Michael, Simon J. Greenhill, Stephen C. Levinson & Russell D. Gray. 2011. Evolved structure of language shows lineage-specific trends in word-order universals. *Nature* 473. 79–82. DOI:10.1038/nature09923

Evans, Nicholas & Stephen C. Levinson. 2009. The myth of language universals: Language diversity and its importance for cognitive science. *Behavioral and Brain Sciences* 32(5). 429–448. DOI:10.1017/S0140525X0999094X

Fischer, Olga. 1992. Syntax. In Norman Blake (ed.), *The Cambridge history of the English language, Vol. 2: 1066–1476*, 207–408. Cambridge: Cambridge University Press. DOI:10.1017/CHOL9780521264754.005

Fischer, Olga & Wim van der Wurff. 2006. Syntax. In Richard Hogg & David Denison (eds.), *A history of the English language*, 109–198. Cambridge: Cambridge University Press. DOI:10.1017/CBO9780511791154.004

Frellesvig, Bjarke. 2010. *A history of the Japanese language*. Cambridge: Cambridge University Press. DOI:10.1017/CBO9780511778322

Gildea, Spike. 1997. Introducing ergative word order via reanalysis: Word order change in the Cariban family. In Joan L. Bybee, John Haiman & Sandra A. Thompson (eds.), *Essays on language function and language type*, 145–163. Amsterdam, Philadelphia: John Benjamins. DOI:10.1075/z.82.10gil

Givón, Talmy. 1971. Historical syntax and synchronic morphology: An archaeologist's field trip. *Chicago Linguistic Society* 7. 394–415.

Greenberg, Joseph H. 1963. Some universals of grammar with particular reference to the order of meaningful elements. In Joseph H. Greenberg (ed.), *Universals of language*, 58–90. Cambridge, MA: MIT Press.

Haspelmath, Martin. 2019. Can cross-linguistic regularities be explained by constraints on change? In Karsten Schmidtke-Bode, Natalia Levshina, Susanne Maria Michaelis & Ilja A. Seržant (eds.), *Explanation in typology: Diachronic sources, functional motivations and the nature of the evidence*, 1–23. Berlin: Language Science Press. DOI:10.5281/zenodo.2583804

Hawkins, John A. 1983. *Word order universals*. New York: Academic Press. DOI:10.1016/C2009-0-21896-4

Hawkins, John A. 1994. *A performance theory of order and constituency*. Cambridge: Cambridge University Press. DOI:10.1017/CBO9780511554285

Hawkins, John A. 2004. *Efficiency and complexity in grammars*. Oxford: Oxford University Press. DOI:10.1093/acprof:oso/9780199252695.001.0001

Heine, Bernd. 2009. From nominal to clausal morphosyntax: Complexity via expansion. In Talmy Givón & Masayoshi Shibatani (eds.), *Syntactic complexity: Diachrony, acquisition, neuro-cognition, evolution*, 23–52. Amsterdam, Philadelphia: John Benjamins. DOI:10.1075/tsl.85.02fro

Heine, Bernd & Tania Kuteva. 2002. *World lexicon of grammaticalization*. Cambridge: Cambridge University Press. DOI:10.1017/CBO9780511613463

Heine, Bernd & Tania Kuteva. 2007. *The genesis of grammar: A reconstruction.* Oxford: Oxford University Press.

Himmelmann, Nikolaus P. 2005. The Austronesian languages of Asia and Madagascar: Typological characteristics. In Alexander Adelaar & Nikolaus P. Himmelmann (eds.), *The Austronesian languages of Asia and Madagascar*, 110–181. London, New York: Routledge. DOI:10.4324/9780203821121

Hopper, Paul J. & Elizabeth Closs Traugott. 2003. *Grammaticalization.* 2nd edn. Cambridge: Cambridge University Press. DOI:10.1017/CBO9781139165525

Kaufman, Daniel. 2009. Austronesian nominalism and its consequences: A Tagalog case study. *Theoretical Linguistics* 35(1). 1–49. DOI:10.1515/THLI.2009.001

Kirby, Simon. 1999. *Function, selection, and innateness: The emergence of language universals.* Oxford: Oxford University Press.

Kirby, Simon & Morten H. Christiansen. 2003. From language learning to language evolution. In Morten H. Christiansen & Simon Kirby (eds.), *Language evolution*, 272–294. Oxford: Oxford University Press. DOI:10.1093/acprof:oso/9780199244843.003.0015

Kirby, Simon & James R. Hurford. 1997. Learning, culture and evolution in the origin of linguistic constraints. In Phil Husbands & Inman Harvey (eds.), *Fourth European Conference on Artificial Life*, 493–502. Cambridge, MA; London: The MIT Press.

Lehmann, Christian. 2015[1982]. *Thoughts on grammaticalization.* 3rd edn. Berlin: Language Science Press. DOI:10.17169/langsci.b88.99

Lynch, John, Malcolm Ross & Terry Crowley. 2002. *The Oceanic languages.* London: Routledge. DOI:10.4324/9780203820384

Ogloblin, Alexander K. 2005. Javanese. In Alexander Adelaar & Nikolaus P. Himmelmann (eds.), *The Austronesian languages of Asia and Madagascar*, 590–624. London, New York: Routledge.

Pinker, Steven. 1994. *The language instinct: How the mind creates language.* New York: HarperCollins.

Roberts, Ian. 2007. *Diachronic syntax.* Oxford: Oxford University Press.

Roberts, Seán & James Winters. 2013. Linguistic diversity and traffic accidents: Lessons from statistical studies of cultural traits. *PloS One* 8(8). e70902. DOI:10.1371/journal.pone.0070902

Sasse, Hans-Jürgen. 2009. Nominalism in Austronesian: A historical typological perspective. *Theoretical Linguistics* 35(1). 167–181. DOI:10.1515/THLI.2009.010

Shinzato, Rumiko. 2011. Nominalization in Okinawan: From a diachronic and comparative perspective. In Foong Ha Yap, Karen Grunow-Hårsta & Janick Wrona (eds.), *Nominalization in Asian languages: Diachronic and typologi-*

cal perspectives, Vol. 1, 445–472. Amsterdam, Philadelphia: John Benjamins. DOI:10.1075/tsl.96.16shi

Starosta, Stanley, Andrew K. Pawley & Lawrence Reid. 1982. The evolution of focus in Austronesian. In Amran Halim, Lois Carrington & Stephen Wurm (eds.), *Papers from the Third International Conference on Austronesian Linguistics, Vol. 2: Tracking the travellers*, 145–170. Canberra: Pacific Linguistics. DOI:10.15144/PL-C75.145

Van Everbroeck, Ezra. 1999. Language type frequency and learnability: A connectionist appraisal. In Martin Hahn & Scott C. Stoness (eds.), *Proceedings of the 21st Annual Conference of the Cognitive Science Society, Vancouver, British Columbia, Canada*, 755–60. Mahwah, NJ: Erlbaum.

Yap, Foong Ha, Karen Grunow-Hårsta & Janick Wrona (eds.). 2011. *Nominalization in Asian languages: Diachronic and typological perspectives, Vol. 1*. Amsterdam, Philadelphia: John Benjamins. DOI:10.1075/tsl.96

Chapter 4

Grammaticalization accounts of word order correlations

Matthew S. Dryer

University at Buffalo

This paper examines the role that grammaticalization plays in explaining word order correlations. It presents some data that only grammaticalization accounts for, but also argues that there are correlations that grammaticalization does not account for. The conclusion is that accounts entirely in terms of grammaticalization or accounts that make no reference to grammaticalization are both inadequate.

1 Introduction

There is extensive literature both on identifying word order correlations (Greenberg 1963; Hawkins 1983; Dryer 1992) and on possible explanations for these correlations. Proposed explanations can be grouped loosely into three types. First, it is proposed that some correlations exist because of some sort of similarity or shared property of the pairs that correlate. An example of this is the hypothesis that the order of object and verb correlates with the order of adposition and noun phrase because both involve a pair of head and dependent. A second type of explanation is in terms of sentence processing (Kuno 1974; Dryer 1992; 2009; Hawkins 1994; 2004; 2014), under which the types that do not conform to the correlations are less frequent because structures containing the two inconsistent types are more difficult to parse. This would be what Haspelmath (2019 [this volume]) calls a functional-adaptive type of explanation. A third line of explanation is in terms of grammaticalization (Givón 1979; Heine & Reh 1984: 241–244; Bybee 1988; Aristar 1991; DeLancey 1994; Collins 2012, Collins 2019 [this volume]). For example it is hypothesized that the reason (or a reason) why the order of adposition and noun phrase correlates with the order of verb and object is that one

Matthew S. Dryer. 2019. Grammaticalization accounts of word order correlations. In Karsten Schmidtke-Bode, Natalia Levshina, Susanne Maria Michaelis & Ilja A. Seržant (eds.), *Explanation in typology: Diachronic sources, functional motivations and the nature of the evidence*, 63–95. Berlin: Language Science Press. DOI:10.5281/zenodo.2583810 grammaticalization source for adpositions is verbs and the order of verb and object remains the same when the verb grammaticalizes as an adposition. This line of explanation is thus crucially based on the diachronic sources of adpositions and hence a type of source-based explanation (Cristofaro 2019 [this volume]).

Despite these competing hypotheses for explaining word order correlations, there is surprisingly little attempt by proponents of an explanation in terms of grammaticalization to argue against other approaches or by proponents of other approaches to argue against grammaticalization. In fact, proponents of other approaches rarely even mention the possible role of grammaticalization. The goal of this paper is to argue that both explanations in terms of grammaticalization and explanations in terms of shared features or processing are needed in explaining word order correlations. I will focus on the pros and cons of grammaticalization explanations, largely ignoring the difference between accounts in terms of shared features and accounts in terms of sentence processing.[1]

In §2, I discuss explanations for correlations involving order of adposition and noun phrase and discuss evidence that only a grammaticalization approach can account for. Namely I examine SVO & GenN languages that have both prepositions and postpositions and show that not only does an approach involving grammaticalization predict languages with both prepositions and postpositions but it also correctly predicts the semantics associated with each type of adposition. In §3, I give reasons why grammaticalization cannot account for all word order correlations, concluding that grammaticalization and other factors conspire to account for some correlations. And in §4, I discuss data involving word order properties of definiteness markers where grammaticalization seems to make the wrong prediction.

2 A grammaticalization account of the correlations with the order of adposition and noun phrase

In this section, I present evidence for a grammaticalization account for correlations involving the order of adposition and noun phrase that only grammaticalization can account for. In §2.1, I discuss evidence of adpositions grammaticalizing from verbs. In §2.2, I discuss evidence of a second grammaticalization source for adpositions, namely head nouns in genitive constructions. The next section,

---

[1]In Dryer (1992), I argue for a processing account over an account in terms of heads and dependents for the various correlations between pairs of elements and the order of verb and object.

§2.3, is, in my view, the most important section of this paper. In that section, I discuss SVO languages which employ GenN word order. Grammaticalization theory predicts that in such languages, if adpositions arise from both grammaticalization sources discussed in §2.1 and §2.2, the language will have both prepositions and postpositions, the former arising from verbs, the latter from head nouns in genitive constructions, with particular semantics associated with each. I present evidence from a number of languages showing that this prediction is borne out.

2.1 Adpositions that grammaticalize from verbs

Let me turn now to one of the best-known word order correlations, between the order of object and verb and the order of adposition and noun phrase, where VO languages tend to have prepositions while OV languages tend to have postpositions (Greenberg 1963; Dryer 1992). Evidence for this correlation is given in Tables 1 and 2. The data for VO languages is given in Table 1. The numbers in Table 1 denote numbers of genera containing languages of the given sort, divided into five large continental areas (Dryer 1989). The more frequent type in each area is enclosed in square brackets.

Table 1: Order of adposition and noun phrase in VO languages

	Africa	Eurasia	Oceania	N.America	S.America	TOTAL
VO & Po	10	6	3	5	15	39
VO & Pr	[37]	[25]	[48]	[27]	15	152

Table 1 shows that prepositions outnumber postpositions in VO languages by a wide margin in four of the five areas, with the fifth area (South America) having an equal number of genera containing languages with prepositions and those containing languages with postpositions. Overall, VO & Pr outnumbers VO & Po by 152 to 39 genera.

The corresponding data for OV languages is given in Table 2. Table 2 shows a stronger preference for postpositions in OV languages than the preference for prepositions in VO languages shown in Table 1, in that Table 2 shows only 11 genera containing OV & Pr languages while Table 1 shows 39 genera containing VO & Po languages. I discuss an explanation for this difference in terms of grammaticalization in §3 below.

Matthew S. Dryer

Table 2: Order of adposition and noun phrase in OV languages

	Africa	Eurasia	Oceania	N.America	S.America	TOTAL
OV & Po	[25]	[45]	[82]	[28]	[41]	221
OV & Pr	3	2	5	0	1	11

An explanation of this correlation in terms of grammaticalization appeals to the fact that verbs are a common source for adpositions, so that when a verb is grammaticalized as an adposition, the order with the verb followed by object is retained as preposition followed by noun phrase, while the order with the object followed by verb is retained as noun phrase plus postposition.

Two examples of this process of grammaticalization in English are the prepositions *including* and *concerning*, as in (1).

(1) English

    a. Four men, including John, arrived.

    b. I will talk to you later concerning your thesis.

Both of these prepositions retain the present participle form ending in *-ing*, coming from the verbs *include* and *concern*.

Grammaticalization of adpositions from verbs is common in many other languages and widely described in the literature. The examples in (2) to (7) illustrate apparent examples of grammaticalization of particular semantic types of adpositions from verbs with particular meanings.

give → for

(2) Efik (Niger-Congo, Delta Cross: Nigeria; Givón 2001: 163)
     nam utom emi **ni**   mi.
     do   work this **give** me
     'Do this **for** me.'

give → to (marking addressee)

(3) Yoruba (Niger-Congo, Defoid: Nigeria; Givón 2001: 163)
     mo sọ **fún** ọ.
     I   said **give** you
     'I said **to** you.'

66

go → to (marking goal of motion)

(4)   Nupe (Niger-Congo, Ebira-Nupoid: Nigeria; Givón 1979: 221)
      ū bīcī **lō** dzūká.
      he ran **go** market
      'He ran **to** the market.'

follow → with (comitative)

(5)   Mandarin Chinese (Sino-Tibetan, Sinitic: China; Li & Thompson 1981:
      423)
      tā bu **gēn**   wǒ jiǎng-hua.
      3SG NEG **follow** 1SG speak-speech
      'He doesn't talk **with** me.'

take → object case marker

(6)   Yatye (Niger-Congo, Idomoid: Nigeria; Givón 2001: 163)
      ìywi **awá utsì** ikù.
      boy **took door** shut
      'The boy shut **the door**.'

be at → at

(7)   Mandarin Chinese (Sino-Tibetan, Sinitic: China; Yu Li, p.c.)
      tā **zài** guō-li chǎo fàn.
      3SG **be.at** pot-in fry   rice
      'He is frying rice **in** the pot.'

The grammaticalization of adpositions from verbs provides a possible basis for
an explanation of the correlation between the order of verb and object and the
order of adposition and noun phrase.

2.2 Adpositions that grammaticalize from head nouns in nominal possessive constructions

Another common grammaticalization source for adpositions (and probably the
more common source) is head nouns in genitive constructions. English has a
number of prepositions that have arisen from head nouns in genitive constructions, including those in (8).

(8) English

   a. in the side of NP → inside NP
   b. by the side of NP → beside NP
   c. by the cause of NP → because of NP

Because these adpositions arose from head nouns in a genitive construction with NGen order, they ended up as prepositions rather than postpositions. The opposite situation arose in Amharic, where the examples in (9) illustrate two postpositions arising from head nouns in a GenN construction.

(9) Amharic (Afro-Asiatic, Semitic: Ethiopia; Givón 1971: 399)

   a. NP + bottom → NP + under
      kä-bet **tač** allä.
      at-house **bottom** is
      'He is **under** the house.'
   b. NP + reason → NP + because of
      bä-issu **mikniyat** näw.
      at-he **reason** is
      'It is **because of** him.'

This type of grammaticalization of adpositions from head nouns in genitive constructions would explain the correlation between the order of noun and genitive and the order of adposition and noun phrase. The data in Tables 3 and 4 provides evidence for this correlation. The data in Table 3 shows GenN languages being overwhelmingly postpositional, while the data in Table 4 shows NGen languages being overwhelmingly prepositional.

Table 3: Order of adposition and noun phrase in GenN languages

	Africa	Euras	Oceania	N.Amer	S.Amer	TOTAL
GenN & Po	[31]	[50]	[73]	[33]	[54]	241
GenN & Pr	2	7	13	3	4	29

Table 4: Order of adposition and noun phrase in NGen languages

	Africa	Euras	Oceania	N.Amer	S.Amer	TOTAL
NGen & Po	7	0	6	0	1	14
NGen & Pr	[34]	[19]	[29]	[19]	[10]	111

2.3 An interesting prediction of grammaticalization accounts for adpositions

Sections §2.1 and §2.2 illustrate two grammaticalization sources for adpositions, one from verbs, the other from head nouns in genitive constructions. In languages which are VO and NGen, both sources will lead to prepositions rather than postpositions. Conversely, in languages which are OV and GenN, both sources will lead to postpositions. But there are many languages which are VO but GenN. Dryer (1997; 2013) shows that although OV languages tend to be GenN and verb-initial languages tend to be NGen, both orders of noun and genitive are common among SVO languages, as shown in Table 5.

Table 5: Order of genitive and noun in SVO languages

	Africa	Euras	Oceania	N.Amer	S.Amer	TOTAL
SVO & GenN	11	11	13	2	[11]	48
SVO & NGen	[41]	[16]	13	[5]	3	78

Table 5 shows that NGen is more common overall than GenN among SVO languages by 78 genera to 48. However, the higher number of genera containing SVO & NGen languages turns out to be entirely due to languages in Africa. Outside Africa, SVO & NGen and SVO & GenN are both found in exactly 37 genera. The general conclusion is that there is no evidence of any preference for NGen order over GenN order among SVO languages.

Because of the two grammaticalization sources for adpositions described in the two preceding sections, grammaticalization theory makes an interesting prediction about SVO & GenN languages. Namely, if adpositions arise in any such languages from both grammaticalization sources, the language should have both prepositions and postpositions, those arising from verbs being prepositions and those arising from nouns being postpositions. The evidence in this section shows that this prediction is borne out.

Matthew S. Dryer

In fact, grammaticalization theory makes more specific predictions about what meanings will be associated with prepositions and what meanings will be associated with postpositions in such languages. The lefthand column in Table 6 summarizes typical meanings associated with adpositions that arise from verbs, while the righthand column summarizes typical meanings associated with adpositions that arise from head nouns in genitive constructions.

Table 6: Typical meanings associated with adpositions

Typical meanings associated with adpositions that come from verbs	Typical meanings associated with adpositions that come from nouns
benefactive ('for')	specific locations like
instrumental ('with')	'under', 'behind', 'in front of'
comitative ('with')	'because of'
similative ('like')	
allative ('to, toward')	
general locations ('at')	
adpositions marking direct objects	

Note that it is typically adpositions denoting specific locations that arise from nouns; adpositions denoting general locations (meaning something like 'at') often arise from verbs. Similarly adpositions associated with motion away from source or towards a location also more often arise from verbs. Grammaticalization theory predicts that in an SVO & GenN language with both prepositions and postpositions, the prepositions will tend to have meanings like those in the lefthand column in Table 6, while the postpositions will tend to have meanings like those in the righthand column. This section shows that these predictions are also borne out.

The first language illustrating how these predictions are borne out is Nǀuuki. The SVO order of Nǀuuki is illustrated in (10), GenN order in (11).

(10)   Nǀuuki (Tuu: South Africa; Collins & Namaseb 2011: 10)
       ǂharuxu ke   ãi Ooe.
       Haruxu DECL eat meat
       'Haruxu is eating meat.'

(11) Nǀuuki (Tuu: South Africa; Collins & Namaseb 2011: 37)
      siso ŋǂona
      Siso knife
      'Siso's knife'

Nǀuuki has both prepositions and postpositions. Examples illustrating the preposition *ŋǀa* are given in (12) and (13), (12) illustrating an instrumental use, (13) a comitative use.

(12) Nǀuuki (Tuu: South Africa; Collins & Namaseb 2011: 25)
      n-a   si laa Ɵoe ŋǀa ŋǂona.
      1SG-DECL IRR cut meat **with knife**
      'I will cut the meat **with a knife**.'

(13) Nǀuuki (Tuu: South Africa; Collins & Namaseb 2011: 25)
      lalaˤe ke sĩĩsen ŋǀa ŋǀaŋgusi.
      lalaˤe DECL work **with Nǀaŋgusi**

      'lalaˤe works **with Nǀaŋgusi**.'

In contrast, example (14) illustrates a postposition *xuu* 'in front of'.

(14) Nǀuuki (Tuu: South Africa; Collins & Namaseb 2011: 80)
      ǀx'esi ǀʔaa sũi   loβa xuu
      necklace go sit.down **child front**
      'The necklace fell **in front of the child**.'

The prepositions and postpositions in Nǀuuki (Collins & Namaseb 2011: 24–25) are listed in Table 7.

Table 7: Prepositions and postpositions in Nǀuuki

Prepositions		Postpositions	
ŋǀa	'instrumental, comitative'	ǁãʔẽ	'in'
ǁa	'like'	xuu	'in front of'
ŋ	'linker'	tsʔii	'behind'
		ǀqhaa	'next to'

Two of the three prepositions, *ŋǀa* 'instrumental, comitative' and *ǁa* 'like', conform to the semantic types of adpositions arising from verbs and the fact that they are prepositions rather than postpositions can be explained if they have arisen from verbs in a VO language. And all four of the postpositions represent specific locations, conforming to what we expect semantically of adpositions arising from head nouns in genitive constructions; the fact that they are postpositions rather than prepositions can be explained in that they have arisen from head nouns in a genitive construction in a GenN language.

A second example is provided by Logba. Like Nǀuuki, Logba is SVO, as illustrated in (15), and GenN, as in (16).

(15)   Logba (Niger-Congo, Kwa: Ghana; Dorvlo 2008: 105)
Setor ó-kpe   i-gbeɖi=é.
Setor sg-peel nc-cassava=DET
'Setor peeled the cassava.'

(16)   Logba (Niger-Congo, Kwa: Ghana; Dorvlo 2008: 71)
Kɔdzo a-klɔ=a
Kɔdzo nc-goat=DET
'Kɔdzo's goat'

Also like Nǀuuki, Logba has both prepositions and postpositions. The preposition *kpɛ* with instrumental or comitative meaning is illustrated in (17).

(17)   Logba (Niger-Congo, Kwa: Ghana; Dorvlo 2008: 96)
Udzi=é   ó-glɛ uzugbo **kpɛ a-futa**.
woman=DET sg-tie head   **with nc-cloth**
'The lady tied her head **with a cloth**.'

In contrast, an example illustrating a postposition *etsi* 'under' is given in (18).

(18)   Logba (Niger-Congo, Kwa: Ghana; Dorvlo 2008: 98)
i-datɔ=a   í-tsi   a-fúta=á   etsi.
nc-spoon=DET sg-be.in **nc-cloth=DET under**
'The spoon is **under the cloth**.'

In Table 8 is a list of the prepositions and postpositions of Logba (Dorvlo 2008: 95, 98). While one of the prepositions has a meaning more commonly associated with adpositions that arise from nouns (*na* 'on'), the other prepositions all have meanings that grammaticalization theory predicts for adpositions arising from verbs and all the postpositions have meanings involving specific locations, the

Table 8: Prepositions and postpositions of Logba

Prepositions		Postpositions	
fɛ	'at'	nu	'inside'
na	'on'	etsi	'under'
kpɛ	'instrumental, comitative'	tsú	'on'
gu	'about'	ité	'in front of'
dzígu	'from'	zugbó	'on'
		yó	'surface contact' (e.g. on a wall)
		anú	'at tip of, at edge of'
		otsoe	'on the side of'
		amá	'behind'

types of meanings that grammaticalization predicts for adpositions that arise from nouns.

The third SVO & GenN language with both prepositions and postpositions is Eastern Kayah Li, a Karenic language in the Sino-Tibetan family spoken in Myanmar and Thailand. The prepositions and postpositions of Eastern Kayah Li are listed in Table 9 (Solnit 1997: 209–214). Apart from three prepositions with unusual meanings ('as much as', 'as big as', 'as long as'), the rest of the prepositions and all of the postpositions have meanings conforming to the semantics typically associated with adpositions arising from verbs and adpositions arising from head nouns in genitive constructions respectively.

The fourth SVO & GenN language exhibiting a similar pattern is Jabem, an Oceanic language in the Austronesian family spoken in Papua New Guinea. In Table 10 is a list of the prepositions and postpositions of Jabem (Dempwolff 1939; Bradshaw & Czobor 2005: 42–44; Ross 2002: 291). While all the postpositions again have meanings denoting specific locations, as we would expect of adpositions arising from head nouns in genitive constructions, three of the prepositions also have meanings of that sort ('next to', 'close to'). In fact, Dempwolff specifically suggests that these prepositions arose from verbs (suggesting, for example, that *tamiŋ* 'next to' comes from a verb meaning 'to be close upon').[2]

---

[2]I base this on Bradshaw & Czobor's (2005) English translation of Dempwolff (1939).

Table 9: Prepositions and postpositions of Eastern Kayah Li

Prepositions		Postpositions	
dɤ	'at'	kū	'inside'
mú	'at'	klɔ	'outside'
bɤ	'at'	khu	'on, above'
bá	'as much as'	kɛ ~ kɛdē	'down inside'
tí	'as big as'	khʌ	'at apex of'
tɤ ~ thɤ	'as long as'	lē	'under, downhill from'
phú ~ hú	'like'	chá	'near'
		ŋē ~ béseŋē	'in front of'
		khjā ~ békhjā	'behind'
		lo	'on non-horizontal surface'
		klē	'in (an area)'
		rɔklē	'beside'
		ple ~ ple kū	'in narrow space between'
		cɔkū	'in middle of, between'
		thɯ	'on edge of'
		təkjā	'in the direction of'

Table 10: Prepositions and postpositions of Jabem

Prepositions		Postpositions	
tamiŋ	'next to, onto'	lêlôm	'inside'
baŋ	'close to'	lôlôc	'on top of'
paŋ	'close to'	làbu	'under'
ŋa	'instrumental'	sawa	'between'
aⁿga	'from'	lùŋ	'in middle of'
		nêm	'in front of'
		mu	'behind'
		gala	'near'
		tali	'at edge of'

In Table 11 to 16 are lists of prepositions and postpositions from six other SVO & GenN languages that have both. All show patterns similar to those in the four languages described above in this section, with the prepositions having meanings associated with adpositions arising from verbs and the postpositions with meanings associated with adpositions arising from nouns.

Table 11: ǂHoã (Kxa: Botswana, Collins & Gruber 2014: 101–105)

Prepositions		Postpositions	
kì	'linker'	na	'in'
ke	'comitative'	za	'by, beside'
		ǁq'am	'above'
		ǂkà	'below'
		ǂ'hàã	'in front of'
		kya"m	'near'

Table 12: Koromfe (Niger-Congo, Gur: Burkina Faso, Mali, Rennison 1997; 2017)

Prepositions		Postpositions	
la	'instrumental, comitative'	nɛ	'benefactive, purpose, about'
hal	'until'	kana	'like'
		dɔba	'on top of'
		hɛrəga	'beside, near'
		hogo	'under'
		jɪka nɛ	'in front of'
		joro	'in, inside'
		bɛllɛ	'behind'
		tʊllɛ	'in the middle of, between'

Table 13: Mandarin Chinese (Sino-Tibetan, Sinitic: China, Li & Thompson 1981)

Prepositions (or coverbs)		Postpositions (or locative particles)	
gēn	'with (comitative)'	shàng	'on top of, above'
gěi	'for' (benefactive)	xià	'below'
bǎ	object marker	lǐ	'in, inside'
duì	'toward'	wài	'outside'
cóng	'from'	qián	'in front of'
zài	'at'	hòu	'behind'
tì	'instead of'	páng	'beside'
bèi	'by'	dōngbu	'east of'
àn	'according to'	zhèr	'this side of'
dào	'to'	qián	'in front of'
		hòu	'behind'
		páng	'beside'
		zhōngjian	'in the centre of'

Table 14: Koyra Chiini (Songhay: Mali, Heath 1999: 104–109)

Prepositions		Postpositions	
nda	'comitative, instrumental'	se	'dative'
bilaa	'without'	ra	'locative'
hal	'until'	ga	'beside, from'
jaa	'since'	doo	'at the place of'
bara	'except'	banda	'behind'
kala	'except'	beene	'above'
		čire	'under'
		kuna	'in'
		jere	'beside'
		jine	'in front of'
		maasu	'inside'
		tenje	'facing'

Table 15: Taba (Austronesian, South Halmahera: Indonesia, Bowden 2001: 109–111)

Prepositions		Postposition	
ada	'comitative, instrumental'	li	'on, in, at'[a]
pake	'instrumental'		
untuk	'benefactive'		
lo	'like'		

[a]The fact that the one postposition in Taba has general locative meaning does not fit the expectations for a postposition in a GenN language. But the fact that it is locative while the prepositions are not does fit loosely. It is possible that it originally had a narrower locative meaning that has become bleached.

Table 16: Dagbani (Niger-Congo, Gur: Ghana, Olawsky 1999)

Prepositions		Postpositions	
ni	'comitative, instrumental'	nyaaŋa	'behind'
jɛndi	'about, concerning'	zuɣu	'on top of'
		gbinni	'under'
		sani	'towards'
		sunsuuni	'in the middle of'
		ni	'in, at, to'
		puuni	'inside'
		polo	'in the direction of'
		lɔŋni	'under'

The languages illustrated in Table 7 to Table 16 above are instances of SVO languages with GenN order and both prepositions and postpositions. Though less common, there are also languages of the opposite sort, OV languages with NGen order and both prepositions and postpositions, where the semantics associated with prepositions and postpositions respectively is the opposite of that found in SVO & GenN languages. An example is Iraqw. Example (19) illustrates the preposition *daandú* 'behind'. That it has grammaticalized from the head noun in a genitive construction is clear from the fact that it occurs in construct state, the morphological form that head nouns take in genitive constructions.

(19) Iraqw (Afro-Asiatic, Cushitic: Tanzania; Mous 1993: 97)
      loo'a i   **daandú**   hunkáy.
      sun   3SBJ **behind.CONSTR cloud**
      'The sun is **behind the cloud.**'

In contrast, example (20) illustrates a postpositional clitic =*i* 'directional' that attaches to the last word in the noun phrase. In (20) it attaches to the noun *do'* 'house', the possessor of *afkú* 'mouth' ('door'), but it is marking the entire noun phrase *afkú do'* 'mouth (door) of the house' as the goal of the motion denoted by the verb *qaas* 'put'.

(20) Iraqw (Afro-Asiatic, Cushitic: Tanzania; Mous 1993: 252)
      famfe'amo u-n   **af-kú**   **do'=i**   qaas-áan.
      snake   MASC.OBJ-EXPEC **mouth-CONSTR.MASC house=DIR** put-1PL
      'Let us put a snake **on the door of the house.**'

In Table 17 is a list of prepositions and postpositions in Iraqw (Mous 1993: 95–107). Setting aside momentarily the first three prepositions in Table 17, the semantics associated with the prepositions and postpositions in Iraqw is the reverse of what we found in (10) to (18) for SVO & GenN languages. Namely, in Table 17, it is the prepositions which denote specific locations, while the postpositions have meanings that are generally associated with adpositions arising from verbs.

The first three prepositions in Table 17 have the same meanings as the first three postpositions in the table. Their meanings are thus ones that we might have expected to be associated with postpositions in an OV language. These prepositions take the form of /a/ plus the corresponding postpositional clitics. Mous (1993: 102) speculates that the /a/ in these forms may have originally been the copula *a*. It is possible that these prepositions have arisen by analogy to other prepositions in the language.

Table 17: Prepositions and postpositions in Iraqw

Prepositions		Postpositions	
ar	'instrumental'	=(a)r	'instrumental, comitative'
as	'because of'	=sa	'because of'
ay	'to'	=i	'to'
dír	'to'	=wa	'from'
amór	'at'		
daandú	'on'		
alá	'behind'		
gurúu	'inside'		
gamú	'under'		
bihháa	'beside'		
tla'á(ng)	'between'		
tsee'á	'outside'		
afíqoomár	'until'		
gawá	'on'		
geerá	'before'		
afá	'at the edge of'		
bará	'in'		

A second instance of an OV & NGen language with both prepositions and post-positions is Kanuri. Example (21) illustrates the locative-instrumental postpositional clitic =*lan* attaching to a postnominal modifier *Musa=be* 'Musa's', marking *fər Musa=be* 'Musa's horse' as an instrumental.[3]

(21) Kanuri (Saharan: Nigeria, Niger; Hutchison 1976: 5)
      [fər   Musa=be]=lan   kadio.
      [horse Musa=GEN]=INS come.PST.3SG
      'He came **on/by Musa's horse**.'

Kanuri also has prepositions, like *suro* 'inside' in (22).

---

[3]There are thus two postpositional clitics in the phonological word *Musa=be=lan* in Table 17, the =*be* marking Musa as possessor of *fər* 'horse' and the =*lan* marking *fər Musa=be* 'Musa's horse' as an instrumental.

(22)   Kanuri (Saharan: Nigeria, Niger; Hutchison 1976: 80)
   suro fato=be=ro   kargawo.
   inside house=GEN=to enter.PST.3SG
   'He went **into the house**.'

Note that *suro* retains its nominal nature in (22), in that its complement *fato* 'house' is marked as a possessor, with the genitive postpositional clitic *=be*, and the entire phrase marked with the postpositional clitic *=ro* 'to', so that (22) could be glossed as 'He went to the inside of the house'. To what extent these locational nouns have grammaticalized as prepositions is not clear. Even if they have not grammaticalized much yet, they illustrate how an OV & NGen language could acquire prepositions.

In Table 18 is a list of prepositions and postpositions of Kanuri (Hutchison 1981: 257–263).

Table 18: Prepositions and postpositions of Kanuri

Prepositions		Postpositions	
bótówò	'next to'	=(là)n	'locative, instrumental'
cî	'at edge of'	=rò	'benefactive, indirect object, to'
dàryé	'at the end of'	=mbèn	'through, towards'
dáwù	'in middle of'		
fúwù	'in front of'		
fərtə	'at base of'		
gəré	'next to'		
kátè	'between'		
kəlâ	'on top of'		
ngáwò	'behind, after'		
sədíà ~ cídíà	'under'		
súró	'inside, during'		

The meanings associated with the prepositions in Kanuri are similar to those of the prepositions in Iraqw, but are also similar to the meanings of the postpositions in the various SVO & GenN languages discussed above. Conversely, the meanings associated with the postpositions in Kanuri are similar to those of the postpositions in Iraqw and also similar to the meanings of the prepositions in the various SVO & GenN languages discussed above.

There is another instance of a language with both prepositions and postpositions that provides an interesting variation of the argument in this section, namely English. While English is predominantly a prepositional language, it has at least two postpositions, *ago* and *notwithstanding*, as in (23).[4]

(23)   English

    a.   I saw him three weeks ago.

    b.   I went to the concert, the doctor's advice notwithstanding.

What is unusual about these two postpositions in English is that although both are apparently grammaticalizations of verbs, they are ones where what is now the object of that postposition was originally the subject of the verb (rather than the object, the more common situation with grammaticalizations from verbs). According to the Merriam Webster online dictionary,[5] *ago* comes from an obsolete verb meaning 'pass' so that *three weeks ago* derives from *three weeks have passed*, where *three weeks* was originally the subject of this verb. And *notwithstanding* comes from *not* plus a form of the verb meaning 'withstand' in the sense of 'providing an obstacle for'; again, what is now the object of the postposition *notwithstanding* was originally the subject of the verbal expression. The fact that these two words arose as postpositions rather than as prepositions reflects the fact that subjects normally preceded the verb, even in earlier varieties of English when word order was more flexible. Again, only a grammaticalization account explains these.

The evidence in this section involves data that only grammaticalization can explain. An explanation in terms of grammaticalization for the correlation between the order of verb and object and order of adposition and noun phrase as well as the correlation between the order of noun and genitive and order of adposition and noun phrase predicts that we should find both prepositions and postpositions in the same language where the former derive from verbs and the latter from head nouns in genitive constructions, as well as predicting the semantic differences between the two types of adposition. The evidence in this section shows how these predictions are borne out. There is no obvious way in which accounts in terms of processing or similarity could explain this data.

---

[4]*Notwithstanding* also occurs as a preposition. The postpositional use is apparently the original use. I suspect that the use as a preposition arose due to its semantic similarity to another preposition *despite*.

[5]https://www.merriam-webster.com/dictionary

3 What grammaticalization does not explain

The preceding section provides evidence that grammaticalization explains, at least partly, the correlation between the order of verb and object and order of adposition and noun phrase as well as the correlation between the order of noun and genitive and order of adposition and noun phrase. In this section, I discuss the question whether grammaticalization fully explains word order correlations and argue that it does not. I first discuss word order correlations for which there does not seem to be any good explanation in terms of grammaticalization. Table 19 provides a list of pairs of elements that are shown by Dryer (1992) to correlate with the order of verb and object, where the verb patterner refers to elements that occur first in these pairs more often among VO languages than among OV languages (and where the object patterner refers to the other member of the pair).

Table 19: Pairs of elements that correlate with the order of verb and object

Verb patterner	Object patterner	Example
verb	adpositional phrase	*slept + on the floor*
verb	manner adverb	*ran + slowly*
copula verb	predicate	*is + a teacher*
'want'	VP	*wants + to see Mary*
noun	relative clause	*movies + that we saw*
adjective	standard of comparison	*taller + than Bob*
complementizer	clause	*that + John is sick*
question particle	sentence	
adverbial subordinator	clause	*because + Bob has left*

For none of these pairs of elements that correlate with the order of verb and object is there a convincing explanation in terms of grammaticalization. For example, the order of verb and adpositional phrase most likely correlates with the order of verb and object because of semantic similarities between these two pairs of elements or because of processing factors. It is hard to imagine an explanation in terms of grammaticalization for this correlation.

I devote the remainder of this section to discussing the correlation between the order of verb and object and the order of noun and genitive. While there have been attempts to explain this correlation in terms of grammaticalization, I claim here that such attempts fall short of providing a plausible explanation.

A good summary of this approach is provided by Collins (2019 [this volume]). However, most of the cases discussed by Collins are highly speculative, especially compared to the evidence for adpositions deriving from verbs or nouns. The arguments involve cases where the constructions now used for main clauses are claimed to have originated from nominalizations (where a construction like *John's seeing Peter* is claimed to have replaced an existing finite construction like *John saw Peter*).[6] Assuming that the word order in nominalizations reflects the order of noun and genitive (an assumption that is probably valid), the new construction will employ an order of verb and object that reflects the order of noun and genitive.[7]

While there probably have been some instances in which a nominalization construction came to be used as the primary construction for main clauses, there is little evidence of this in most families and the correlation between the order of verb and object and the order of noun and genitive seems far too strong to be explained purely in this way. Consider the data in Table 20 on the relative frequency of the different orders of noun and genitive in OV languages.

Table 20 shows that GenN order outnumbers NGen by 247 to 25 genera, a ratio of almost 10-to-1. The evidence for nominalizations coming to be used as main clauses is far too meagre to account for such a strong correlation.

It should be noted that the order of noun and genitive correlates with the order of verb and object less strongly than the order of adposition and noun phrase correlates with either the order of verb and object or the order of noun

---

[6]Some of Collins' arguments are particularly unconvincing. He cites data from Angas showing nominalizations being used for complements of the verb meaning 'want'. But this only shows that some languages express such complements using nominalizations; it provides no evidence of nominalizations coming to be used as main clauses. He also cites the large number of Austronesian languages as evidence for the frequency by which nominalizations become main clauses. But quite apart from the fact that Collins provides no evidence to support his claim that it is generally accepted that nominalizations came to be used as main clauses in Austronesian, the size of the family is not relevant; what is relevant is the number of instances of changes of this sort. A number of proposals that main clause constructions originated as nominalizations are based largely on the fact that the same case marker is used for both possessors and subjects (or transitive subjects). But there are many ways by which this can arise without nominalizations coming to be used as main clauses.

[7]It will also determine the order of verb and subject, especially for intransitive verbs. There are issues arising here that are beyond the scope of this paper. And while I find the evidence that grammaticalization explains the correlation between the order of verb and object and the order of noun and genitive unconvincing, I must concede that it would account for the large number of SVO & GenN languages. In other words, it would account for the fact that the order of noun and genitive is one of the few orders that correlates not only with the order of verb and object but also with the order of verb and subject (Dryer 2013).

Table 20: Order of noun and genitive in OV languages

	Africa	Euras	Oceania	N.Amer	S.Amer	TOTAL
OV & GenN	[26]	[46]	[87]	[34]	[54]	247
OV & NGen	13	1	10	0	1	25

and genitive: Tables 1 and 2 above show a particularly strong correlation between the order of verb and object and the order of adposition and noun phrase; Tables 3 and 4 show an even stronger correlation between the order of noun and genitive and the order of adposition and noun phrase. But the large number of SVO & GenN languages shows that the correlation between the order of verb and object and the order of noun and genitive is less strong.

One possible explanation for why the correlation between the order of verb and object and the order of noun and genitive is weaker is that all three of these correlations are due in part to factors other than grammaticalization (such as the processing explanations of Dryer 1992 and Hawkins 1994; 2004; 2014), but that grammaticalization augments the correlation between the order of verb and object and the order of adposition and noun phrase as well as the correlation between the order of noun and genitive and the order of adposition and noun phrase. In other words, it may be a mistake to try to choose between grammaticalization and other factors in explaining word order correlations; they may conspire to lead to these stronger correlations.

In fact, data presented by Dryer (1992; 2013) suggests that the correlation between the order of verb and object and the order of adposition and noun phrase as well as the correlation between the order of noun and genitive and the order of adposition and noun phrase are stronger than most of the correlations in Table 19 above. Since there do not appear to be promising explanations for those correlationsin terms of grammaticalization, the fact that the two correlations involving adpositions are particularly strong suggests again that both grammaticalization and other factors play a role in explaining those correlations.

Note also that grammaticalization explains the fact mentioned above in §2.1 that the preference for postpositions among OV languages is stronger than the preference for prepositions among VO languages. Namely, OV languages are overwhelmingly GenN so that both sources for adpositions lead to postpositions in OV languages. In contrast there are many SVO languages with GenN order. In such languages the adpositions derived from head nouns will be postpositions, so that (assuming some such languages lack adpositions derived from verbs) we expect to find SVO languages with postpositions.

4 Order of noun and definiteness marker

In this section, I discuss a different type of problem for grammaticalization accounts of word order correlations. In the cases discussed in §3, grammaticalization simply fails to predict a word order correlations which can be shown to be real. In the case discussed in this section, grammaticalization makes a prediction that turns out not to hold, involving the order of definiteness marker and noun.

The most common grammaticalization source for markers of definiteness appears to be demonstratives. In fact my database contains 102 instances of languages that use demonstratives as markers of definiteness, compared to 274 languages with markers of definiteness that are distinct from demonstratives. Both the order of definiteness marker and noun and the order of demonstrative and noun exhibit weak correlations with the order of verb and object, but what is surprising from the perspective of grammaticalization is that they exhibit opposite correlations. Namely, definiteness markers *precede* the noun more often in VO languages than in OV languages, while demonstratives *follow* the noun more often in VO languages than in OV languages.

Consider first definiteness markers in VO languages. Table 21 provides data on the order of definiteness marker and noun in VO languages. The last line in Table 21 gives the proportion of the number on the first line as a proportion of the sum of the number on the first line and the number on the second line. For example, the .21 on the third line in Table 21 under Africa represents 8 as a proportion of 39 (the sum of 8 and 31). I use these proportions in the discussion below.

Table 21: Order of noun and definiteness marker in VO languages

	Africa	Euras	Oceania	N.Amer	S.Amer	TOTAL
VO & DefN	8	[11]	[16]	[17]	[7]	59
VO & NDef	[31]	3	13	8	0	55
Proportion DefN	.21	.79	.55	.68	1.00	$\bar{x}$=.64

Table 21 shows the two orders of definiteness marker and noun to be about equally common among VO languages, with DefN order found in languages in 59 genera and NDef order found in languages in 55 genera. This is a case, however, where the total numbers of genera are somewhat misleading, since one area, Africa, exhibits a very different pattern from what we find in the other four areas. In Africa, genera containing VO languages in which the definiteness marker follows the noun outnumber genera containing VO languages in which the definiteness marker precedes the noun by 31 to 8. In the other four areas, in contrast, it is more common among VO languages for the definiteness marker to precede the noun; in fact, in three of the areas (Eurasia, North America, and South America), DefN order is more than twice as common as NDef order. The mean of the proportions over the five areas, namely .64, also reflects a preference for DefN order among VO languages. Another way to see this is that if we exclude Africa, DefN outnumbers NDef among VO languages by 51 to 24.[8]

Table 22 provides comparable data on the order of definiteness marker and noun among OV languages. We again find only a small difference, though it is NDef that outnumbers DefN among OV languages, by 53 genera to 38.

Table 22: Order of noun and definiteness marker in OV languages

	Africa	Euras	Oceania	N.Amer	S.Amer	TOTAL
OV & DefN	3	[9]	15	4	[7]	38
OV & NDef	[12]	5	[23]	[9]	4	53
Proportion DefN	.20	.64	.39	.31	.64	$\bar{x}$=.44

But what is revealing is to compare the proportions from the last lines of Tables 21 and 22, given in Table 23.

Table 23: Proportion of genera containing DefN languages among VO vs. OV languages

	Africa	Eurasia	Oceania	N.America	S.America	Mean
VO	[.21]	[.79]	[.55]	[.68]	[1.00]	.64
OV	.20	.64	.39	.31	.64	=.44

Here we find that although the margin of difference in Africa is very small, it is still the case that the proportion of genera containing DefN languages is greater among VO languages in all five areas. This gives us reason to conclude that there

---

[8]The higher preference for NDef order among VO languages in Africa reflects a general difference between Africa and the rest of the world in that postnominal modifiers are more common in Africa than elsewhere (Dryer 2010). Table 20 above shows a similar difference between Africa and the rest of the world: while GenN outnumbers NGen among OV languages overall by almost 10-to-1, the ratio in Africa is only 2-to-1 and over half (13 out of 25) of the genera containing OV & NGen languages are in Africa.

is a correlation, albeit a weak one, between the order of verb and object and the order of definiteness marker and noun, with the definiteness marker preceding the noun more often among VO languages than among OV languages.

Given the fact that the most common grammaticalization source for definiteness markers appears to be demonstratives, we might expect to find a similar correlation between the order of verb and object and the order of demonstrative and noun. We do find a clear trend, but it is the opposite correlation. Namely while definiteness markers precede the noun more often among VO languages compared to OV languages, demonstratives tend to follow the noun more often among VO languages compared to OV languages.

Tables 24 to 26 provide data supporting this. Table 24 provides relevant data for VO languages. It shows that although NDem order is slightly more common than DemN order, by 118 genera to 92, this order is more common in only three of the five areas (and in fact, if we exclude Africa, it is DemN order that is more common among VO languages, by 84 genera to 66).

Table 24: Order of noun and demonstrative in VO languages

	Africa	Euras	Oceania	N.Amer	S.Amer	TOTAL
VO & DemN	8	12	24	[24]	[24]	92
VO & NDem	[52]	[16]	[31]	12	7	118
Proportion DemN	.13	.43	.44	.67	.77	$\bar{x}=.49$

However, Table 25 shows that among OV languages, DemN order is about twice as common as NDem order, by 181 genera to 95, although there are two areas where NDem is more common among OV languages.

Table 25: Order of noun and demonstrative in OV languages

	Africa	Euras	Oceania	N.Amer	S.Amer	TOTAL
OV & DemN	16	[44]	45	[30]	[46]	181
OV & NDem	[18]	6	[57]	6	8	95
Proportion DemN	.47	.88	.44	.83	.85	$\bar{x}=.70$

Again, it is useful to compare the proportions from the last lines of Tables 24 and 25, shown in Table 26.

Table 26: Proportion of genera containing DemN languages among VO vs. OV languages

	Africa	Eurasia	Oceania	N.America	S.America	Mean
VO	.13	.43	.44	.67	.77	.49
OV	[.43]	[.88]	.44	[.83]	[.85]	.70

Table 26 shows that the proportion of genera containing DemN languages is higher among OV languages in four areas while the proportion is the same in the fifth area (Oceania).[9] There is thus a clear trend in the opposite direction from what we found for the order of definiteness marker and noun. Given that the most common grammaticalization source for definiteness markers appears to be demonstratives, this contrast is quite surprising.

I have no explanation for the source of this difference between definiteness markers and demonstratives. But I will share some interesting data from particular languages that conforms to this difference. First, there are a few languages in which the same form is used as a demonstrative and as a marker of definiteness, but this form occurs on different sides of the noun, depending on its function. In Swahili, the forms that are used as distal demonstratives when following the noun function as markers of definiteness when they precede the noun, as shown in (24). Since Swahili is SVO, this difference conforms to the contrast in the crosslinguistic data shown above.

(24)   Swahili (Niger-Congo, Bantoid; Ashton 1947: 59)

    a. m-tu   **yu-le**
       NC_1-man NC_1-**that**

       'that man'

    b. **yu-le**   m-tu
       NC_1-DEF NC_1-man

       'the man'

In Abui, we find the opposite situation: the form *do* functions as a demonstrative when it precedes the noun, as in (25a), but as a marker of definiteness when it follows the noun, as in (25b).

---

[9]If we compute the proportions to three decimal places, DemN is also higher among OV languages compared to VO languages in Oceania (by .441. to .434). However, this difference is too small to base any conclusion on.

(25)   Abui (Timor-Alor-Pantar: Indonesia; Kratochvíl 2007: 111, 114)

    a.   **do**   sura
       this book
      'this book (near me)'

    b.   kaai **do**
       dog DEF
      'the dog (I just talked about)'

Significantly, Abui is an OV language, so the fact that Abui exhibits the opposite pattern from what we saw in Swahili again conforms to the crosslinguistic pattern described above.

The situation in Ute is similar to that in Abui. Namely Ute is OV and the word *'u* functions as a demonstrative when it precedes the noun, as in (26a), but as a marker of definiteness when it follows the noun, as in (26b).

(26)   Ute (Uto-Aztecan: United States; Givón 2011: 50, 38)

    a.   **'ú**   kava   sá-gha-rʉ-mʉ   qhárʉ-kwa-pʉga.
       that.SBJ horse.SBJ white-have-NMLZ-ANIM.SBJ run-go-REM
      'That white horse ran away.'

    b.   ta'wa-chi   **'u**   sivaatu-chi   paqha-qa.
       man-ANIM.SBJ **DEF.SBJ** goat-ANIM.OBJ kill-ANT
      'The man killed a goat.'

The situation in Loniu is somewhat different. In Loniu, the definiteness marker and demonstrative are similar in form, though not identical, with *iy* as the definiteness marker and *iyɔ* as the demonstrative. The two in fact can co-occur as in (27), with the definiteness marker preceding the noun, and the demonstrative following the noun.

(27)   Loniu (Austronesian, Oceanic: Papua New Guinea; Hamel 1994: 100)
    iy   amat iyɔ
    DEF man this
    'this man'

Again, since Loniu is VO, this order difference conforms to the crosslinguistic pattern described above.

And we find similar phenomena in cases where the definiteness marker and demonstrative are completely different in form but can co-occur, with one preceding the noun and one following. In Kana, the definiteness marker precedes the noun while the demonstrative follows, as in (28).

(28)   Kana (Niger-Congo, Delta Cross: Nigeria; Ikoro 1996: 70)
        ló   bárí āmā
        DEF fish this
        'this fish'

Since Kana is VO, this conforms to the crosslinguistic pattern. Contrast this with the situation in Kwoma (Washkuk), which is OV, and in this case it is the demonstrative that precedes the noun and the definiteness marker that follows, as in (29).

(29)   Kwoma (Sepik: Papua New Guinea; Kooyers 1974: 49)
        kata ma   rii
        that man DEF
        'that man'

These differences between demonstratives and definiteness markers are a puzzle if demonstratives are the primary grammaticalization source for definiteness markers. It should be emphasized, however, that although definiteness markers and demonstratives exhibit very different patterns in terms of how they correlate with the order of verb and object, it is still the case that they correlate with each other, i.e. that the order of definiteness marker and noun and the order of demonstrative and noun correlate. This is shown in Tables 27 and 28, excluding languages where the definiteness marker is the same as the demonstrative. Table 27 shows that among DefN languages with definiteness markers that are distinct from demonstratives, it is approximately twice as common for the demonstrative to precede the noun as well, by 41 genera to 20.

Table 27: Order of noun and demonstrative in DefN languages

	Africa	Euras	Oceania	N.Amer	S.Amer	TOTAL
DefN & DemN	3	[7]	[12]	[11]	[8]	41
DefN & NDem	[4]	3	7	3	3	20

Conversely, Table 28 shows that among NDef languages with definiteness markers that are distinct from demonstratives, it is much more common for the demonstrative to follow the noun as well, by 67 genera to 11.

Table 28: Order of noun and demonstrative in NDef languages

	Africa	Euras	Oceania	N.Amer	S.Amer	TOTAL
NDef & DemN	4	3	2	1	1	11
NDef & NDem	[33]	[6]	[19]	[8]	1	67

While grammaticalization probably plays some role in explaining this correlation, it seems likely that the clear semantic similarity between definiteness markers and demonstratives plays a role as well. There is also a correlation between the order of definiteness marker and noun and the order of indefinite marker and noun, a correlation that is presumably due to semantic similarity or processing, not grammaticalization.

5 Conclusion

I have argued that there is evidence that any approach to explaining word order correlations that ignores the role of grammaticalization is inadequate. At the same time, I have argued that while grammaticalization plays a role in explaining some correlations, a pure grammaticalization approach fails as well.

Although I have focused my discussion of SVO & GenN languages on those with both prepositions and postpositions, further research is needed on SVO & GenN languages with prepositions as the only or dominant type or with postpositions as the only or dominant type. Grammaticalization theory would predict that SVO & GenN languages with prepositions will be ones where the primary source of adpositions is verbs, while SVO & GenN languages with postpositions will be ones where the primary source of adpositions is head nouns in genitive constructions. I suspect that this is true and if so, it would further bolster the argument that grammaticalization plays an important role in explaining correlations involving adpositions. One reason to suspect it is true is the geographical distribution of the two types of languages. My database includes 21 genera containing SVO & GenN languages with prepositions and 13 of these genera (almost two thirds of them) are in an area stretching from China and Southeast Asia through Austronesian. The fact that so many of the SVO & GenN languages are in this region is significant since my impression is that the grammaticalization of adpositions from verbs is especially common in this region. Conversely, my database includes 19 genera containing SVO & GenN languages with postpositions and only two of these genera are in the region mentioned above stretching from China through Austronesian where SVO & GenN & Pr languages are common. I suspect that this is because outside that region, it is more common for adpositions to grammaticalize from nouns. However, this is a matter for future research.

Abbreviations

The paper abides by the Leipzig Glossing Rules. Additional abbreviations include the following ones:

ANIM	animate	EXPEC	expectational
ANT	anterior	NC	noun class
CONSTR	construct state	REM	remote

Acknowledgements

I am indebted to Lea Brown, Karsten Schmidtke-Bode and members of the audience at the 2015 meeting of the DGfS (the German Linguistic Society) for comments on an earlier version of this paper. I also acknowledge funding from The Social Sciences and Humanities Research Council of Canada, the National Science Foundation (in the United States), the Max Planck Institute for Evolutionary Anthropology (in Leipzig, Germany) and the Humboldt Foundation (in Germany).

References

Aristar, Anthony R. 1991. On diachronic sources and synchronic pattern: An investigation into the origin of linguistic universals. *Language* 67(1). 1–33.

Ashton, Ethel O. 1947. *Swahili grammar (including intonation)*. 2nd edn. London: Longman, Green & Co.

Bowden, John. 2001. *Taba: description of a South Halmahera language* (Pacific Linguistics). Canberra: The Australian National University.

Bradshaw, Joel & Francisc Czobor. 2005. *Otto Dempwolff's grammar of the Jabêm language in New Guinea*. Hawai'i: University of Hawai'i Press.

Bybee, Joan L. 1988. The diachronic dimension in explanation. In John A. Hawkins (ed.), *Explaining language universals*, 350–379. Oxford: Blackwell.

Collins, Chris & Jeff Gruber. 2014. *A grammar of ǂHõã with vocabulary, recorded utterances and oral texts*. Cologne: Rüdiger Köppe.

Collins, Chris & Levi Namaseb. 2011. *A grammatical sketch of N|uuki with stories*. Cologne: Rüdiger Köppe.

Collins, Jeremy. 2012. The evolution of the Greenbergian word order correlations. In Thomas C. Scott-Phillips, Mónica Tamariz, Erica A. Cartmill & James R. Hurford (eds.), *The evolution of language: 9th international conference*, 72–79. Singapore: World Scientific. DOI:10.1142/9789814401500_0010

Collins, Jeremy. 2019. Some language universals are historical accidents. In Karsten Schmidtke-Bode, Natalia Levshina, Susanne Maria Michaelis & Ilja A. Seržant (eds.), *Explanation in typology: Diachronic sources, functional motivations and the nature of the evidence*, 47–61. Berlin: Language Science Press. DOI:10.5281/zenodo.2583808

Cristofaro, Sonia. 2019. Taking diachronic evidence seriously: Result-oriented vs. source-oriented explanations of typological universals. In Karsten Schmidtke-Bode, Natalia Levshina, Susanne Maria Michaelis & Ilja A. Seržant (eds.), *Explanation in typology: Diachronic sources, functional motivations and the nature of the evidence*, 25–46. Berlin: Language Science Press. DOI:10.5281/zenodo.2583806

DeLancey, Scott. 1994. Grammaticalization and linguistic theory. In *Proceedings of the 1993 Mid-America Linguistics Conference and Conference on Siouan/Caddoan Languages*, 1–22. Boulder: Dept. of Linguistics, University of Colorado.

Dempwolff, Otto. 1939. *Grammatik der Jabêm-Sprache auf Neuguinea*. Hamburg: Friederichsen, de Gruyter.

Dorvlo, Kofi. 2008. *A grammar of logba (ikpana)*. Leiden: Leiden University (Doctoral dissertation).

Dryer, Matthew S. 1989. Large linguistic areas and language sampling. *Studies in Language* 13(2). 257–292. DOI:10.1075/sl.13.2.03dry

Dryer, Matthew S. 1992. The Greenbergian word order correlations. *Language* 68(1). 81–138. DOI:10.1353/lan.1992.0028

Dryer, Matthew S. 1997. On the six-way word order typology. *Studies in Language* 21(1). 69–103. DOI:10.1075/sl.21.1.04dry

Dryer, Matthew S. 2009. The branching direction theory of word order correlations revisited. In Sergio Scalise, Elisabetta Magni & Antonietta Bisetto (eds.), *Universals of language today*, 185–208. Dordrecht: Springer. DOI:10.1007/978-1-4020-8825-4_10

Dryer, Matthew S. 2010. Noun-modifier order in Africa. In Osamu Hieda, Christa König & Hirosi Nakagawa (eds.), *Geographical typology and linguistic areas: With special reference to Africa*, 287–311. Amsterdam, Philadelphia: John Benjamins. DOI:10.1075/tufs.2.23dry

Dryer, Matthew S. 2013. On the six-way order typology, again. *Studies in Language* 37(2). 267–301. DOI:doi.org/10.1075/sl.37.2.02dry

Givón, Talmy. 1971. Historical syntax and synchronic morphology: An archaeologist's field trip. *Chicago Linguistic Society* 7. 394–415.

Givón, Talmy. 1979. *On understanding grammar.* New York: Academic Press. DOI:10.1075/z.213

Givón, Talmy. 2001. *Syntax: An introduction. Vol. I.* Amsterdam, Philadelphia: John Benjamins. DOI:10.1075/z.syn1

Givón, Talmy. 2011. *Ute reference grammar.* Amsterdam, Philadelphia: John Benjamins. DOI:10.1075/clu.3

Greenberg, Joseph H. 1963. Some universals of grammar with particular reference to the order of meaningful elements. In Joseph H. Greenberg (ed.), *Universals of language*, 58–90. Cambridge, MA: MIT Press.

Hamel, Patricia J. 1994. *A grammar and lexicon of Loniu, Papua New Guinea* (Pacific Linguistics). Canberra: The Australian National University. DOI:10.15144/PL-C103

Haspelmath, Martin. 2019. Can cross-linguistic regularities be explained by constraints on change? In Karsten Schmidtke-Bode, Natalia Levshina, Susanne Maria Michaelis & Ilja A. Seržant (eds.), *Explanation in typology: Diachronic sources, functional motivations and the nature of the evidence*, 1–23. Berlin: Language Science Press. DOI:10.5281/zenodo.2583804

Hawkins, John A. 1983. *Word order universals.* New York: Academic Press. DOI:10.1016/C2009-0-21896-4

Hawkins, John A. 1994. *A performance theory of order and constituency.* Cambridge: Cambridge University Press. DOI:10.1017/CBO9780511554285

Hawkins, John A. 2004. *Efficiency and complexity in grammars.* Oxford: Oxford University Press. DOI:10.1093/acprof:oso/9780199252695.001.0001

Hawkins, John A. 2014. *Cross-linguistic variation and efficiency.* Oxford: Oxford University Press. DOI:10.1093/acprof:oso/9780199664993.001.0001

Heath, Jeffrey. 1999. *A grammar of Koyra Chiini: The Songhay of Timbuktu.* Berlin: Mouton de Gruyter. DOI:10.1515/9783110804850

Heine, Bernd & Mechthild Reh. 1984. *Grammaticalization and reanalysis in African languages.* Hamburg: Helmut Buske.

Hutchison, John P. 1976. *Aspects of Kanuri syntax*. Bloomington: Indiana University (Doctoral dissertation).

Hutchison, John P. 1981. *A reference grammar of the Kanuri language*. Madison: African studies program, University of Wisconsin.

Ikoro, Suanu M. 1996. *The Kana language*. Leiden: Rijksuniversiteit te Leiden (Doctoral dissertation).

Kooyers, Orneal. 1974. Washkuk grammar sketch. In *Grammatical studies in three languages of Papua New Guinea* (Workpapers in Papua New Guinea linguistics 6), 5–74. Ukarumpa: Summer Institute of Linguistics.

Kratochvíl, František. 2007. *A grammar of Abui: a Papuan language of Alor*. Utrecht: LOT.

Kuno, Susumu. 1974. The position of relative clauses and conjunctions. *Linguistic Inquiry* 5(1). 117–136.

Li, Charles N. & Sandra A. Thompson. 1981. *Mandarin Chinese: A functional reference grammar*. Berkeley: University of California Press.

Mous, Marten. 1993. *A grammar of Iraqw*. Hamburg: Helmut Buske.

Olawsky, Knut J. 1999. *Aspects of Dagbani grammar with special emphasis on phonology and morphology*. Munich: Lincom.

Rennison, John R. 1997. *Koromfe*. London, New York: Routledge.

Rennison, John R. 2017. Koromfe-English/French/German dictionary. https://www.univie.ac.at/linguistics/personal/john/dict_A4.pdf.

Ross, Malcolm. 2002. Jabêm. In John Lynch, Malcolm Ross & Terry Crowley (eds.), *The Oceanic languages*, 270–296. Richmond: Curzon.

Solnit, David B. 1997. *Eastern Kayah Li: Grammar, texts and glossary*. Honululu: University of Hawai'i Press.

Chapter 5

Preposed adverbial clauses: Functional adaptation and diachronic inheritance

Holger Diessel

University of Jena

In the historical literature it is commonly assumed that subordinate clauses are derived from paratactic sentences. However, while this assumption is not implausible for certain types of postposed adverbial clauses, there is no obvious connection between preposed adverbial clauses and parataxis. This paper investigates the diachronic development of preposed adverbial clauses from a cross-linguistic perspective. Drawing on data from a typological and diachronic database, it is shown that preposed adverbial clauses evolve from various diachronic sources that are semantically and structurally similar to the target construction (e.g. adpositional phrases, pre- and postnominal relative clauses, juxtaposed sentences). Considering the factors behind these developments, the paper argues that while the occurrence of preposed adverbial clauses can be explained by general cognitive processes of language use, the internal structure of preposed adverbial clauses, notably the position of the subordinator, is primarily determined by grammaticalization.

1 Introduction

It is a standard assumption of historical linguistics that syntactic structures often develop from structurally independent elements in discourse (Givón 1979). An oft-cited example is the diachronic development of subordinate clauses from paratactic sentences. As Lehmann (1988) and others have shown, there is a cline of clause linkage ranging from the combination of two structurally independent sentences in discourse to tightly organized bi-clausal structures in which one clause is syntactically dependent on the other one. Building on this observation, it is commonly assumed that subordinate clauses have evolved from independent sentences or parataxis (e.g. Hopper & Traugott 2003: 176–184). However,

Holger Diessel. 2019. Preposed adverbial clauses: Functional adaptation and diachronic inheritance. In Karsten Schmidtke-Bode, Natalia Levshina, Susanne Maria Michaelis & Ilja A. Seržant (eds.), *Explanation in typology: Diachronic sources, functional motivations and the nature of the evidence*, 97–122. Berlin: Language Science Press. DOI:10.5281/zenodo.2583812 while this assumption appears to be plausible for many postposed subordinate clauses, there is no obvious connection between parataxis and preposed subordinate clauses.

Clause combining in discourse has a backwards orientation. Paratactic sentences are usually related to previous sentences, as evidenced by the occurrence of anaphoric pronouns and clause linkers that connect the current sentence to participants and propositions of the preceding sentence or discourse (1).

(1) *John$_i$* was accepted to Harvard. *Therefore, he$_i$* moved to Boston.

Like independent sentences, complex sentences are processed with a backwards orientation if the subordinate clause follows the main clause (e.g. *John$_i$ moved to Boston, because he$_i$ was accepted to Harvard*). However, unlike paratactic sentences, preposed subordinate clauses have an inherent forward orientation in that pronouns and clause linkers are related to elements of the upcoming main clause (2).

(2) *Because he$_i$* was accepted to Harvard, *John$_i$* moved to Boston.

Considering the projective force of preposed subordinate clauses, it is unclear if and how these structures have evolved from clause combining strategies in discourse. It is the purpose of this paper to investigate the diachronic developments of preposed subordinate clauses from a cross-linguistic perspective. Specifically, the paper is concerned with the development of preposed adverbial clauses.

Following Cristofaro (2003), adverbial clauses are here defined as part of a biclausal construction consisting of a main clause and a subordinate clause in which the event designated by the subordinate clause specifies the circumstances under which the event of the main clause takes place. Several typological studies have investigated the positional patterns of adverbial clauses (e.g. Greenberg 1963; Diessel 2001; Schmidtke-Bode 2009; Diessel & Hetterle 2011; Hetterle 2015); but they are either based on small and biased samples or concentrate on particular adverbial relations (e.g. purpose or cause). In the current study, we will be concerned with four general semantic types of adverbial clauses (i.e. adverbial clauses of time, condition, cause and purpose) based on data from a genetically and geographically dispersed convenience sample of 100 languages. The languages come from 85 genera (which maximally include two languages) and six large geographical areas (i.e. Eurasia, Africa, South East Asia and Oceania, Australia and New Guinea, North America, South America) (cf. Dryer 1992). The bulk of the data were gathered from reference grammars and other published sources, supplemented by information from native speakers and language specialists.[1]

The paper is divided into three parts. The first part describes the cross-linguistic distribution of preposed adverbial clauses in the 100 language sample; the second part provides an overview of the main diachronic paths to preposed adverbial clauses; and the third part considers the developments described in light of the debate about functional and diachronic explanations for language universals that takes center stage in the present volume.

2 Cross-linguistic patterns

Let us begin with some general observations regarding the position of subordinate clauses. Subordinate clauses are dependent categories of an associated element. Three basic types of subordinate clauses are commonly distinguished: (i) complement clauses, which are dependent categories of a complement-taking verb or predicate, (ii) relative clauses, which are dependent categories of a noun or noun phrase, and (iii) adverbial clauses, which may be seen as dependent categories of a main clause or main clause predicate.

The position of all three types of subordinate clauses relative to the associated element correlates with the position of other dependent categories relative to the so-called head, but the correlations are skewed in particular directions (Diessel 2001). As Greenberg (1963) already noted, the order of relative clause and noun correlates with that of object and verb, but there is a predominance of postnominal relative clauses. In VO languages, relative clauses are almost always postposed to the associated N(P), but in OV languages we find both prenominal and postnominal relatives (cf. Dryer 2005).

The order of complement clause and verb is similar. As Schmidtke-Bode & Diessel (2017) have shown, although object complement clauses usually serve the same syntactic function as object NPs, they do not always occur in the same structural position as nominal objects. In VO languages, complement clauses follow the verb with almost no exception, but in many OV languages they are postposed to the main verb, as for instance in Persian, Epena Pedee and Supyire. There is thus a general tendency for both relative and complement clauses to follow the associated category, which may be due to the oft-noted trend for long and heavy constituents to follow short ones (cf. Behaghel 1932).

---

[1]A list of languages included in the sample is given in the Appendix.

However, adverbial clauses are different. Although adverbial clauses are long constituents, they often precede the main clause. As Diessel (2001) observed (based on data from a small and biased sample), in VO languages, adverbial clauses occur both before and after the associated main clause, but in some OV languages, there is a general tendency to prepose all adverbial clauses. This tendency is also evident in the current sample (cf. Table 1).

Table 1: The order of adverbial clause (AC) and main clause (MC) and the order of verb and object

	Languages in which all types of ACs (usually) precede the MC	Languages in which ACs are commonly pre- and postposed	Languages in which all types of ACs (usually) follow the MC	Total
VO	-	40	-	40
VO/OV	-	8	-	8
OV	31	21	-	52
Total	31	69	-	100

As can be seen, most of the languages of the current sample make common use of both pre- and postposed adverbial clauses, but in more than half of all OV languages, adverbial clauses are usually preposed to the main clause. In Japanese, for instance, there is a very strong tendency to prepose adverbial clauses (though in spoken Japanese, adverbial clauses sometimes follow the main clause as afterthoughts; cf. Ford & Mori 1994).

Generalizing across the data in Table 1, we may say that while the order of adverbial clause and main clause correlates with that of object and verb, the occurrence of preposed adverbial clauses is cross-linguistically predominant. However, on closer inspection we find that the predominance of preposed adverbial clauses is mainly due to certain semantic types of adverbial clauses that precede the main clause in both VO and OV languages. Consider the data in Table 2, which show that the positional patterns of adverbial clauses correlate with their meaning.

Note that the frequencies in Table 2 are based on constructions rather than on languages. Since some languages have multiple adverbial clause constructions of the same semantic type, Table 2 includes a larger number of constructions than languages. Note also that this table concerns both adverbial clauses that are tied to a specific position by linguistic convention and adverbial clauses that are sta-

Table 2: The meaning and position of adverbial clause constructions in a sample of 100 languages

	Preposed	Pre- and postposed	Postposed	Total
Condition	94 [91.3%]	9 [8.7%]	0 [0%]	103
Time	119 [59.8%]	68 [34.2%]	12 [6.0%]	199
Cause	40 [38.8%]	24 [21.2%]	49 [43.4%]	113
Purpose	33 [28.7%]	19 [16.5%]	63 [54.8%]	115
Total	286	120	124	530

tistically biased to precede or follow the main clause. In the latter case, some of the data in Table 2 are based on frequency counts from linguistic corpora, but more often these data are based on field workers' judgements regarding the position of adverbial clauses. While expert judgements are less reliable than corpus counts, they provide a reasonable estimate as to how main and adverbial clauses are arranged in a particular language.[2]

As can be seen, conditional clauses typically precede the main clause (cf. Greenberg 1963: Universal 14), though in many languages, conditional clauses can also be postposed to the main clause. Like conditional clauses, temporal clauses tend to precede the main clause, but temporal clauses follow the main clause more often than conditionals. The position of temporal clauses varies with the nature of the temporal link they encode. For instance, temporal clauses denoting a prior event, i.e. an event that precedes the one in the main clause, are more often preposed than temporal clauses denoting a posterior event. In English, for example, *after-* and *since-*clauses denote a prior event and precede the main clause more often than adverbial clauses denoting a posterior event such as *before-* and *until-*clauses (cf. Diessel 2008). The same tendency has been observed in several other languages of the current sample (e.g. in German, Supyire, Abun, Nkore Kiga, Noon, and Taba).

Moreover, and this is particularly striking, there is a general tendency to prepose adverbial clauses that correspond to English *when-*clauses. Like *after* and *since, when* can denote a prior event, but it can also indicate a link between events that occur simultaneously (Diessel 2008). However, regardless of the temporal re-

---

[2]Psycholinguistic evidence suggests that while speakers have difficulties to estimate the absolute frequencies of linguistic elements, their judgements of relative linguistic frequencies are quite reliable (Hasher & Zacks 1984).

lationship that is expressed by a *when*-clause, there is a tendency for temporal *when*-clauses to precede the main clause. In fact, in a substantial number of languages *when*-clauses are generally preposed to the main clause in the current sample (i.e. Abun, Supyire, Yagua, Trumai, Motuna).

Finally, cause and purpose clauses tend to follow the main clause. Table 2 shows that there are 40 adverbial clause constructions of cause and 33 adverbial clause constructions of purpose that precede the main clause, but most of these constructions occur in languages like Japanese, in which all adverbial clauses are preposed to the main clause regardless of their meaning. Generalizing across these findings we may conclude that the cross-linguistic tendency to prepose adverbial clauses is mainly due to the fact that conditional clauses and certain types of temporal clauses, notably *when*-clauses, precede the main clause regardless of the order of other syntactic constituents.

Interestingly, a number of studies suggest that the position of adverbial clauses does not only correlate with the semantic link between main clauses and adverbial clauses, but also with aspects of their internal structure. Of particular importance here is the position of the subordinator (cf. Diessel 2001; Schmidtke-Bode 2009; Hetterle 2015). Across languages, adverbial clauses are often marked by subordinate conjunctions that typically appear at the beginning or end of the subordinate clause. Dryer (1992) showed that the position of the subordinator correlates with the order of verb and object: In VO languages, adverbial clauses usually occur with initial subordinators, but in OV languages they often include a final marker. However, the position of the subordinator does not only correlate with the order of verb and object, it also correlates with the position of the adverbial clause. Consider the data in Table 3, which is restricted to adverbial clauses with free subordinating morphemes.[3]

As can be seen, adverbial clauses that follow the main clause or that are flexible with regard to their position typically occur with an initial marker. There are languages in which postposed and flexible adverbial clauses include a final marker, but this is relatively rare (and mainly found in certain areas, e.g. South America). By contrast, preposed adverbial clauses are frequently marked by a final subordinator, especially in languages in which all adverbial clauses precede the main clause, as for instance in Amele, Burmese, Japanese, Korafe, Korean, Santali, Slave, Turkish, Wappo, Warao, and Menya. Only conditional clauses and temporal *when*-clauses are commonly preposed and often marked by an initial subordinator (in languages in which other semantic types of adverbial clauses are flexible or postposed to the main clause).

---

[3]Since adverbial clause constructions that do not include a free subordinating morpheme are disregarded, Table 3 includes only a subset of the adverbial clause constructions in Table 2.

Table 3: The position of free subordinators in pre- and postposed adverbial clauses

	Preposed		Flexible (no preference)		Postposed		
	Initial	Final	Initial	Final	Initial	Final	Total
Condition	34	22	5	-	-	-	61
Time	20	47	43	5	7	3	125
Cause	2	26	11	6	37	4	86
Purpose	-	20	2	4	38	4	68
Total	56	115	61	15	82	11	340

3 Diachronic sources

Having described the positional patterns of adverbial clauses (and adverbial subordinators), let us now consider their diachronic evolution. Where do preposed adverbial clauses come from? In the historical literature, syntactic development is commonly described as a process that leads from a source construction A to a target construction B, but this scenario is not always appropriate to characterize syntactic change (cf. Givón 1991; Van de Velde et al. 2013). Since subordinate clauses are complex grammatical units, they are usually related to several other constructions, e.g. other types of subordinate clauses, certain types of phrasal constituents and independent sentences. Since all of these constructions can influence the development of a particular adverbial clause, it is not always possible to trace adverbial clauses to one specific source. However, while the diachronic developments of adverbial clauses are (usually) influenced by several constructions, in many cases there is one construction that is so closely related to a certain type of adverbial clause that it can be seen as the primary determinant, or source, of that clause. For instance, many postposed adverbial clauses are so similar to paratactic sentences that it seems reasonable to assume that parataxis has a significant impact on the development of (many) postposed subordinate clauses. However, while the development from parataxis provides a plausible scenario for the rise of (many) postposed adverbial clause, it does not explain where preposed adverbial clauses come from.

Since preposed adverbial clauses are thematically related to the ensuing discourse, there is no obvious connection to parataxis unless we assume that preposed adverbial clauses are based on postposed subordinate clauses that were fronted after they developed from paratactic sentences. However, there is no evidence for this scenario. The diachronic developments of adverbial clauses have been examined in a large number of studies (e.g. Haiman 1985; Haspelmath 1989; Givón 1991; Genetti 1991; Harris & Campbell 1995; Frajzyngier 1996; Disterheft & Viti 2010), but although fronting appears to provide a plausible scenario for the development of preposed adverbial clauses, there is almost no evidence for this scenario in the historical literature. On the contrary, what previous studies suggest is that adverbial clauses usually occur in the same position as their diachronic sources. In what follows, we consider four common source constructions for preposed adverbial clauses.

First, while preposed adverbial clauses are unlikely to have evolved from paratactic sentences through fronting, there is one common diachronic path that leads from independent sentences in discourse to complex sentences with preposed adverbial clauses. As Haiman (1985: 39–70) observed, in many languages conditional relations are expressed by juxtaposed clauses that have the same structure as two simple sentences, as in the following examples from Vietnamese (3), Mapudungun (4) and Wambaya (5).

(3) Vietnamese (Austro-Asiatic, Viet-Muong; Haiman 1985: 45)
[Không có màn], không chịu nôi.
not   be net   not   bear can
'If there's no net, you can't stand it.'

(4) Mapudungun (Araucanian; Smeets 2008: 184)
[Aku-wye-fu-l-m-i],   pe-pa-ya-fwi-y-m-i.
arrive-PLPF-IPD-COND-2-SG see-hither-IRR-OBJ-IND-2-SG
'If you had arrived (by then), you would have seen him.'

(5) Wambaya (West Barkly; Nordlinger 1998: 219)
[Yabu ng-uda   gijilulu]   jiyawu ng-uda.
have 1SG.A-NACT.PST money.IV(ACC) give   1SG.A-NACT.PST
'If I'd had the money I would have given (it to her).'

While some of these languages have conditional markers (e.g. Vietnamese *nêu* 'if'), conditional relations are commonly expressed by unmarked sentences that have the same structure as main clauses: they include finite verb forms, occur with the same arguments and adjuncts as independent sentences, and do not include an (obligatory) subordinate marker. Note, however, that while these constructions look like independent sentences, they are intonationally bound to the ensuing clause and sometimes constrained with regard to verb inflection. The conditional clause in Mapudungun, for instance, takes a mood suffix that is optional in main clauses but obligatory in conditionals. Moreover, in some languages these constructions occur with a topic or focus marker that one might analyze as a subordinator, such as the focus clitic at the end of the protasis in example (6) from Mangarayi.

(6) Mangarayi (Isolate; Merlan 1982: 22)
     [ña-yaŋ-gu=**bayi**] wawg wa-ñan-mi   biwin-gana.
     2SG-go-DI-FOC   follow IRR-1SG>2SG-AUX behind-ABL
     'If you go, I will follow (after) you.'

In addition to conditional clauses, preposed temporal clauses are sometimes based on juxtaposed sentences (e.g. in Lao, Vietnamese, Taba, Tetun, Gooniyandi); but preposed cause and purpose clauses are usually based on other types of constructions. Adpositional phrases, for instance, are often closely related to (preposed) cause and purpose clauses. Consider, for instance, the following examples from Turkish (7) and Amele (8), in which cause and purpose clauses are marked by benefactive postpositions.

(7) Turkish (Turkic; Kornfilt 1997: 74)
     Hasan [kitab-ı san-a   ver-diğ-im   **için**] çok kız-dı.
     Hasan book-ACC you-DAT give-F.NMLZ-1SG for   very angry-PST
     'Hasan got very angry because I gave the book to you.'

(8) Amele (Nuclear Trans New Guinea, Madang; Roberts 1987: 58)
     [Ija sab faj-ec   **nu**] h-ug-a.
     1SG food buy-INF/NMLZ for come-1SG-PST
     'I came to buy food.'

Note that the adverbial clauses in both examples are expressed by nominalizations. While adpositions and case affixes are also found with finite clauses, they are especially frequent with nominalized clauses, suggesting that nominalization provides a link between adpositional phrases and fully developed (subordinate) clauses (cf. Deutscher 2009; Heine 2009).

Adverbial clauses that are morphologically related to adpositional phrases are widely used to express semantic relations of cause and purpose. In addition, certain types of temporal clauses denoting a prior or posterior event are often strikingly similar to (temporal) adpositional phrases (e.g. English *after-, since-* and *before*-clauses) (Blake 1999; Hetterle 2015); but conditional clauses and temporal *when*-clauses are only rarely marked by adpositions.

Apart from juxtaposed sentences and adpositional phrases, relative clauses provide a very frequent source for (preposed) adverbial clauses. The development is well-known from English. As Hopper & Traugott (2003) have shown, temporal *while*-clauses have evolved from a relative or appositive construction that modified a generic head noun meaning 'time' (9).

(9) Old English (Indo-European, Germanic; Hopper & Traugott 2003: 90)
  & wicode Þær Þa   **hwile**   [Þe man Þa burg   worthe
  and lived   there that.DAT time.DAT that one that fortress worked.on
  & getimbrode].
  and built

  '... and camped there at the time that/while the fortress was worked on and built.'

Similar types of adverbial clauses occur in many other languages of the current sample (e.g. in Mayogo (10) and Toqabaqita (11)). Sometimes the subordinator is based on a generic noun, and sometimes it is based on a relative marker (as for instance many of the adverbial subordinators in Tamasheq; cf. Heath 2005: 660).

(10) Mayogo (Niger-Congo, Ubangi; Sawka 2001: 153)
  [**Nedhinga** u a-zʉ   'he], ndɨlɨ-e   a-sɨ   kuto.
  while/time 3PL PST-eat thing child-REF PST-sleep down

  'While they ate something, this child slept on (the) floor.'

(11) Toqabaqita (Austronesian, Oceanic; Lichtenberk 2008: 1173)
  [**Si** **manga na** kero   fula   mai], keko   qono qa-daroqa
  PRTT time   REL 3DU.NON.FUT arrive VENT 3DU.SEQ sit   SBEN-3DU.PERS

  'When (lit. 'the time that') they arrived, they sat (down) ...'

The development is especially frequent with temporal *when*- and *while*-clauses, but there are also other semantic types of adverbial clauses that are based on relative clauses in my data. In German, for instance, cause and condition clauses are marked by adverbial subordinators (i.e. *weil* and *falls*) that are based on nominal heads of relative or appositive clauses meaning 'time (span)' and 'case'. Moreover, at least 25 languages of the current sample have conditional clauses based on temporal *when/while*-clauses (which at least in some cases are ultimately based on relative clauses). Note that this development does not only involve postnominal relatives but also prenominal and internally headed relative clauses, as illustrated by the following examples from Amele (12), Korean (13) and Jamsay (14).[4]

(12)   Amele (Nuclear Trans New Guinea, Madang; Roberts 1987: 57)
[Ija cabi   meul ceh-ig-en   **sain eu na**] ma ca ceta ca   mun
1SG garden new plant-1SG-FUT **time that at**   taro add yam add   banana
ca manin ca   ceh-ig-en.
add bean   add plant-1SG-FUT
'When I plant my new garden, I will plant taro, yam, banana and beans.'

(13)   Korean (Isolate; Sohn 1994: 70)
Na-nun [pi-ka   w-ass-ul   **ttay-(ey)**] ttena-ss-ta.
I-TC   rain-NOM come-PST-PROSP time-at   leave-PST-DECL
'I left when it had rained.'

(14)   Jamsay (Dogon; Heath 2008: 559)
[Wárú **dògùrù** ù   gô:-Ø]   ...
farming time   2SG.SBJ go:out.PFV-PTCP.NON.HUMAN
'At the time when you (first) went out to do the farming, ...'

Finally, preposed adverbial clauses are also often influenced by complement clauses. In Middle English, for instance, adverbial subordinators were frequently accompanied by the complementizer *that (e.g. after that, since that, gif that)*, which is still commonly used in result clauses (cf. *so that*). Likewise, in Chalcatongo Mixtec, most adverbial clauses are marked by the complementizer *xa=*, which also appears in complement and relative clauses (Macaulay 1996: 156–168). Moreover, there is a well-known path that leads from quotative constructions, which in many languages are similar to complement clauses, to adverbial clauses. In particular, purpose and cause clauses are sometimes derived from quotatives (cf. Güldemann 2008).

Quotative constructions consist of a "quote index", including a "quotative marker", and a "quote clause" of direct speech that often shows little evidence for embedding (cf. Güldemann 2008). In many cases, the quotative marker is a general verb of saying (e.g. 'say', 'speak'), but it can also be a marker of similarity (e.g. 'like') or a manner deictic (e.g. 'so'). Although quote clauses are often not embedded in the associated clause, the quotative verb takes the quote clause as some

---

[4] According to Epps (2009), Hup has adverbial clauses that are based on headless relative clauses.

kind of semantic argument, which typically occurs in the same position as a direct object.[5] When this happens in OV languages, the consequence is that quote clauses precede the quotative verb. If these constructions are extended into the domain of adverbial subordination, the adverbial clause is preposed to the main clause (or main verb) and marked by a clause-final subordinator that is ultimately based on the quotative verb, as in the following examples from Aguaruna (15) and Lezgian (16).

(15) Aguaruna (Jivaroan; Overall 2009: 175)
Nuwa-na   [yumi ʃikika-ta   **tu-sã**]   awɨma-wa.
woman-ACC water draw.ASP-IMP say-SUB.3.SS send.ASP-NON.A/S>A/S
"When (they) sent a woman to draw water, ….' (lit. 'saying "draw some water, ..."')

(16) Lezgian (Nakh-Daghestanian; Haspelmath 1993: 390)
Bazar.di-n   juǧ ada-z   [tars-ar   awa-č   **luhuz**] tak'an
Sunday-GEN day he-DAT lesson-PL be.in-NEG saying hateful
x̂a-nwa-j.
become-PRF-PST
'He hated Sunday because there were no lessons.'

Table 4 provides an overview of the various sources for preposed adverbial clauses considered in this section. Let me emphasize that this table simplifies in several ways. First, as pointed out above, the development of adverbial clauses is usually influenced by multiple constructions so that there are often several source constructions (though one of them is often dominant). Second, there are frequent diachronic connections between the various semantic types of adverbial clauses that are not indicated in Table 4 except for the development of temporal *when/while*-clauses into conditional clauses, which is particularly frequent. Third, there is reason to assume that postposed adverbial clauses can influence the structure of preposed adverbial clauses through analogical extension (cf. Traugott 1985). Fourth, in addition to the eight source constructions shown in Table 4,

---

[5]Munro (1982) and Güldemann (2008) point out that quote clauses do not generally occur in the same position as direct objects, which is one reason why these researchers argue that quote clauses are not (always) complements. However, while quote clauses are often less tightly integrated into a clause (or VP) than direct objects, they are related to object complement clauses by family resemblance and since object complement clauses pattern with object NPs, there is also a tendency for quote clauses to occur in the same position as direct objects (see Schmidtke-Bode & Diessel 2017 for some discussion of the relationship between quote clauses, object complement clauses and nominal objects from a cross-linguistic perspective).

Table 4: Frequent source constructions of preposed adverbial clauses

Condition	juxtaposed sentences (Haiman 1985)
	temporal *when/while*-clauses (Traugott 1985)
Time	adpositional phrases / nominalizations (Genetti 1991)
	pre- and postnominal relative clauses (Givón 1991)
Cause	adpositional phrases / nominalizations (Genetti 1991)
	quotative / complement constructions (Ebert 1991)
Purpose	adpositional phrases / nominalizations (Schmidtke-Bode 2009)
	quotative / complement constructions (Güldemann 2008)

there are other (less frequent) source constructions of preposed adverbial clauses that have been disregarded. And finally, there is evidence that constructional change typically proceeds in a local fashion that is driven by language users' experience with particular lexical expressions (e.g. Givón 1991), but this has been ignored in the above discussion. In order to account for all of these factors, one would need a different theoretical approach — perhaps some kind of network model, in which adverbial clauses are linked to various other types of constructions that simultaneously affect their use and their development (see Diessel 2015 for some discussion of such a model). However, in what follows we concentrate on the idealized developments that are summarized in Table 4.

4 Discussion: Functional adaptation and/or persistence

To recapitulate, we have seen that the occurrence of preposed adverbial clauses correlates with the position of other grammatical categories and the semantic relationship between main and adverbial clause (§2), and we have seen that condition, time, cause and purpose clauses develop from, or under the influence of, a wide range of constructions (§3). Concluding the paper, let us ask what leads to the development and cross-linguistic distribution of preposed adverbial clauses.

Many linguistic typologists assume that language universals are motivated by semantic and pragmatic factors that influence the diachronic developments of linguistic structure. On this view, cross-linguistic regularities are functional adaptations to communication and processing (e.g. Foley & Van Valin 1984; Dik 1989; Hawkins 2004). However, as particularly Cristofaro (2019 [this volume]) and

Collins (2019 [this volume]) argue, there is an alternative approach that stresses the importance of diachronic inheritance, or persistence, for the rise of language universals. In this approach, cross-linguistic tendencies, or statistical universals, are the by-product of diachronic processes that are NOT immediately motivated by functional-adaptive factors. In the remainder of this paper, I argue that the cross-linguistic tendencies in the linear organization of adverbial clauses are the result of both functional aspects of language use and persistence effects of grammaticalization.

PREPOSED ADVERBIAL CLAUSES IN HEAD-FINAL LANGUAGES. Given that clause combining in discourse has a strong backwards orientation, one might wonder why adverbial clauses are not generally postposed. However, there are several reasons why languages prepose adverbial clauses. To begin with, above we have seen that the positional patterns of adverbial clauses vary with their meaning, but in some rigid OV languages, they are consistently preposed to the main clause, suggesting that the order of main and adverbial clauses is part of the traditional VO/OV typology (cf. Diessel 2001).

There are numerous proposals in the literature to explain correlations between the order of verb and object and that of other grammatical categories. Especially prominent is Hawkins' processing approach, in which word order correlations are explained by general principles of syntactic processing that are assumed to influence both language use and language change (cf. Hawkins 1994; 2004). Specifically, Hawkins proposed that head-final or OV languages tend to prepose dependent categories, including subordinate clauses, because syntactic structures with consistent dependent-head orders are easier to process, and thus more strongly preferred, than structures with mixed or inconsistent dependent-head orders (see Dryer 1992 for a similar explanation).

The processing approach provides a straightforward explanation for the dominant use of preposed adverbial clauses in OV languages, but as Krifka (1985) and others have noted, word order correlations can also be explained by analogy or similarity. There is abundant evidence from psycholinguistic research that speakers tend to arrange semantically or formally similar expressions in parallel positions (see Pickering & Ferreira 2008 for a review of psycholinguistic research on the influence of structural priming on linear order). Like objects, adverbial clauses are dependent categories, but other than that, adverbial clauses do not seem to have much in common with object NPs, making it rather unlikely that analogy and similarity account for this correlation. However, if we broaden the perspective and include other types of constructions into the analysis, there is reason to assume that the correlation between adverbial clauses and object NPs is due to analogical pressure that affects a whole network of constructions.

To begin with, adverbial clauses are often similar to adpositional phrases functioning as adjuncts, and since the latter are usually similar to object NPs, adverbial clauses are also related to direct objects (via adjuncts). As Dryer (1992) showed, there is a very strong tendency to place nominal objects and (certain semantic types of) adjuncts on the same side of the verb and since adverbial clauses pattern like adjunct phrases, they also pattern with object NPs.

Moreover, in many languages, adverbial clauses are expressed by the same or very similar types of constructions as complement clauses. Since complement clauses are also related to object NPs, we may hypothesize that the ordering correlation between complex sentences including adverbial clauses and verb phrases including nominal objects is (also) mediated by constructions including complement clauses, as the latter share properties with both of them.

Thus, while adverbial clauses do not have much in common with object NPs, they are similar to adpositional phrases and complement clauses, which in turn are similar to nominal objects, suggesting that OV (or head-final) languages prepose adverbial clauses in analogy to (preposed) adpositional phrases and complement clauses (17).

(17)

$$\text{NP–V} \underset{\text{PP–V}}{\overset{\text{CC–V}}{\rightleftharpoons}} \text{AC–V}$$

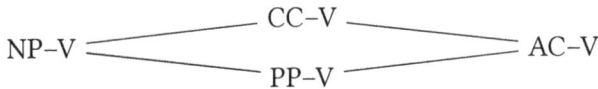

PREPOSED ADVERBIAL CLAUSES IN HEAD-INITIAL LANGUAGES. Analogy is one factor that can motivate the occurrence of preposed adverbial clauses in head-final languages, but since the occurrence of preposed adverbial clauses is not restricted to head-final languages, analogy alone is not sufficient to explain why adverbial clauses are commonly preposed. As we have seen, certain semantic types of adverbial clauses, notably conditional clauses and temporal *when*-clauses, precede the main clause in both head-initial and head-final languages. In order to explain these patterns, we have to consider the semantic and discourse-pragmatic properties of adverbial clauses.

As Chafe (1984), Givón (1984) and many others have pointed out, preposed adverbial clauses serve particular discourse-organizing functions. They provide a thematic ground or orientation for subsequent information, as evidenced by the fact that preposed adverbial clauses are often marked as topics (Haiman 1978). In addition, there are particular conceptual motivations to prepose certain semantic types of adverbial clauses. Conditional clauses, for instance, exhibit a strong tendency to precede the main clause, as conditionals are used to create a particular conceptual framework for the semantic interpretation of associated clauses (Diessel 2005), and some temporal clauses precede the main clause for reasons of iconicity (Diessel 2008).

Considering the semantic and discourse-pragmatic functions of preposed adverbial clauses, we may hypothesize that these functions do not only influence speakers' use of a particular clause order (where there is synchronic choice) but also the development of preposed adverbial clauses in language change or language evolution. In particular, the initial stages of the development seem to be motivated by semantic and discourse-pragmatic factors. For instance, as we have seen, adverbial clauses are often based on relative clauses and adpositional phrases, which in VO languages usually follow the main verb (if we disregard center-embedded RCs), but may be fronted in order to provide an orientation, or topic, for the unfolding sentence. When the fronted constructions are routinely used for discourse-organizing functions, they may develop into preposed adverbial clauses with the same or similar functions.

Assuming that preposed adverbial clauses inherit their discourse functions from fronted relative clauses, adpositional phrases and similar constructions, one might argue that while discourse considerations motivate the use of the various source constructions, they do not immediately motivate the extension of these constructions to adverbial clauses, which seems to be a consequence of automatization, semantic bleaching and formal reduction rather than of discourse processing. However, since grammaticalization is a gradual process with no sharp division between source and target, I would contend that the influence of discourse is not restricted to the initial uses of the source constructions but affects the entire course of the development. After all, automatization, semantic bleaching and formal reduction are driven by frequency of language use, which in turn is driven by the need to use fronted relative clauses, adpositional phrases or (incipient) adverbial clauses for particular discourse purposes.

Thus, while one cannot say that preposed adverbial clauses have evolved to fill a functional gap within the linguistic system, it is still reasonable to conceive of them as functional adaptations to particular discourse environments, as preposed adverbial clauses develop under the continuing influence of discourse considerations.

INITIAL AND FINAL SUBORDINATORS. Let us finally turn to the correlation between the position of adverbial clauses and that of the subordinator. Recall that while postposed adverbial clauses are commonly introduced by a clause-initial conjunction, preposed adverbial clauses often occur with a final marker. In particular, in languages in which adverbial clauses are generally preposed to the main clause, the subordinator typically occurs at the end of the adverbial clause. There are two general explanations for the position of adverbial subordinators in pre- and postposed subordinate clauses: one refers to processing, the other to grammaticalization.

In Hawkins' (1994; 2004) processing approach, the positional patterns of adverbial subordinators are explained by two general principles. To simplify, one principle predicts that the subordinator occurs at the boundary to the main clause because linear structures of this type have a short "recognition domain" that is easy to process and thus more highly preferred than structures with a long recognition domain. And the second principle predicts that there is a general tendency to place the subordinator at the beginning of the subordinate clause (regardless of clause order), because initial subordinators prevent the parser from misinterpreting subordinate clauses as main clauses (see also Diessel 2005: 455–459).

Hawkins' theory provides a good fit to the data, but lacks a diachronic dimension. As it stands, it is completely unclear how the word orders that are explained by syntactic processing in this approach have evolved in language history. Haspelmath (2019 [this volume]) argues that functional explanations do not need diachronic evidence if they correctly predict the typological data; but I disagree with this view because functional explanations can turn out to be spurious when we consider how particular phenomena have evolved.

In fact, there is evidence that the above described correlation between the position of the subordinator and the position of the subordinate clause is just a by-product of grammaticalization processes that are not immediately influenced by syntactic processing. That grammaticalization can have an impact on the linear organization of syntactic constituents has been observed in previous research (Li & Thompson 1974). In fact, a number of studies have argued that (some) word order correlations are due to persistence effects in grammaticalization (e.g. Givón 1975, Aristar 1991; Bybee 2010; Collins 2012; see also Collins 2019 [this volume] and Dryer 2019 [this volume]).

For instance, according to Bybee (2010: 111), the correlation between the order of verb and object and that of verb and auxiliary does not need a particular functional explanation, as auxiliaries are usually derived from the main verb of a complement construction that includes an infinitive, or some other type of verb, as verbal complement (e.g. 'want' INFINITIVE). If the verb precedes the verbal complement of a complex VP in the diachronic source, the auxiliary precedes the main verb in the target construction; but if the verb follows the verbal complement in the diachronic source, the auxiliary is postposed to the main verb in the target construction. As a consequence of these developments, the order of auxiliary and verb correlates with that of verb and object (18).

(18) $[\text{VERB} \quad [\text{VERB}]_{\text{OBJ}}]_{\text{VP}}$ $[[\text{VERB}]_{\text{OBJ}} \quad \text{VERB}]_{\text{VP}}$
       ↓   ↓   ↓   ↓
     $[\text{AUX} \quad \text{VERB}]_{\text{VP}}$ $[\text{VERB} \quad \text{AUX}]_{\text{VP}}$

It is conceivable that the correlation between the position of adverbial subordinators and that of adverbial clauses is also due to persistence effects of grammaticalization. For instance, above we have seen that purpose clauses in Amele and cause/purpose clauses in Turkish are marked by a clause-final subordinator that also serves as a benefactive adposition in postpositional phrases. Since postpositional phrases usually precede all other constituents in Amele and Turkish (and most other head-final languages), it is a plausible hypothesis that the occurrence of final subordinators in these constructions is related to the fact that they are based on postpositions (of preposed adpositional constructions).

(19) $[[\ \text{NP}\ ] \quad \text{P}]_{\text{PP}}$ $[\ ...\ \text{v}\ ...\ ]_{\text{S}}$
       ↓   ↓   ↓
     $[[...\ \text{s}\ ...\ \text{SUB}]_{\text{AC}} \quad [\ ...\ \text{v}\ ...\ ]_{\text{MC}}]$

In other cases, final subordinators are based on quotative verbs, as for instance, in some temporal and causal clauses of Aguaruna and Lezgian ((15)-(16)). Here again, the final position of the subordinator is likely to be a consequence of grammaticalization. Since quotative clauses precede the quote verb in Aguaruna and Lezgian (and many other head-final languages), the final position of the subordinator is readily explained by the fact that it evolved from a quotative verb that followed the quote clause in the source construction.

(20) $[[\text{QUOTE}]\ \text{v}]$ $[\ ...\ \text{v}\ ...\ ]_{\text{SIMPLE S}}$
       ↓   ↓   ↓
     $[[...\ \text{s}\ ...\ \ \text{SUB}]_{\text{AC}} \quad [\ ...\ \text{v}\ ...\ ]_{\text{MC}}]_{\text{COMPLEX S}}$

Crucially, while Hawkins' processing approach can also account for the main trends in the data, it cannot explain the exceptional cases. For instance, while postposed and flexible adverbial clauses are usually marked by initial subordinators (as predicted by Hawkins), there are 26 postposed (and flexible) adverbial clause constructions in the data in which the subordinator comes at the end of the adverbial clause, as in example (21) from Yagua.

(21) Yagua (Peba-Yaguan; Payne & Payne 1990: 340)
     Deerá-miy sąąniy-yąą   [sa-tįįysįa **túunu**].
     child-COLL shout-DISTRIB 3SG-play   while
     'The children are shouting while they play.'

While the existence of these structures flies in the face of Hawkins' processing account, it has a straightforward diachronic explanation. As Payne & Payne (1990: 340) point out, the subordinate conjunction comes at the end of the adverbial clause in (21) because *túunu* 'while' has evolved from a postposition meaning 'side', and since postpositional phrases follow the verb in Yagua, the resulting adverbial clause includes a clause-final marker.

Considering these examples, we may hypothesize that grammaticalization accounts for the occurrence of final subordinators in preposed adverbial clauses. However, since adverbial subordinators are derived from a wide range of sources, it is unclear at this point if the grammaticalization account is sufficient to explain the cross-linguistic data. Moreover, even if it turns out that the position of the subordinator is primarily determined by grammaticalization, this does not necessarily exclude the possibility that processing also affects the position of the subordinator as an independent factor. More research is needed to determine the role of grammaticalization (and processing) on the development of word order correlations, but I suspect that the cross-linguistic distribution of initial and final subordinators is primarily caused by grammaticalization rather than by Hawkins' principles of syntactic processing.

5 Conclusion

To summarize the main points of this paper, we have seen that the position of adverbial clauses correlates with the meaning of adverbial relations and the position of other grammatical categories that are similar to adverbial clauses. Since preposed adverbial clauses include a forward orientation that deviates from the dominant backwards orientation of clause combining in discourse, there is no obvious (diachronic) connection between preposed adverbial clauses and independent sentences. Only conditional and some temporal clauses that precede the main clause are (often) based on juxtaposed sentences that are oriented towards the subsequent clause. All other semantic types of preposed adverbial clauses develop from, or under the influence of, other (source) constructions: adpositional phrases and nominalizations, pre- and postnominal relative clauses, internally headed relatives, and quotative constructions.

The positional patterns of adverbial clauses can be explained by functional and cognitive processes that influence both speakers' choice of a particular clause order in language use and the diachronic developments of pre- and postposed adverbial clauses from certain source constructions. Some of these processes affect the whole class of adverbial clauses (e.g. the discourse-organizing function that motivates the occurrence of preposed adverbial clauses), others are only relevant for certain semantic types of adverbial relations (e.g. iconicity of sequence). Crucially, while the positional patterns of adverbial clauses are motivated by functional and cognitive aspects of language use, the position of the adverbial subordinator may just be a by-product of grammaticalization. Like the positional patterns of auxiliaries and other grammatical markers that evolved through grammaticalization, the positional patterns of adverbial subordinators seem to be determined by the position of their diachronic sources. Since the various source constructions tend to occur in reverse orders in VO and OV languages, it is not improbable that the position of adverbial subordinators correlates with that of other grammatical categories in head-initial and head-final languages because of persistence effects in grammaticalization. However, more research is needed to investigate the cognitive and diachronic mechanisms behind these correlations.

Abbreviations

The paper abides by the Leipzig Glossing Rules. Additional or deviant abbreviations include:

AC	adverbial clause	PLPF	pluperfect
ASP	aspect	PROSP	prospective
COLL	collective	PRTT	partitive
DI	desiderative-intentional (mood)	REF	referential
DISTRIB	distributive	S	sentence/clause
IPD	impeditive	SBEN	self-benefactive
MC	main clause	SEQ	sequential
MID	middle voice	SS	same subject
NACT	non-actual (irrealis) mood	TC	topic-contrast
PART	particle	VENT	ventive
PERS	personal		

Appendix: Language sample

AFRICA: Fongbe, Hausa, Jamsay, Kana, Khwe, Konso, Koyra Chiini, Krongo, Lango, Mayogo, Mbay, Nkore Kiga, Noon, Supyire, Tamasheq.
NORTH AND CENTRAL AMERICA: Choctaw, (Barbareño) Chumash, Kiowa, Lakota, (Chalcatongo) Mixtec, Musqueam, Ojibwe, Purépecha, Rama, Slave, Tepehua, (Jamul) Tiipay, Tümpisa Shoshone, Tzutujil, Wappo, West Greenlandic.

SOUTH AMERICA: Aguaruna, Awa Pit, Barasano, Cavineña, Epena Pedee, Hup, Jarawara, Kwazá, Mapudungun, Matsés, Mekens, Mosetén, Ndyuka, (Huallaga) Quechua, Tariana, Trumai, Urarina, Warao, Wariˈ, Yagua, Yuracaré.

EURASIA: Abkhaz, Ainu, (Gulf) Arabic, Basque, Evenki, French, Georgian, German, Hungarian, Japanese, Korean, Lezgian, Malayalam, Marathi, Persian, Santali, Serbo-Croatian, Turkish, (Kolyma) Yukaghir.

SOUTH-EAST ASIA AND OCEANIA: Burmese, Hmong Njua, Begak Ida'an, (Karo) Batak, Lao, Mandarin Chinese, Dolakha Newar, Qiang, Semelai, Taba, Tetun, Toqabaqita, Tukang Besi, Vietnamese, Yakan.

AUSTRALIA AND NEW GUINEA: Gooniyandi, Imonda, Kayardild, Kewa, Korafe, Lavukaleve, Mali, Mangarayi, Menya, Motuna, Martuthunira, Ungarinjin, Wambaya, Yimas

References

Aristar, Anthony R. 1991. On diachronic sources and synchronic pattern: An investigation into the origin of linguistic universals. *Language* 67(1). 1–33.

Behaghel, Otto. 1932. *Deutsche Syntax: Eine geschichtliche Darstellung. Vol. 4: Worstellung, Periodenbau.* Heidelberg: Winter.

Blake, Barry J. 1999. Nominal marking on verbs: Some Australian cases. *Word* 50(3). 299–317. DOI:10.1080/00437956.1999.11432490

Bybee, Joan L. 2010. *Language, usage and cognition.* Cambridge: Cambridge University Press. DOI:10.1017/CBO9780511750526.011

Chafe, Wallace. 1984. How people use adverbial clauses. In *Annual Meeting of the Berkeley Linguistics Society*, vol. 10, 437–449. DOI:10.3765/bls.v10i0.1936

Collins, Jeremy. 2012. The evolution of the Greenbergian word order correlations. In Thomas C. Scott-Phillips, Mónica Tamariz, Erica A. Cartmill & James R. Hurford (eds.), *The evolution of language: 9th international conference*, 72–79. Singapore: World Scientific. DOI:10.1142/9789814401500_0010

Collins, Jeremy. 2019. Some language universals are historical accidents. In Karsten Schmidtke-Bode, Natalia Levshina, Susanne Maria Michaelis & Ilja A. Seržant (eds.), *Explanation in typology: Diachronic sources, functional motivations and the nature of the evidence*, 47–61. Berlin: Language Science Press. DOI:10.5281/zenodo.2583808

Cristofaro, Sonia. 2003. *Subordination.* Oxford: Oxford University Press. DOI:10.1093/acprof:oso/9780199282005.001.0001

Cristofaro, Sonia. 2019. Taking diachronic evidence seriously: Result-oriented vs. source-oriented explanations of typological universals. In Karsten Schmidtke-Bode, Natalia Levshina, Susanne Maria Michaelis & Ilja A. Seržant (eds.), *Ex-*

planation in typology: Diachronic sources, functional motivations and the nature of the evidence, 25–46. Berlin: Language Science Press. DOI:10.5281/zenodo.2583806

Deutscher, Guy. 2009. Nominalization and the origin of subordination. In Talmy Givón & Masayoshi Shibatani (eds.), *Syntactic complexity: Diachrony, acquisition, neuro-cognition, evolution*, 199–214. Amsterdam, Philadelphia: John Benjamins. DOI:10.1075/tsl.85.08nom

Diessel, Holger. 2001. The ordering distribution of main and adverbial clauses: A typological study. *Language* 77(3). 433–455. DOI:10.1353/lan.2001.0152

Diessel, Holger. 2005. Competing motivations for the ordering of main and adverbial clauses. *Linguistics* 43(3). 449–470. DOI:10.1515/ling.2005.43.3.449

Diessel, Holger. 2008. Iconicity of sequence: A corpus-based analysis of the positioning of temporal adverbial clauses in English. *Cognitive linguistics* 19(3). 465–490. DOI:10.1515/COGL.2008.018

Diessel, Holger. 2015. Usage-based construction grammar. In Ewa Dąbrowska & Dagmar Divjak (eds.), *Handbook of Cognitive Linguistics*, 295–321. Berlin, New York: De Gruyter Mouton. DOI:10.1515/9783110292022-015

Diessel, Holger & Katja Hetterle. 2011. Causal clauses: A cross-linguistic investigation of their structure, meaning, and use. In Peter Siemund (ed.), *Linguistic universals and language variation*, 23–54. Berlin, New York: Mouton de Gruyter. DOI:10.1515/9783110238068.23

Dik, Simon C. 1989. *The theory of functional grammar. Part 1: The structure of the clause.* Dordrecht: Foris.

Disterheft, Dorothy & Carlotta Viti. 2010. Subordination. In Silvia Luraghi & Vit Bubenik (eds.), *Continuum companion to historical linguistics*, 230–249. London: Continuum.

Dryer, Matthew S. 1992. The Greenbergian word order correlations. *Language* 68(1). 81–138. DOI:10.1353/lan.1992.0028

Dryer, Matthew S. 2005. Relationship between the order of object and verb and the order of relative clause and noun. In Martin Haspelmath, Matthew S. Dryer, Bernard Comrie & David Gil (eds.), *The world atlas of language structures*, 390–393. Oxford: Oxford University Press.

Dryer, Matthew S. 2019. Grammaticalization accounts of word order correlations. In Karsten Schmidtke-Bode, Natalia Levshina, Susanne Maria Michaelis & Ilja A. Seržant (eds.), *Explanation in typology: Diachronic sources, functional motivations and the nature of the evidence*, 63–95. Berlin: Language Science Press. DOI:10.5281/zenodo.2583810

Ebert, Karen H. 1991. Vom verbum dicendi zur Konjunktion – ein Kapitel universaler Grammatikalisierung. In Walter Bisang & Peter Rinderknecht (eds.), *Von Europa bis Ozeanien, von der Antonymie zum Relativsatz: Gedenkschrift für Meinrad Scheller*, 75–95. Zürich: Universität Zürich.

Epps, Patience. 2009. Escape from the noun phrase: From relative clause to converb and beyond in an Amazonian language. *Diachronica* 26(3). 287–318. DOI:10.1075/dia.26.3.01epp

Foley, William A. & Robert D. Jr. Van Valin. 1984. *Functional syntax and universal grammar*. Cambridge: Cambridge University Press.

Ford, Cecilia E. & Junko Mori. 1994. Causal markers in Japanese and English conversations: A cross-linguistic study of interactional grammar. *Pragmatics* 4(1). 31–61. DOI:10.1075/prag.4.1.03for

Frajzyngier, Zygmunt. 1996. *Grammaticalization of the complex sentence: A case study in Chadic*. Amsterdam, Philadelphia: John Benjamins. DOI:10.1075/slcs.32

Genetti, Carol. 1991. From postposition to subordination in Newari. In Elizabeth Closs Traugott & Bernd Heine (eds.), *Approaches to Grammaticalization. Vol. II*, 227–256. Amsterdam, Philadelphia: John Benjamins. DOI:10.1075/tsl.19.2.13gen

Givón, Talmy. 1975. Serial verbs and syntactic change: Niger-Congo. In Charles N. Li (ed.), *Word order and word order change*, 47–112. Austin: University of Texas Press.

Givón, Talmy. 1979. *On understanding grammar*. New York: Academic Press. DOI:10.1075/z.213

Givón, Talmy. 1984. *Syntax: A functional-typological introduction. Vol. I*. Amsterdam, Philadelphia: John Benjamins. DOI:10.1075/z.17

Givón, Talmy. 1991. The evolution of dependent clause morpho-syntax in Biblical Hebrew. In Elizabeth Closs Traugott & Bernd Heine (eds.), *Approaches to grammaticalization. Vol. II: Focus on types of grammatical markers*, 257–329. Amsterdam, Philadelphia: John Benjamins. DOI:10.1075/tsl.19.2.14giv

Greenberg, Joseph H. 1963. Some universals of grammar with particular reference to the order of meaningful elements. In Joseph H. Greenberg (ed.), *Universals of language*, 58–90. Cambridge, MA: MIT Press.

Güldemann, Tom. 2008. *Quotative indexes in African languages: A synchronic and diachronic survey*. Berlin, New York: Mouton de Gruyter. DOI:10.1515/9783110211450

Haiman, John. 1978. Conditionals are topics. *Language* 54(3). 564–589. DOI:10.2307/412787

Haiman, John. 1985. *Natural syntax.* Amsterdam, Philadelphia: John Benjamins.

Harris, Alice C. & Lyle Campbell. 1995. *Historical syntax in cross-linguistic perspective.* Cambridge: Cambridge University Press. DOI:10.1017/CBO9780511620553

Hasher, Lynn & Rose T. Zacks. 1984. Automatic processing of fundamental information: The case of frequency of occurrence. *American Psychologist* 39(12). 1372–1388. DOI:10.1037/0003-066X.39.12.1372

Haspelmath, Martin. 1989. From purposive to infinitive - A universal pathway of grammaticalization. *Folia Linguistica Historica* X(1–2). 287–310. DOI:10.1515/flih.1989.10.1-2.287

Haspelmath, Martin. 1993. *A grammar of Lezgian.* Berlin, New York: Mouton de Gruyter. DOI:10.1515/9783110884210

Haspelmath, Martin. 2019. Can cross-linguistic regularities be explained by constraints on change? In Karsten Schmidtke-Bode, Natalia Levshina, Susanne Maria Michaelis & Ilja A. Seržant (eds.), *Explanation in typology: Diachronic sources, functional motivations and the nature of the evidence,* 1–23. Berlin: Language Science Press. DOI:10.5281/zenodo.2583804

Hawkins, John A. 1994. *A performance theory of order and constituency.* Cambridge: Cambridge University Press. DOI:10.1017/CBO9780511554285

Hawkins, John A. 2004. *Efficiency and complexity in grammars.* Oxford: Oxford University Press. DOI:10.1093/acprof:oso/9780199252695.001.0001

Heath, Jeffrey. 2005. *A grammar of Tamashek (Tuareg of Mali).* Berlin: Mouton de Gruyter. DOI:10.1515/9783110909586

Heath, Jeffrey. 2008. *A grammar of Jamsay.* Berlin: Mouton de Gruyter. DOI:10.1515/9783110207224

Heine, Bernd. 2009. From nominal to clausal morphosyntax: Complexity via expansion. In Talmy Givón & Masayoshi Shibatani (eds.), *Syntactic complexity: Diachrony, acquisition, neuro-cognition, evolution,* 23–52. Amsterdam, Philadelphia: John Benjamins. DOI:10.1075/tsl.85.02fro

Hetterle, Katja. 2015. *Adverbial clauses in cross-linguistic perspective.* Berlin, New York: Mouton de Gruyter. DOI:10.1515/9783110409857

Hopper, Paul J. & Elizabeth Closs Traugott. 2003. *Grammaticalization.* 2nd edn. Cambridge: Cambridge University Press. DOI:10.1017/CBO9781139165525

Kornfilt, Jaklin. 1997. *Turkish.* Berlin: Mouton de Gruyter.

Krifka, Manfred. 1985. Harmony or consistency? review of john a. hawkins, word order universals. *Theoretical Linguistics* 12(1). 73–94. DOI:10.1515/thli.1985.12.1.73

Lehmann, Christian. 1988. Towards a typology of clause linkage. In John Haiman & Sandra A. Thompson (eds.), *Clause combining in grammar and discourse*, 181–225. Amsterdam, Philadelphia: John Benjamins. DOI:10.1075/tsl.18.09leh

Li, Charles N. & Sandra A. Thompson. 1974. Historical change of word order: A case study in Chinese and its implications. In John M. Anderson & Charles Jones (eds.), *Historical linguistics, Vol. 1*, 199–217. Amsterdam: North Holland.

Lichtenberk, Frantisek. 2008. *A grammar of Toqabaqita*. Berlin: Mouton de Gruyter. DOI:10.1515/9783110199062

Macaulay, Monica Ann. 1996. *A grammar of Chalcatongo Mixtec*. Berkeley: University of California Press.

Merlan, Francesca. 1982. *Mangarayi*. Amsterdam: North Holland.

Munro, Pamela. 1982. On the transitivity of 'say' verbs. In Paul J. Hopper & Sandra A. Thompson (eds.), *Studies in transitivity*, 301–318. New York: Academic Press. DOI:10.1080/07268609408599507

Nordlinger, Rachel. 1998. *A grammar of Wambaya, Northern Territory (Australia)* (Pacific Linguistics). Canberra: The Australian National University.

Overall, Simon. 2009. The semantics of clause linkage in Aguaruna. In R. M. W. Dixon & Alexandra Y. Aikhenvald (eds.), *The semantics of clause linkage: A cross-linguistic typology*, 167–192. Oxford: Oxford University Press.

Payne, Doris L. & Thomas E. Payne. 1990. Yagua. In Desmond C. Derbyshire & Geoffrey K. Pullum (eds.), *Handbook of Amazonian languages. Vol II*, 249–471. Berlin: Mouton de Gruyter. DOI:10.1515/9783110860382

Pickering, Martin J. & Victor S. Ferreira. 2008. Structural priming: A critical review. *Psychological Bulletin* 134(3). 427–459. DOI:10.1037/0033-2909.134.3.427

Roberts, John. 1987. *Amele*. London: Croom Helm.

Sawka, Kenneth. 2001. *Aspects of Mayogo grammar*. Arlington: University of Texas (MA thesis).

Schmidtke-Bode, Karsten. 2009. *A typology of purpose clauses*. Amsterdam, Philadelphia: John Benjamins. DOI:10.1075/tsl.88

Schmidtke-Bode, Karsten & Holger Diessel. 2017. Cross-linguistic patterns in the structure, function, and position of (object) complement clauses. *Linguistics* 55(1). 1–38. DOI:10.1515/ling-2016-0035

Smeets, Ineke. 2008. *A grammar of Mapuche*. Berlin: Mouton de Gruyter. DOI:10.1515/9783110211795

Sohn, Ho-Min. 1994. *Korean*. London: Routledge.

Traugott, Elizabeth Closs. 1985. Conditional markers. In John Haiman (ed.), *Iconicity in syntax*, 289–307. Amsterdam, Philadelphia: John Benjamins. DOI:10.1075/tsl.6.14clo

Van de Velde, Freek, Hendrik De Smet & Lobke Ghesquière. 2013. On multiple
source constructions in language change. *Studies in Language* 37(3). 473–489.
DOI:10.1075/bct.79

Chapter 6

Attractor states and diachronic change in Hawkins's "Processing Typology"

Karsten Schmidtke-Bode
Leipzig University and Friedrich Schiller University Jena

This paper provides an assessment of John Hawkins's (2004; 2014) programme of explaining cross-linguistic regularities in terms of functional-adaptive principles of efficient information processing. In the first part of the paper, I systematize how such principles may possibly affect the diachronic development of languages, and I argue that evidence for efficient coding can be obtained primarily from the actualization process, rather than the innovation stage that is at the focus of purely source-based approaches to explaining universals. In the second part of the paper, I present a small case study on a specific prediction made in Hawkins (2014), concerning the typology and diachrony of article morphemes. This will allow us to carve out both strengths and weaknesses of Hawkins's programme in its current manifestation.

1 Introduction

In debating the role of source- and result-oriented explanations in typology, a research programme that merits discussion is John Hawkins's approach to cross-linguistic variation, laid out most comprehensively in Hawkins (1994; 2004; 2014). The overarching hypothesis of these works is that many cross-linguistic generalizations about grammatical structure can be explained as adaptations to efficient information processing ("processing typology", see Hawkins 2007). In a nutshell, Hawkins argues that efficient information processing can be achieved by (i) "minimizing domains" in which certain semantic and syntactic relations are processed, (ii) "minimizing forms" whenever their information content is recoverable from the context or long-term statistical knowledge, (iii) arranging elements in such a way that the ultimate message can be transmitted as rapidly

Karsten Schmidtke-Bode. 2019. Attractor states and diachronic change in Hawkins's "Processing Typology". In Karsten Schmidtke-Bode, Natalia Levshina, Susanne Maria Michaelis & Ilja A. Seržant (eds.), *Explanation in typology: Diachronic sources, functional motivations and the nature of the evidence*, 123–148. Berlin: Language Science Press. DOI:10.5281/zenodo.2583814 and accurately as possible, i.e. without delays, false predictions, backtracking, etc. These efficiency principles are thus attractors that are assumed to affect linguistic choices in usage events and ultimately also the conventionalized shapes of grammars.

Hawkins's programme is one of the most systematic attempts to ground typological data in psycholinguistic research and to link it to the arena of language use; in this spirit, it is similar, for example, to the work of Bybee (1985; 2010) and Croft (2001; 2003). Moreover, Hawkins's "performance-grammar-correspondence hypothesis", according to which grammatical rules are basically crystallized usage preferences, echoes one of the key tenets of the usage-based theory of language (Langacker 1987; Kemmer & Barlow 2000). And some specific efficiency principles, such as the "minimization of forms" in proportion to their degree of predictability, even have exact parallels in other functional-typological works (e.g. Haiman 1983; Croft 2003; Haspelmath 2008).

At the same time, however, Hawkins's work is not always received uncritically within usage-based linguistics. Among other things, it is couched in a formal phrase-structure architecture that appears to presuppose the existence of many grammatical categories (see Diessel 2016); some of its principles have been criticized for not being truly domain-general but perhaps specific to language (such as a pressure for short constituent recognition domains, see Bybee 2010); and crucially in the present context, Hawkins has also been criticized for neglecting or underestimating the diachronic dimension behind the phenomena he attempts to explain (e.g. Cristofaro 2017; Collins 2019 [this volume]). But to the extent that Hawkins does make reference to historical developments, the nature and plausibility of his diachronic claims are worth investigating in more detail, which is precisely what the present contribution aims to do.

To this end, the first part of the paper develops a systematization, in the usage-based framework, of how Hawkins's functional-adaptive principles possibly affect the diachronic development of languages. I argue that there is solid evidence for efficient information processing in the moulding of grammar, suggesting that there is a place for result-oriented processes, beside source determination, in accounting for typological distributions. In the second part of the paper, I exemplarily focus on a diachronic prediction made in Hawkins (2014), according to which languages of different word-order types show markedly different propensities for grammaticalizing definite articles (the prediction will be formulated more precisely as we go along). This miniature case study will not only serve as a testing ground for this specific efficiency-based hypothesis, but also allow us to identify some general merits and potential problems of processing typology.

2 The diachronic dimension in processing typology

In the usage-based approach, language change is conceived as a multi-step process (Croft 2000; 2006; Aitchison 2013) that starts by breaking a convention in the form of a linguistic innovation ("altered replication"), followed by the spread of that innovation through both the linguistic system ("diffusion") and the speech community ("propagation"). Hawkins's publications contain a number of indications as to how his efficiency principles influence innovation, diffusion and propagation processes. I will tackle each of them briefly, in reverse order, as this reflects an increasing degree of explicitness of the respective proposals.[1]

As for PROPAGATION processes, Hawkins is usually reticent with regard to the forces that implement efficient structures, even though the central diachronic mechanism in his programme is that of "selection": Efficient variants are said to be selected relatively more frequently than their inefficient counterparts, until they may ultimately oust the inefficient ones completely. It is in this way, Hawkins argues, that preferred patterns in performance can conventionalize into grammatical rules, although he concedes in Hawkins (2014: 10) that it is presently poorly understood how exactly this "translation from performance to grammar" works. Now, if one subscribes to the view that propagation is entirely driven by sociolinguistic forces like prestige, solidarity and the resulting accommodation (e.g. Croft 2000; Cristofaro 2017; Cristofaro 2019 [this volume]), it remains mysterious, indeed, how Hawkins's very idea of selection processes can fit in.

On the other hand, there are well-known accounts of language change in which propagation is not exclusively a social phenomenon: Keller's (1994) "Invisible Hand" theory, for example, leaves room for functional considerations in the selection process. Some of Keller's classic examples of invisible-hand processes, such as the emergence of a traffic jam or a short-cutting footpath do not, in fact, involve social motives: People follow a certain course of action because they primarily consider its functional advantages, regardless of the sociolinguistic profile of the person whose behaviour they adopt. Cristofaro (2017) claims that there is no empirical evidence at all for this scenario in linguistics, but this assessment is overly pessimistic: Rosenbach (2008), in a detailed examination of evolutionary accounts of language change, concludes that "the evidence available does not speak for the *exclusive* role of social factors in the selection process" (Rosenbach

---

[1]Although the present section is specifically about Hawkins's work, it actually applies to "functional-adaptive constraints" (Haspelmath 2019 [this volume]) more generally, not least because Hawkins's processing typology draws on and incorporates similarly-minded principles from many other functionalist typologists (e.g. Greenberg, Comrie, Keenan, Givón, Haiman, Croft, Haspelmath, etc.).

2008: 44; emphasis in original). Therefore, I currently see no reason to dismiss a priori a theory in which both social and functional selection pressures can be operative in propagation (see also Haspelmath 1999; Nettle 1999; Enfield 2014 for similar positions).[2] On this view, then, Hawkins's efficiency principles are relevant to, and hence at least partially drive, the propagation process, although empirical evidence that clearly disentangles functional and social selection processes is, of course, very hard to come by (see also Seiler 2006).

The empirical picture is clearer, in my view, when it comes to DIFFUSION or ACTUALIZATION processes, i.e. the spread of an innovation through the linguistic system.[3] Although Hawkins himself does not speak of diffusion or actualization, the process is actually highly germane to his research, as many of the phenomena he discusses in support of his efficiency theory are cases of limited diffusion. In relativization, for example, a well-known pattern is for resumptive pronouns, once they have been innovated, not to spread across the entire range of relativization sites, but to be restricted to certain sections of Keenan & Comrie's (1977) accessibility hierarchy (as in Hausa, Hebrew, Welsh and many other languages). Similarly, when object case markers develop and spread within the linguistic system, they typically end up being confined to animate, definite or pronominal objects, rather than being extended across the board (see, e.g., Sinnemäki 2014 for a quantitative study).

Many other cases of such differential marking are collected in Haspelmath (2008) and subsumed by Hawkins (2004; 2014) under his "Minimize Forms" principle: The marker in question is applied to those environments that require more processing effort, and is left out economically elsewhere. Processing effort, in turn, may be related to various factors, notably constraints on working memory

---

[2]Note that recent mathematical models of language change (e.g. Blythe & Croft 2012) clearly show that selection as such is a crucial element of propagation processes, in as far as alternative models of propagation that do not rely on a weighting of linguistic variants (e.g. Trudgill 2004) do not produce the empirical patterns of propagation that have been established in historical linguistics and sociolinguistics. However, Blythe & Croft (2012) also concede that their model cannot distinguish between social and functional factors in selection, i.e. it leaves open which of these is more vital in the propagation process or how they possibly interact.

[3]The term DIFFUSION is best-known in the context of "lexical diffusion" (Wang 1969), which refers to the successive spread of a phonetic or morphosyntactic innovation to different lexical items (e.g. the Progressive construction to more and more lexical verbs, or final consonant devoicing to all relevant words). In the present paper, I am using the term diffusion in a broader sense, comprising also the application of an innovated grammatical marker or construction to a new morphosyntactic environment (e.g. the extension of *all but* in its historically younger sense 'almost' from adjectival uses (*This was all but remarkable*) to verbal environments (*He all but fell down*), see De Smet 2012). Diffusion is thus synonymous with the term ACTUALIZATION (Timberlake 1977, Andersen 2001 and many others, most recently De Smet 2012).

(e.g. longer processing domains correlating with resumptive pronouns) and the relative unexpectedness ('surprisal') of a given configuration (see Norcliffe et al. 2015 on memory- and expectation-based processing in cross-linguistic perspective). For example, discourse participants and animate entities are more likely to be subjects than objects, hence it is precisely these kinds of objects that are more surprising. Paired with the Hawkinsian assumption of efficiency on the part of the speaker, it is also only these objects that need to be marked overtly. A similar surprisal-based account is provided by Haig (2018) to explain "why differential object indexation is an attractor state" (Haig 2018: 781) in the grammaticalization of object pronouns.

In Hawkins's programme, then, all of these cases are amenable to an explanation in terms of efficient information processing. I believe that this account is presently superior to purely source-oriented typologies such as Cristofaro's, for the following reasons.

Firstly, there is solid evidence for efficiency where the occurrence of a particular marker is optional. This can be observed, for example, with variable relativizers that, other things being equal, show up less frequently when a relative clause is statistically expected given the previous co-text, and vice versa (Wasow et al. 2011). As Fox & Thompson (2007) observe, a sentence like

(1)   This was the ugliest set of shoes [I ever saw in my life].

would sound "quite awkward" (Wasow et al. 2011: 181) if the relative clause were introduced by *that*; according to Wasow et al., this is precisely because a relative clause is expected in this context, which is in turn why relative *that* tends to be omitted efficiently. Jaeger (2010) shows that similar predictability effects account for a large portion of the variability of the English complementizer *that*.

Importantly, the same kinds of effect also show up in psycholinguistic experimentation, and in languages other than English. For example, recent studies have shown that optional case marking in Japanese, optional indexation in Yucatec Maya relative clauses or optional plural marking in an artificial language exhibit an efficient distribution in the participants' linguistic behaviour, other things being tightly controlled for (Kurumada & Jaeger 2015; Norcliffe & Jaeger 2016; Kurumada & Grimm 2017). All of these synchronic effects are independent of the historical source of the respective marker. In other words, no matter how a particular relativizer emerges, it comes to be applied in ways that are consonant with Hawkins's efficiency predictions. And as, for example, Seržant (2019 [this volume]) shows, such optional marking can conventionalize into more fixed grammatical patterns over time.

Secondly, to the extent that the "Minimize Form" effects are typologically sound (i.e. independent of geographical and genetic affiliations), they are in contrast with a powerful principle that we observe elsewhere in grammars, viz. the potent force of analogy (see Gentner & Smith 2012; Blevins & Blevins 2009). Analogy is the driving force behind lexical diffusion, and where it runs to (near) completion, the result is a productive grammatical rule in the traditional sense. Time and again, historical studies show just how sweeping analogical extension can be: By incremental diffusion processes, English has conventionalized a rule that every main clause requires an overt subject, and every lexical verb now needs *do*-support if it is to occur in an interrogative clause. In other languages, split alignment systems are gradually being eliminated in favour of unified marking: for example, younger speakers of Choctaw (Muskogean: USA) are in the process of re-shaping split intransitivity into a nominative-accusative system with consistent coding for the S argument (Broadwell 2006: 140); and Creissels (2018) argues more generally that there are strong analogical pressures on languages to regain consistent alignment patterns if these get disrupted by grammaticalization processes.[4]

In view of these analogical forces, one may wonder why systems of differential resumption, differential object marking or differential possessive marking exist quite pervasively, and in highly systematic ways. In Cristofaro's account, they are persistence effects, i.e. they are all due to the fact that the unmarked meanings are perceived as incompatible with the source construction. For example, when an object marker originates from a topic marker, it is expected to be restricted to object NPs whose properties are most closely associated with topicality (or topicworthiness), such as pronominal, animate and definite entities, and not to apply elsewhere. In fact, Dalrymple & Nikolaeva (2011) argue that such erstwhile topic markers are often extended to animate and/or definite objects, thus diffusing in principled ways to create DOM patterns that may plausibly be linked to the source construction. However, given the powers of analogy, why does diffusion stop there? If it is really the source construction pulling its weight here, one may wonder why it does not do so in many other cases.

Just consider what is perhaps the textbook example of a development that standardly overrides effects from the source construction, namely diffusion processes in grammaticalization. It is by analogical extension that the *going-to*-future has spread to inanimate subjects (*The icicle is going to break off.*), and that the French negative marker *pas* has been extended beyond contexts of directed motion (*Je*

---

[4]For example, "many languages in which the grammaticalization of a new TAM form resulted in [tense-based split ergative alignment] have undergone a subsequent evolution that can be characterized as regularization under the pressure of analogy" (Creissels 2018: 81).

ne vais pas. 'I'm not going.' > *Je ne sais pas.* 'I don't know.'). In other words, if analogy works in many other instances of grammaticalization, why not in those cases that involve differential marking? Siding with Hawkins (and Haspelmath 2019 [this volume]) here, I find it convincing that an attractor state of efficient coding shapes the development of grammatical systems, especially in light of the behavioural evidence cited above.

Thirdly, while I agree with Cristofaro (2019 [this volume])) that functional principles should be "visible" in the diachronic development of particular structures, I find her interpretation of this requirement too narrow: She demands that the alleged motivations be present at the innovation stage of a grammatical construction and hence directly influence its emergence. But as we have just seen, it is often during the actualization phase that functional-adaptive principles are operative, regardless of how or why a given marker originated in the first place (see also Seržant 2019 [this volume]).

Interestingly, while Joan Bybee is now often cited as a representative of source-oriented typology, her relevant publications reveal a broader perspective than Cristofaro's: "Identifying the causal mechanisms [that lead to typological generalizations] requires a detailed look at *all* the properties of a change – including its directionality, gradualness, spread through the community and through the lexicon" (Bybee 2008: 108; see also Bybee 1988). Crucially, it is precisely in lexical-diffusion processes that many of her well-known frequency effects apply: For example, Bybee's "conserving effect" of token frequency explains why highly entrenched main verbs like *speak, think* and *mean* resisted the innovative *do*-support in *wh*-questions for a long time (e.g. *What spekest thou?*, see Ogura 1993), or why the change from *-th* to *-s* in the third-person of English verbs affected the most frequent verbs last (notably *hath* and *doth*, see van Gelderen 2014: 172). In a similar vein, I would thus argue that the diffusion or actualization stage is highly relevant for the kinds of effect that lead to efficient typological marking patterns.

In conclusion, I consider Hawkins's account (and functional-adaptive motivations of similar kinds) capable of explaining why certain changes do *not* happen – particularly, why we find that analogical extensions are systematically brought to a halt even though they are so commonly carried through in other domains of grammar.[5]

---

[5] See also Smith (2001) for a similar view: He investigates the diachronic development of agreement loss in Romance participles and argues that while parsing principles cannot be held responsible for the *rise* of participial agreement, they did play a role in its gradual disappearance. Specifically, Smith claims that agreement was retained longest in those environments where it was most beneficial for processing. Therefore, "functionality is here acting as a brake on actualization" (Smith 2001: 214), just as I argued more generally above.

Let us finally turn to the realm of INNOVATION, i.e. Hawkins's suggestions as to why, where and when certain grammatical structures emerge. A central concept here is that of correlated evolution: When a language changes in one part of the grammar, Hawkins often expects to see "ripple effects" (Hawkins 2014: 88) in domains that are linked to the changing subsystem by certain efficiency principles. For example, since Hawkins assumes that phrases of different types (VPs, PPs, NPs, etc.) show harmonic ordering patterns to allow efficient sentence processing, a change from OV to VO is predicted to engender innovations in PPs and NPs as well (see Dunn et al. 2011 and the papers in *Linguistic Typology* 15(2) for ample discussion of this issue). In the present context, perhaps the most interesting claim with regard to innovation is that efficiency principles can predict the occurrence of grammaticalization: While many grammaticalization paths are universal "attractor trajectories" (Bybee & Beckner 2015) – open to all languages with similar source constructions due to the same mechanisms of reanalysis –, Hawkins's efficiency principles predict under which structural conditions (e.g. in which language "types") particular events of grammaticalization are more or less likely to happen. In the remainder of this paper, I will briefly discuss a specific example of such a hypothesis developed by Hawkins (2014).

3 A test case for processing typology

In his (2014) monograph, Hawkins examines the structure of noun phrases (NPs) from a processing perspective. Across the world's languages, NPs often contain elements in addition to the head noun that, in Hawkins's view, can function as processing cues to the recognition (or online "construction") of an NP, such as articles, classifiers and related morphemes.[6] Hawkins argues that such elements are more efficient in VO languages than in OV languages: As illustrated schematically in Figure 1, an additional NP constructor C in a VO language can shorten the domain for the construction of the VP (V+NP), especially if N is delayed by

---

[6]Although Hawkins frames the idea of "online construction" in terms of syntactic trees, nodes and categories, the basic intuition behind it is functional in nature: Translated into the usage-based parlance of, e.g., Croft (2001), Beckner & Bybee (2009) or Bates & MacWhinney (1989), Hawkins's idea is that a referential expression should be recognizable as such, based on reliable cues in the speech stream. Referential expressions (or NPs, for that matter) are arguably best cued by nouns and determiners, and the construction of an NP is thus facilitated by the early availability of such "constructing categories" within the string of units that ultimately belong to the NP. More generally, I believe that Hawkins is thus actually quite compatible with usage-based and construction-grammatical conceptions of processing, even though he uses terminology that is closely associated with generative syntax.

intervening material (e.g. in AP-N sequences like *the very delicious meal*). In an OV language, by contrast, additional NP constructors lengthen this dependency domain, no matter where they occur in the NP:

VO languages	**OV languages**
$_{VP}$ [V $_{NP}$ [N ...]]	[[... N ... C] $_{NP}$ V] $_{VP}$
$_{VP}$ [V $_{NP}$ [C ... N ...]]	[[... C ... N] $_{NP}$ V] $_{VP}$
|-----|	|--------|

Figure 1: V-NP processing in VO- and OV-languages (adapted from Hawkins 2014: 125)

From these considerations, one might derive the following prediction:

(2)   While all languages have source constructions for articles (notably demon-stratives for definite articles and the numeral 'one' for indefinite articles), the grammaticalization of these sources into more general NP markers should be a more productive historical process in VO languages than in OV languages. As a result, the synchronic typological distribution of arti-cles is significantly different in the two language types.

As a matter of fact, Hawkins' (2014) prediction is narrower in scope: He applies it only to definite articles, and only to independent definite articles (i.e. words and clitics rather than affixes). The following examples illustrate the language types that are expected to be frequent according to (2):

(3)   a.   VO with definite article
          Maori (Austronesian, Oceanic; Bauer 1993: 256)
          I   kite ia   i   te   whare.
          T/A see 3SG OBJ DET house
          'She saw the house.'

      b.   OV without definite article
          Lezgian (Nakh-Daghestanian, Lezgic; Haspelmath 1993: 343)
          Ada-z   balk'an aku-na.
          he-DAT horse   see-AOR
          'He saw the horse.'

In support of the hypotheses in (2), Hawkins cites some of Dryer's (2005) *WALS* data, which show, indeed, that definite-article words are relatively more frequent in VO-languages (more on the data below).

Hawkins's approach, as illustrated by this specific example, has a number of assets: For instance, it emphasizes the importance of the linear dimension of language, which tightly constrains production and parsing processes but which tended to be neglected by (at least early) cognitive-linguistic and construction-based approaches to grammar (see also Diessel 2011 for a similar critique). Hawkins's work is clearly pioneering here, and in the recent usage-based literature, related notions like contextual predictability, informativity and projective links have come to take a highly prominent place (see, e.g., Gahl & Garnsey 2004; Levy 2008; Auer 2009). Furthermore, Hawkins's diachronic thinking adds a new dimension to classic research in grammaticalization. As Good (2008: 7) points out, work on grammaticalization typically offers "permissive explanations [...], that is, it focuses on particular grammaticalization paths without, in general, accounting for what factors will cause one language, but not another, to instantiate those paths." Hawkins's approach elevates this "permissive" nature of explanation to what Good (ibid.) calls a "probabilistic" one: It attempts to explain why certain grammaticalization processes are set in motion only (or preferably) in certain language types or at certain points in time (see also Hawkins 1986; 2012 for representative work along these lines).

But just how convincing are such claims and the empirical support that Hawkins provides for them? In the present case, I have a number of reservations about the picture drawn in Hawkins (2014).

To begin with, I do not quite see why the hypothesis is restricted to the development of definite articles, as indefinite articles should qualify equally well as NP constructors. Similarly, Hawkins's preoccupation with word-based processing (which is prominent throughout his 2014 book), to the neglect of affixes with identical functions, is not sufficiently motivated. In addition to the problem that free and bound markers are very hard to distinguish consistently for cross-linguistic comparison (Haspelmath 2011), it remains unclear if there is a measurable psycholinguistic difference between word- and affix-processing. As long as there is no evidence for the view that free and bound definiteness markers are parsed in fundamentally different ways, we should rather take a more embracing approach to the data and ask whether VO- and OV-languages differ in their propensity to grammaticalize article morphemes from their respective source constructions.

With these considerations in mind, the first step of the empirical assessment is, just like in Hawkins (2014), to examine the typological distribution of article morphemes. Dryer's *WALS* data, in their most recent version, are set out in Table 1.

Table 1: Distribution of articles in different word-order types (Dryer 2013a,c)

	VO	OV	ndo	Totals	
Distinct ART word	144	52	14	210	
DEF affix	49	33	6	88	ART
DEM used as ART	30	33	5	68	
Only INDEF ART	20	24	0	44	
No ART	70	111	14	195	NO ART
Totals	313	253	39	605	

For the purposes of testing our revised version of Hawkins's hypothesis, we need to discard the languages without a dominant order of V and O ("ndo"), and we basically conflate the figures in the first four rows of Table 1 and contrast them with those in the final row. In other words, (i) we consider both free and bound definiteness morphemes; (ii) we include those languages which are beginning to use a demonstrative like an article (row 3, see Dryer 2013a for details) – thus incorporating cases of incipient grammaticalization; (iii) we include languages with indefinite articles only.[7] The conflated form of the data thus looks like in Table 2.

The distribution in Table 2 looks conspicuously skewed, but of course these are raw data that are not controlled for genetic and areal effects.[8] Therefore, what Hawkins's (2014) analysis clearly needs to be augmented with (in this case as well as virtually all others in his book) is proper statistical modelling according to contemporary standards (see, e.g., Bickel 2011). To this end, I am seeking converging evidence from two complementary quantitative approaches to the data, namely mixed-effects logistic regression (see also Cysouw 2010; Jaeger et al. 2011) and

---

[7]Some readers may object to this way of grouping the data. For example, one might reasonably argue that languages in which demonstratives are used with some article-like functions should *not* be said to have "proper" articles (yet). However, even when such languages are classified differently for statistical purposes, the results remain the same in many respects (see supplementary material SM3.2).

[8]For similar raw data, see also Dryer (2009), who endorses Hawkins's processing explanation.

Table 2: Distribution of articles in different word-order types (reorganized)

	VO	OV	Totals
ART morph	243	142	385
No ART morph	70	111	181
Totals	313	253	566

Bickel's (2011; 2013) Family Bias Method (which is particularly suitable to testing hypotheses formulated in diachronic terms). In the supplementary materials to this paper[9], I offer a more detailed, non-technical introduction to the Family Bias Method (SM1), as well as the statistical properties of all models (SM2–5). For reasons of space, I here confine myself to describing some major results of the analyses.[10]

Figure 2 shows that there is a significant effect of word order on the occurrence of articles in a mixed-effects regression model (β = -0.73, p < 0.001).[11] Although the model is not particularly good overall, probably missing important further predictors (R^2_c = 0.14, C = 0.72), Hawkins's hypothesized effect is clearly present, as the probability of *not* having articles (y-axis) increases significantly as we go from VO to OV (x-axis).

In the Family Bias estimations, too, it turns out that, among those families that do not just show a chance distribution of articles, VO families are about 2.6 times more likely to develop articles than OV families. This is illustrated in Table 3, and Figure 3 shows that this effect is stable (i.e. never reversed) across all six macro areas. In sum, the global typological picture is consistent with Hawkins's processing account, even when tested against a more comprehensive data set and with more rigorous modes of examination.

---

[9]See http://www.kschmidtkebode.de/publications or http://doi.org/10.5281/zenodo.2577480.

[10]All statistical analyses were performed in *R* 3.3.1 (*R* Development Core Team 2016). I am grateful to Taras Zakharko and Balthasar Bickel for making their Family Bias algorithm freely available (Zakharko & Bickel 2011ff.).

[11]All regression analyses I performed are based on generalized linear mixed-effects models that include genealogical and macro-areal dependencies as random effects (see SM3). The model in Figure 2, for example, contains by-family and by-area random intercepts for the distribution of articles, while a by-area random slope for the word-order effect did not improve the model significantly and was hence excluded from the final model.

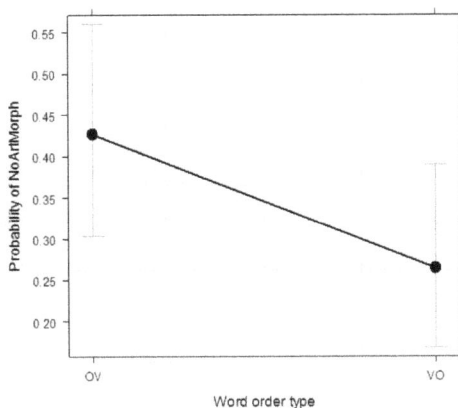

Figure 2: Effect of word order type on the probability of (not) having articles in a mixed-effects model (see SM3 for details)

Table 3: (Rounded) family biases for articles in different word-order types (N_{total} = 217 genetic units, 99 of which are estimated to be "biased" (as opposed to internally diverse); Fisher exact test, p = 0.039)

	VO	OV	Totals
ART morph	50	19	69
No ART morph	15	15	30
Totals	**65**	**34**	**99**

Recall, however, that a second prediction of this account is that articles are especially useful in those VO languages that have modifiers before the head noun in NPs (*a very delicious meal*). One would thus expect, for example, that the grammaticalization of articles is particularly productive in VO languages with ADJ-N order, and, from an efficiency perspective, less so in those with N-ADJ order. I tested this by examining the order of nouns and adjectives (Dryer 2013b) in all VO languages in the same sample as above (N_{total} = 278 languages).

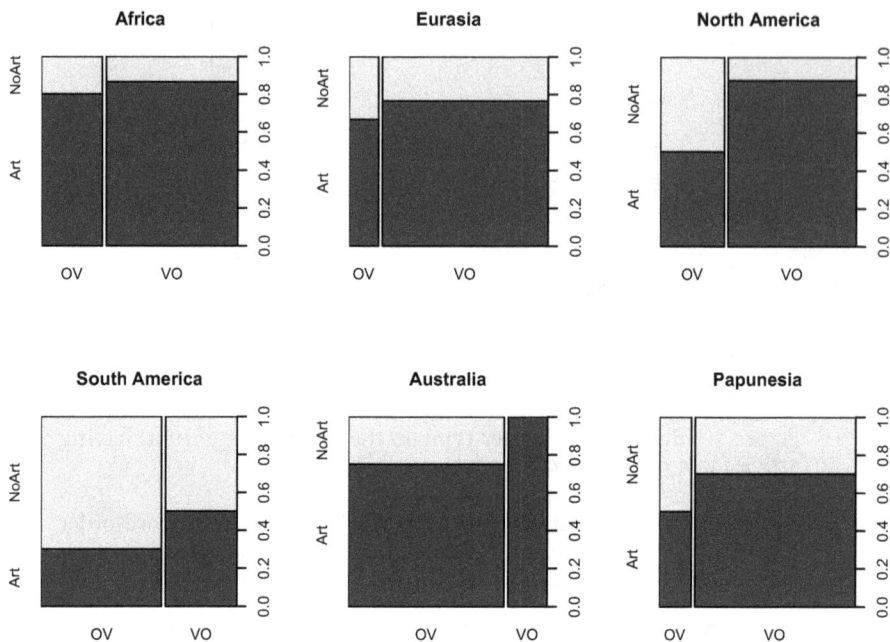

Figure 3: Family biases by macro area (see SM2 for details)

Across several different statistical models (and operationalizations of the hypothesis, see SM4), I did not find support for Hawkins's efficiency hypothesis. In one analysis, for example, I probed whether article words are more likely in VO languages with ADJ-N order than in those with N-ADJ order. Figure 4 shows that this is neither the case for definite articles nor for articles in general.[12]

Clearly, this picture does not speak for a critical processing pressure being at work. And the same conclusion actually carries over to OV languages: It is true that, to the extent that these languages show a reduced propensity for developing articles, they manage to keep NP processing domains slightly shorter; but there

---

[12]Moreover, if we look at VO languages which are beginning to use a demonstrative as a definite article (N = 26 in Dryer 2013a), Hawkins's account would lead us to expect that such incipient grammaticalization is particularly frequent in the constellation DEM-N and ADJ-N (and again less frequent if N precedes both the ADJ and the DEM). Now, of the 26 languages in question, 22 are N-DEM and four are DEM-N. It is the latter type that is interesting here, and we find that two of these four languages are ADJ-N and the other two N-ADJ. Again, no clear pattern along Hawkinsian lines can be detected here.

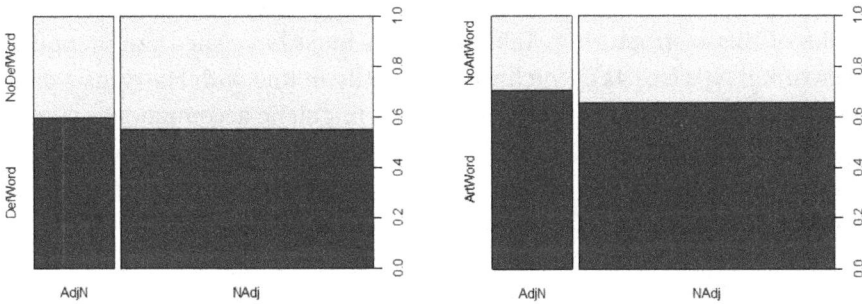

Figure 4: Occurrence of articles in VO languages depending on the position of adjectives (left plot: definiteness words only; right plot: all article-like words; for the corresponding mixed-effects models, see SM4)

are several indications that this pressure cannot be particularly strong.

First, our Family Bias calculations show, in addition to the findings from above, that *none* of the large OV families in the sample actually exhibits a significant bias (towards or against articles) in the first place; they are all internally diverse, i.e. with no more than chance distributions of articles (Table 4).[13]

Table 4: Distribution of biases (for or against) articles among large families in the sample (N_{total} = 29 genetic units)

	VO	OV	Totals
significantly biased	12	0	12
internally diverse	6	11	17
Totals	**18**	**11**	**29**

Second, from a more qualitative perspective, there is suggestive evidence that a potential efficiency motivation in OV languages is easily overridden by other factors. For example, Ross (2001) discusses an interesting case of an intense contact situation in which the Austronesian language Takia adapted its VO syntax

---

[13]Bickel (2013) suggests that the (minimum) strength of a universal pressure can be calculated on the basis of the proportion of biased families k among all families of a particular kind n (here: OV families): $\hat{s} = (k+1)/(n+2)$. Based on the figures in Table 4, we obtain $\hat{s}_{(OV)} = (0+1)/(11+2) = 0.077$. This estimate is so small in magnitude that one is forced to conclude that there is no particular pressure at all on OV languages with regard to the development of articles.

to the OV structure of its Papuan contact language Waskia. Ross argues that, in the wake of this restructuring, Takia speakers must have shed the prenominal article word in NPs (see 4a), which would be fully in line with Hawkins's prediction. At the same time, however, the degree of linguistic accommodation was so intense that Takia speakers also did something else: They grammaticalized a postnominal deictic element into a postnominal demonstrative with some article-like functions, reproducing exactly the article pattern in Waskia (see 4b-c).

(4)   a. Proto-Western Oceanic (Ross 2001: 142)

          a   tam^{w}ata a-ña

          DET man   that-3SG

          'that man'

    b. Takia (Austronesian, Oceanic; Ross 2001: 140)

          Waskia   tamol **an**

          Waskian man **that**

          'that Waskia man'

    c. Waskia (Nuclear Trans New Guinea, Madang; Ross 2001: 140)

          Waskia kadi **mu**

          Waskia man **that**

          'that Waskia man'

In other words, Takia speakers chose precisely the diachronic route that Hawkins would predict to be disfavoured, which goes to show that the alleged processing pressure cannot have been very strong, after all. In this connection, one may also recall that our regression model from above, while bringing out a significant global effect from word order type, did not provide a particularly good fit to the data. The substantial amount of variation in the data that it cannot account for must thus be attributed to other, possibly stronger factors.[14]

---

[14]Diachronic research has actually put forward a number of plausible candidates for such factors. A prominent one since at least Vennemann (1975) is the loss of a case system and the concomitant rigidification of constituent order, which favours the development of articles to express information-structural distinctions that were previously coded by a more flexible word order (see also Hawkins 2004; Hewson & Bubenik 2006; Fischer 2010; Carlier & Lamiroy 2014). Another possible factor is the loss of an aspectual system (Abraham 1997; Leiss 2000; 2007). However, especially the former type of explanation is often viewed critically (e.g. Selig 1992 on Romance; McColl Millar 2000 on English; Leiss 2000 on Germanic), and there is currently no proposal as to how various factors may conspire to explain the synchronic distribution of articles (see also Lüdtke 1991). For some further information and preliminary typological analyses of these factors, interested readers are kindly referred to SM5.

We conclude, then, that Hawkins (2014) correctly predicts a global difference between OV- and VO-languages in the development of articles. But the present analysis also revealed some challenges for this account. Therefore, it still needs to be established by future research whether the global correlation between word order type and the absence of articles really reflects a *causal* connection between these two phenomena, and whether this could be attributed to efficient information processing. If it turns out that Hawkins is correct, the findings in the present section suggest that we would be dealing with a 'weak universal pressure' in the sense of Seržant (2019 [this volume]) or a "weak cognitive bias" with "significant population-level consequences" (Thompson et al. 2016: 4530).

4 Concluding remarks

The present contribution has taken a closer look at John Hawkins's "processing typology", a research programme that fully subscribes to functional-adaptive motivations for grammatical structure. In the first part of the paper, I discussed where such motivations are possibly operative in diachronic change. In my view, a case can be made for Hawkins's efficiency considerations in the process of actualization, i.e. when a linguistic innovation comes to be extended to a principled, cross-linguistically similar subset of potential application sites (as in differential flagging and indexing, relativization, etc.). In this respect, I consider Hawkins's account as superior to purely source-oriented explanations of grammatical patterns. Of course, this does not deny that persistence accounts are relevant to typological patterns – they clearly are; but it argues against persistence as the sole or perhaps even the dominant explanatory principle for grammatical universals.

A more ambitious but also undoubtedly more problematic move is to link parsing and efficiency to certain innovation processes, such as when a particular grammaticalization channel is predicted to be set in motion only under specific structural conditions. In the brief case study presented here, we saw that Hawkins's NP processing hypothesis provides a neat match to the global typological data, even when these are analyzed in more rigorous and hence more appropriate ways than in Hawkins (2014). On the other hand, the details of neither the typological picture nor individual diachronic studies produce evidence for a strong pressure on languages to develop into the predicted directions. Therefore, the hypothesis that speakers of OV languages are significantly less inclined than speakers of VO languages to grammaticalize additional NP constructors, remains plausible but currently rather weakly substantiated.

What we would need to see to make it more convincing is a triangulation of (i) typological data that are large enough to take several alternative predictor variables from the literature into account (e.g. case and aspect systems, the presence of other NP constructors such as classifiers), (ii) diachronic data from languages that have undergone (or are in the process of undergoing) changes in basic word order, (iii) behavioural evidence, such as psycholinguistic experimentation with artificial languages (e.g. along the lines of Culbertson et al. 2012; see also Levshina 2019 [this volume]). As a matter of fact, a particularly strong aspect of Hawkins's work (especially in Hawkins 2004; 2014) is that it generally attempts precisely this kind of methodological cross-fertilization; but for the domain at issue here, such an approach has yet to be fleshed out in sufficient detail.

Abbreviations

The paper follows the Leipzig Glossing Rules. Additional abbreviation: T/A = tense/aspect marker

Acknowledgements

The research for this paper was carried out in the context of the project *Form-frequency correspondences in grammar* at Leipzig University. The support of the European Research Council (ERC Advanced Grant 670985, Grammatical Universals) is gratefully acknowledged. I would like to thank John Hawkins, Mark Dingemanse, the co-editors of the present volume as well as the audiences of the Diversity Linguistics Conference (Leipzig, March 2017), the 3rd Usage-Based Linguistics Conference (Jerusalem, July 2017) and the Syntax of the World's Languages VIII Conference (Paris, September 2018) for very helpful feedback on previous versions of this paper. The usual disclaimers apply.

References

Abraham, Werner. 1997. The interdependence of case, aspect, and referentiality in the history of German: The case of the verbal genitive. In Ans van Kemenade & Nigel Vincent (eds.), *Parameters of morphosyntactic change*, 29–61. Cambridge: Cambridge University Press.

Aitchison, Jean. 2013. *Language change: Progress or decay?* 4th edn. Cambridge: Cambridge University Press. DOI:10.1017/CBO9780511809866.018

Andersen, Henning (ed.). 2001. *Actualization: Linguistic change in progress.* Amsterdam, Philadelphia: John Benjamins. DOI:10.1075/cilt.219

Auer, Peter. 2009. On-line syntax: Thoughts on the temporality of spoken language. *Language Sciences* 31. 1–13. DOI:10.1016/j.langsci.2007.10.004

Bates, Elizabeth & Brian MacWhinney. 1989. Functionalism and the competition model. In Brian MacWhinney & Elizabeth Bates (eds.), *The cross-linguistic study of sentence processing*, 3–73. New York: Cambridge University Press.

Bauer, Winifred. 1993. *Maori.* Abingdon; New York: Routledge.

Beckner, Clay & Joan L. Bybee. 2009. A usage-based account of constituency and reanalysis. *Language Learning* 59(1). 27–46. DOI:10.1111/j.1467-9922.2009.00534.x

Bickel, Balthasar. 2011. Statistical modeling of language universals. *Linguistic Typology* 15. 401–413. DOI:10.1515/lity.2011.027

Bickel, Balthasar. 2013. Distributional biases in language families. In Balthasar Bickel, Lenore A. Genoble, David A. Peterson & Alan Timberlake (eds.), *Language typology and historical contingency*, 415–444. Amsterdam, Philadelphia: John Benjamins. DOI:10.5167/uzh-86870

Blevins, James P. & Juliette Blevins (eds.). 2009. *Analogy in grammar: Form and acquisition.* Oxford: Oxford University Press. DOI:10.1093/acprof:oso/9780199547548.001.0001

Blythe, Richard A. & William Croft. 2012. S-curves and the mechanisms of propagation in language change. *Language* 88(2). 269–304. DOI:10.2307/23251832

Broadwell, George Aaron. 2006. *A Choctaw reference grammar.* Lincoln; London: University of Nebraska Press.

Bybee, Joan L. 1985. *Morphology: A study of the relation between meaning and form.* Amsterdam, Philadelphia: John Benjamins. DOI:10.1075/tsl.9

Bybee, Joan L. 1988. The diachronic dimension in explanation. In John A. Hawkins (ed.), *Explaining language universals*, 350–379. Oxford: Blackwell.

Bybee, Joan L. 2008. Formal universals as emergent phenomena: The origins of structure preservation. In Jeff Good (ed.), *Linguistic universals and language change*, 108–121. Oxford: Oxford University Press. DOI:10.1093/acprof:oso/9780199298495.003.0005

Bybee, Joan L. 2010. *Language, usage and cognition.* Cambridge: Cambridge University Press. DOI:10.1017/CBO9780511750526.011

Bybee, Joan L. & Clay Beckner. 2015. Emergence at the cross-linguistic level: Attractor dynamics in language change. In Brian MacWhinney & William O'Grady (eds.), *The handbook of language emergence*, 183–200. Oxford: Blackwell. DOI:10.1002/9781118346136.ch8

Carlier, Anne & Béatrice Lamiroy. 2014. The grammaticalization of the prepositional partitive in Romance. In Silvia Luraghi & Tuomas Huumo (eds.), *Partitives and related categories*, 477–519. Berlin: Mouton de Gruyter. DOI:10.1515/9783110346060.477

Collins, Jeremy. 2019. Some language universals are historical accidents. In Karsten Schmidtke-Bode, Natalia Levshina, Susanne Maria Michaelis & Ilja A. Seržant (eds.), *Explanation in typology: Diachronic sources, functional motivations and the nature of the evidence*, 47–61. Berlin: Language Science Press. DOI:10.5281/zenodo.2583808

Creissels, Denis. 2018. The Obligatory Coding Principle in diachronic perspective. In Sonia Cristofaro & Fernando Zúñiga (eds.), *Typological hierarchies in diachrony and diachrony*, 59–109. Amsterdam, Philadelphia: John Benjamins. DOI:10.1075/tsl.121.02cre

Cristofaro, Sonia. 2017. Implicational universals and dependencies. In Nick J. Enfield (ed.), *Dependencies in language: On the causal ontology of linguistic systems*, 9–22. Berlin: Language Science Press. DOI:10.5281/zenodo.573777

Cristofaro, Sonia. 2019. Taking diachronic evidence seriously: Result-oriented vs. source-oriented explanations of typological universals. In Karsten Schmidtke-Bode, Natalia Levshina, Susanne Maria Michaelis & Ilja A. Seržant (eds.), *Explanation in typology: Diachronic sources, functional motivations and the nature of the evidence*, 25–46. Berlin: Language Science Press. DOI:10.5281/zenodo.2583806

Croft, William. 2000. *Explaining language change: An evolutionary approach.* London: Harlow. DOI:10.1075/jhp.6.1.09rau

Croft, William. 2001. *Radical Construction Grammar: Syntactic theory in typological perspective*. Oxford: Oxford University Press. DOI:10.1093/acprof:oso/9780198299554.001.0001

Croft, William. 2003. *Typology and universals*. 2nd edn. Cambridge: Cambridge University Press. DOI:10.1017/CBO9780511840579

Croft, William. 2006. Evolutionary models and functional-typological theories of language change. In Ans van Kemenade & Bettelou Los (eds.), *The handbook of the history of English*, 68–91. Oxford: Blackwell. DOI:10.1002/9780470757048.ch4

Culbertson, Jennifer, Paul Smolensky & Géraldine Legendre. 2012. Learning biases predict a word order universal. *Cognition* 122(3). 306–329. DOI:10.1016/j.cognition.2011.10.017

Cysouw, Michael. 2010. Dealing with diversity: Towards an explanation of NP-internal word order frequencies. *Linguistic Typology* 14(2–3). 253–286. DOI:10.1515/lity.2010.010

Dalrymple, Mary & Irina Nikolaeva. 2011. *Objects and information structure.* Cambridge: Cambridge University Press. DOI:10.1017/CBO9780511993473

De Smet, Hendrik. 2012. The course of actualization. *Language* 88(3). 601–633. DOI:10.1353/lan.2012.0056

Diessel, Holger. 2011. Review article of *Language, usage and cognition* by Joan L. Bybee. *Language* 87(4). 830–844. DOI:10.2307/41348862

Diessel, Holger. 2016. *Word order correlations: Grammaticalization, nominalization, and analogy.* Paper presented at the Workshop on Mechanisms of Grammatical Change, Wissenschaftskolleg zu Berlin.

Dryer, Matthew S. 2005. Definite articles. In Martin Haspelmath, Matthew S. Dryer, David Gil & Bernard Comrie (eds.), *The world atlas of language structures*, 154–157. Oxford: Oxford University Press.

Dryer, Matthew S. 2009. The branching direction theory of word order correlations revisited. In Sergio Scalise, Elisabetta Magni & Antonietta Bisetto (eds.), *Universals of language today*, 185–208. Dordrecht: Springer. DOI:10.1007/978-1-4020-8825-4_10

Dryer, Matthew S. 2013a. Definite articles. In Matthew S. Dryer & Martin Haspelmath (eds.), *The world atlas of language structures online*. Leipzig: Max Planck Institute for Evolutionary Anthropology. http://wals.info/chapter/37, accessed 2016-12-12.

Dryer, Matthew S. 2013b. Order of adjective and noun. In Matthew S. Dryer & Martin Haspelmath (eds.), *The world atlas of language structures online*. Leipzig: Max Planck Institute for Evolutionary Anthropology. http://wals.info/chapter/87, accessed 2016-12-18.

Dryer, Matthew S. 2013c. Order of object and verb. In Matthew S. Dryer & Martin Haspelmath (eds.), *The world atlas of language structures online*. Leipzig: Max Planck Institute for Evolutionary Anthropology. http://wals.info/chapter/83, accessed 2018-12-12.

Dunn, Michael, Simon J. Greenhill, Stephen C. Levinson & Russell D. Gray. 2011. Evolved structure of language shows lineage-specific trends in word-order universals. *Nature* 473. 79–82. DOI:10.1038/nature09923

Enfield, N. J. 2014. *Natural causes of language: Frames, biases, and cultural transmission.* Berlin: Language Science Press. DOI:10.17169/langsci.b48.77

Fischer, Susann. 2010. *Word-order change as a source of grammaticalisation.* Amsterdam, Philadelphia: John Benjamins. DOI:10.1075/la.157

Fox, Barbara A. & Sandra A. Thompson. 2007. Relative clauses in English conversation: Relativizers, frequency, and the notion of construction. *Studies in Language* 31(2). 293–326. DOI:10.1075/sl.31.2.03fox

Gahl, Susanne & Susan M. Garnsey. 2004. Knowledge of grammar, knowledge of usage: Syntactic probabilities affect pronunciation variation. *Language* 80(4). 748–775. DOI:10.1353/lan.2004.0185

Gentner, Dedre & Linda Smith. 2012. Analogical reasoning. In Vilayanur S. Ramachandran (ed.), *Encyclopedia of human behavior*, 2nd edn., 130–136. Amsterdam: Elsevier. DOI:10.1007/978-3-319-47829-6_1076-1

Good, Jeff. 2008. Introduction. In Jeff Good (ed.), *Linguistic universals and language change*, 1–19. Oxford: Oxford University Press. DOI:10.1093/acprof:oso/9780199298495.003.0001

Haig, Geoffrey. 2018. The grammaticalization of object pronouns: Why differential object indexing is an attractor state. *Linguistics* 56(4). 781–818. DOI:10.1515/ling-2018-0011

Haiman, John. 1983. Iconic and economic motivation. *Language* 59(4). 781–819. DOI:10.2307/413373

Haspelmath, Martin. 1993. *A grammar of Lezgian*. Berlin, New York: Mouton de Gruyter. DOI:10.1515/9783110884210

Haspelmath, Martin. 1999. Optimality and diachronic adaptation. *Zeitschrift für Sprachwissenschaft* 18(2). 180–205. DOI:10.1515/zfsw.1999.18.2.180

Haspelmath, Martin. 2008. Creating economical morphosyntactic patterns in language change. In Jeff Good (ed.), *Language universals and language change*, 185–214. Oxford: Oxford University Press. DOI:10.1093/acprof:oso/9780199298495.003.0008

Haspelmath, Martin. 2011. The indeterminacy of word segmentation and the nature of morphology and syntax. *Folia Linguistica* 45(1). 31–80. DOI:10.1515/flin.2011.002

Haspelmath, Martin. 2019. Can cross-linguistic regularities be explained by constraints on change? In Karsten Schmidtke-Bode, Natalia Levshina, Susanne Maria Michaelis & Ilja A. Seržant (eds.), *Explanation in typology: Diachronic sources, functional motivations and the nature of the evidence*, 1–23. Berlin: Language Science Press. DOI:10.5281/zenodo.2583804

Hawkins, John A. 1986. *A comparative typology of English and German: Unifying the contrasts*. London, Sydney: Croom Helm. DOI:10.4324/9781315687964

Hawkins, John A. 1994. *A performance theory of order and constituency*. Cambridge: Cambridge University Press. DOI:10.1017/CBO9780511554285

Hawkins, John A. 2004. *Efficiency and complexity in grammars.* Oxford: Oxford University Press. DOI:10.1093/acprof:oso/9780199252695.001.0001

Hawkins, John A. 2007. Processing typology and why psychologists need to know about it. *New Ideas in Psychology* 25. 87–107. DOI:10.1016/j.newideapsych.2007.02.003

Hawkins, John A. 2012. The drift of English towards invariable word order from a typological and Germanic perspective. In Terttu Nevalainen & Elizabeth C. Traugott (eds.), *The Oxford handbook of the history of English*, 622–632. Oxford: Oxford University Press. DOI:10.1093/oxfordhb/9780199922765.013.0053

Hawkins, John A. 2014. *Cross-linguistic variation and efficiency.* Oxford: Oxford University Press. DOI:10.1093/acprof:oso/9780199664993.001.0001

Hewson, John & Vit Bubenik. 2006. *From case to adposition: The development of configurational syntax in Indo-European languages.* Amsterdam, Philadelphia: John Benjamins. DOI:10.1075/cilt.280

Jaeger, T. Florian. 2010. Redundancy and reduction: How speakers manage syntactic information density. *Cognitive Psychology* 61(1). 23–62. DOI:10.1016/j.cogpsych.2010.02.002

Jaeger, T. Florian, Peter Graff, William Croft & Daniel Pontillo. 2011. Mixed effect models for genetic and areal dependencies in linguistic typology. *Linguistic Typology* 15(2). 281–320. DOI:10.1515/lity.2011.021

Keenan, Edward L. & Bernard Comrie. 1977. Noun phrase accessibility and universal grammar. *Linguistic Inquiry* 8(1). 63–99.

Keller, Rudi. 1994. *Language change: The invisible hand in language.* London: Routledge.

Kemmer, Suzanne & Michael Barlow. 2000. Introduction: A usage-based conception of language. In Michael Barlow & Suzanne Kemmer (eds.), *Usage-based models of language*, vii–xxviii. Stanford, CA: Center for the Study of Language & Information.

Kurumada, Chigusa & Scott Grimm. 2017. Communicative efficiency in language production and learning: Optional plural marking. In *Proceedings of the 39th Annual Meeting of the Cognitive Science Society*, 2500–2506. http://www.sas.rochester.edu/lin/sgrimm/publications/Kurumada%20Grimm2017.pdf, accessed 2017-7-3.

Kurumada, Chigusa & T. Florian Jaeger. 2015. Communicative efficiency in language production: Optional case-marking in Japanese. *Journal of Memory and Language* 83. 152–178. DOI:10.1016/j.jml.2015.03.003

Langacker, Ronald W. 1987. *Foundations of Cognitive Grammar. Vol. I: Theoretical prerequisites.* Stanford: Stanford University Press.

Leiss, Elisabeth. 2000. *Artikel und Aspekt: Die grammatischen Muster von Definitheit.* Berlin: Mouton de Gruyter. DOI:10.1515/9783110825961

Leiss, Elisabeth. 2007. Covert patterns of definiteness/indefiniteness and aspectuality in Old Icelandic, Gothic, and Old High German. In Elisabeth Stark, Elisabeth Leiss & Werner Abraham (eds.), *Nominal determination: Typology, context constraints and historical emergence,* 73–102. Amsterdam, Philadelphia: John Benjamins. DOI:10.1075/slcs.89.06lei

Levshina, Natalia. 2019. Linguistic Frankenstein, or How to test universal constraints without real languages. In Karsten Schmidtke-Bode, Natalia Levshina, Susanne Maria Michaelis & Ilja A. Seržant (eds.), *Explanation in typology: Diachronic sources, functional motivations and the nature of the evidence,* 203–221. Berlin: Language Science Press. DOI:10.5281/zenodo.2583820

Levy, Roger. 2008. Expectation-based syntactic comprehension. *Cognition* 106. 1126–1177. DOI:10.1016/j.cognition.2007.05.006

Lüdtke, Helmut. 1991. Überlegungen zur Entstehung des bestimmten Artikels im Romanischen. *Linguistica* 31. 81–97. DOI:10.4312/linguistica.31.1.81-97

McColl Millar, Robert. 2000. Some suggestions for explaining the origin and development of the definite article in English. In Olga Fischer, Anette Rosenbach & Dieter Stein (eds.), *Pathways of change: Grammaticalization in English,* 275–310. Amsterdam, Philadelphia: John Benjamins. DOI:10.1075/slcs.53.14mil

Nettle, Daniel. 1999. *Linguistic diversity.* Oxford: Oxford University Press.

Norcliffe, Elizabeth, Alice C. Harris & T. Florian Jaeger. 2015. Cross-linguistic psycholinguistics and its critical role in theory development: Early beginnings and recent advances. *Language, Cognition and Neuroscience* 30(9). 1009–1032. DOI:10.1080/23273798.2015.1080373

Norcliffe, Elizabeth & T. Florian Jaeger. 2016. Predicting head-marking variability in Yucatec Maya relative clause production. *Language and Cognition* 8. 167–205. DOI:10.1017/langcog.2014.39

Ogura, Mieko. 1993. The development of periphrastic *do* in English: A case of lexical diffusion in syntax. *Diachronica* X. 51–85. DOI:10.1075/dia.10.1.04ogu

R Development Core Team. 2016. *R: a language and environment for statistical computing.* Vienna: R Foundation for Statistical Computing. http://www.r-project.org.

Rosenbach, Anette. 2008. Language change as cultural evolution: Evolutionary approaches to language change. In Regine Eckardt, Gerhard Jäger & Tonjes Veenstra (eds.), *Variation, selection, development: Probing the evolutionary model of language change,* 23–74. Berlin, New York: Mouton de Gruyter. DOI:10.1515/9783110205398.1.23

Ross, Malcolm. 2001. Contact-induced change in Oceanic languages in North-West Melanesia. In Alexandra Y. Aikhenvald & R. M. W. Dixon (eds.), *Areal diffusion and genetic inheritance*, 134–166. Oxford: Oxford University Press.

Seiler, Guido. 2006. The role of functional factors in language change: An evolutionary approach. In Ole Nedergaard Thomsen (ed.), *Competing models of linguistic change, evolution and beyond*, 163–182. Amsterdam, Philadelphia: John Benjamins. DOI:10.1075/cilt.279.11sei

Selig, Maria. 1992. *Die Entwicklung der Nominaldeterminanten im Spätlatein: Romanischer Sprachwandel und lateinische Schriftlichkeit.* Tübingen: Narr.

Seržant, Ilja A. 2019. Weak universal forces: The discriminatory function of case in differential object marking systems. In Karsten Schmidtke-Bode, Natalia Levshina, Susanne Maria Michaelis & Ilja A. Seržant (eds.), *Explanation in typology: Diachronic sources, functional motivations and the nature of the evidence*, 149–178. Berlin: Language Science Press. DOI:10.5281/zenodo.2583816

Sinnemäki, Kaius. 2014. A typological perspective on differential object marking. *Linguistics* 52(2). 281–313. DOI:10.1515/ling-2013-0063

Smith, John Charles. 2001. Markedness, functionality and perseveration in the actualization of a morphosyntactic change. In Henning Andersen (ed.), *Actualization: Linguistic change in progress*, 203–224. Amsterdam, Philadelphia: John Benjamins. DOI:10.1075/cilt.219.10smi

Thompson, Bill, Simon Kirby & Kenny Smith. 2016. Culture shapes the evolution of cognition. *PNAS* 113(16). 4530–4535. DOI:10.1073/pnas.1523631113

Timberlake, Alan. 1977. Reanalysis and actualization in syntactic change. In Charles N. Li (ed.), *Mechanisms of syntactic change*, 141–177. Austin: University of Texas Press.

Trudgill, Peter. 2004. *New-dialect formation: The inevitability of colonial Englishes.* Edinburgh: Edinburgh University Press.

van Gelderen, Elly. 2014. *A history of the English language.* Amsterdam, Philadelphia: John Benjamins. DOI:10.1075/z.183

Vennemann, Theo. 1975. An explanation of drift. In Charles Li (ed.), *Word order and word order change*, 269–305. Austin: University of Texas Press.

Wang, William S-Y. 1969. Competing changes as a cause of residue. *Language* 45(1). 9–25. DOI:10.2307/411748

Wasow, Thomas, T. Florian Jaeger & David M. Orr. 2011. Lexical variation in relativizer frequency. In Horst J. Simon & Heike Wiese (eds.), *Expecting the unexpected: Exceptions in grammar*, 175–195. Berlin, New York: Mouton de Gruyter. DOI:10.1515/9783110219098.175

Zakharko, Taras & Balthasar Bickel. 2011ff. *Familybias: Family bias estimation. R package.* https://github.com/IVS-UZH, accessed 2016-11-17.

Chapter 7

Weak universal forces: The discriminatory function of case in differential object marking systems

Ilja A. Seržant
Leipzig University

Standard typological methods are designed to test hypotheses on strong universals that broadly override all other competing universal and language-specific forces. In this paper, I argue that there exist also weak universal forces. Weak universal forces systematically operate in the course of development but then interact with, or are even subsequently overridden by, other processes such as analogical extension, persistence effects from the source function, etc. This, in turn, means that there can be statistically significant evidence for violations at the synchronic level and, accordingly, only a weak positive statistical signal. But crucially, the absence of statistical prima-facie evidence for such forces does not amount to evidence for their absence. The assumption that there are also weak universal forces that affect language evolution goes in line with the view that human cognition in general and language acquisition in particular are constrained by probabilistic biases of different range, including weak ones (cf. Thompson et al. 2016). By way of example, the present paper claims that the discriminatory function of case in differential object marking (DOM) systems is a weak universal: It keeps appearing in historically, synchronically and typologically very divergent constellations but is often overridden by other processes in further developments and is, therefore, not significant at the synchronic level in a large sample.

1 Introduction

In this paper, I adopt a dynamic approach to universals (Greenberg 1978) and, accordingly, the following definition of a universal:

Ilja A. Seržant. 2019. Weak universal forces: The discriminatory function of case in differential object marking systems. In Karsten Schmidtke-Bode, Natalia Levshina, Susanne Maria Michaelis & Ilja A. Seržant (eds.), *Explanation in typology: Diachronic sources, functional motivations and the nature of the evidence*, 149–178. Berlin: Language Science Press. DOI:10.5281/zenodo.2583816

(1) A dynamic definition of universals
     principled preferences that affect how languages change over time
     (Bickel 2011: 401).

I conceive of these preferences as statistical tendencies (cf. Bickel 2011) rather than "inviolable constraints" on language in Kiparsky (2008). This definition singles out those universals that are not predetermined by the historical origin of the structures in question, thus resembling Haspelmath's "functional-adaptive constraints" on language (Haspelmath 2019 [this volume]). Universal forces of this kind produce structures that occur with "overwhelmingly greater than chance frequency" or "well more than chance frequency" (Greenberg 1963: 62, 64, *passim*), and they thus allow for exceptions. The number of such exceptions, in turn, is indicative of the *strength* of a universal force.

Strong universal forces reveal themselves as universal on both of the methodological approaches used in typology: on the *static* and on the *dynamic* approach (see Greenberg 1969 for these notions). The former crucially relies on the relative frequency in the synchronic distribution across languages, while the latter is based on the relative frequency of the relevant changes across languages from a proto-stage (STAGE 0) into the synchronic stage (STAGE 1).[1] A typical characteristic of strong universals is that the dynamic and the static evidence for these universals converge. For example, the force that ALL LANGUAGES MUST HAVE VOWELS (Comrie 1989: 19) finds solid evidence for universality on the static approach, in the sense that one would hardly find a spoken language violating this universal, i.e. a language without any vowels. The dynamic approach will equally show that, despite various language-specific processes such as vowel reduction strategies and even vowel loss, these never succeed to such an extent as to yield a language without any vowel, because no other universal or language-specific force may override this universal force in any type of language change.

Another strong universal – albeit somewhat weaker than the former – concerns inflection: IF THERE IS ANY INFLECTION IN NOUNS, THERE IS ALSO SOME INFLECTION IN PRONOUNS (Moravcsik 1993; Plank et al. 2002ff.). A still weaker universal – a number of exceptions can be found in the literature (cf. Handschuh 2014) – concerns case marking: IN A LANGUAGE WITH CASE, THE ZERO-MARKED CASE TENDS TO BE THE ONE THAT MARKS THE SUBJECT OF INTRANSITIVE VERBS (Greenberg 1963: 95).

---

[1] Note that the static approach, too, assumes that the synchronic distributions are the result of diachronic changes that have led to them (cf. Haspelmath 2019 [this volume]). It is, therefore, only methodologically but not ideologically synchronic.

Thus, there is gradience in the strengths of universals and, accordingly, in the number of exceptions found at STAGE 1 with each universal. By entertaining the idea of gradience a bit further, one may also think of a force that systematically operates in the development of a particular category across languages, i.e. in the transition between STAGE 0 and STAGE 1, and is, therefore, a universal according to the definition in (1) above. However, this universal is not strong enough to override competing internal and/or universal forces to remain visible at STAGE 1. A universal of this kind is referred to as *weak universal force*:

(2) Definition of a weak universal force
     A weak universal is a force that systematically exerts an impact in the his-
     torical development from STAGE 0 into STAGE 1 in a particular (grammatical)
     domain; this impact is found across geographic areas and genealogical af-
     filiations in the diachrony with significant frequency, but may be marginal
     and heavily restricted or not be visible at all in the synchronic layer (STAGE
     1).

The synchronic effects of a weak universal force often reside in marginal sub-domains or are overridden altogether by some other, stronger processes (cf. Bickel 2014: 117). This, in turn, means that there will be a significant number of violations and only a weak positive statistical signal (if at all). As a result, the standard methodologies that rely on the relative frequency in the prima-facie data will provide disproof of universality.

To give an example, Hammarström (2015) argues on the basis of 5,230 languages that there is a universal trend for SVO word order across languages (cf. Gell-Mann & Ruhlen 2011; Maurits & Griffiths 2014), henceforth, the SVO UNIVERSAL. Having said this, he claims that "the universal is not the only, nor the most important factor" constraining the synchronic distribution; the most important factor responsible for the current distribution is the order of the immediate ancestor, i.e. inheritance. The following figures illustrate this point: SOV is much more widespread than SVO across language families, with 65.1% SOV vs. 16.2% SVO,[2] but a change from SOV to SVO and from VSO to SVO is significantly more probable than the respective reverse changes (Croft 2003: 234; Maurits & Griffiths 2014). Hammarström (2015) shows that the pressure to retain the inherited word order accounts for 78% of the sample, while the universal SVO accounts for only 14% of the static evidence. The SVO UNIVERSAL is thus a weak universal in

---

[2]SOV (43.3%) is attested only slightly more frequently than SVO (40.2%) if the genealogical bias
  is not controlled for (cf. Dryer 2013). This effect is just due to a few large families with SVO
  (Hammarström 2015).

the sense that it cannot so easily force a language to change into SVO against the pressure of inheritance.

In what follows, I argue that the *discriminatory function* of flagging is a weak universal despite apparent counterevidence. I illustrate this with qualitative data and arguments about how different motivations may lead to a result that is easily misinterpreted if taken at face value. In order to do so, I first introduce the *(global) discriminatory function* and the related phenomenon of *local disambiguation* (§2). §3 exemplifies various differential object marking (DOM) systems and how the discriminatory function interacts with other, stronger forces in each of them. Finally, §4 provides a discussion of the phenomenon of weak universals and conclusions.

2 The (global) discriminatory function

Since a transitive clause has two arguments (A and P), it must be ensured that the hearer will be able to discern which of the arguments should be interpreted as A and P, respectively. Moreover, other potential misinterpretations, such as one NP modifying the other NP – if both are adjacent to each other – or both NPs being coordinated (without a conjunction), should be excluded. There are many ways in which the discriminatory function may be implemented in a particular language or even in a particular sentence, with flagging being one of them:

(3) Definition of the global discriminatory function of P flagging (economy subsumed)
     In a transitive clause, the A and the P argument must be sufficiently disambiguated, e.g. by word order, agreement, voice, world knowledge, and it is only if they are not that there is dedicated P flagging.

A number of researchers have argued that there is only little or no evidence for (A or P) flagging systems being driven by the discriminatory function as defined in (3) cross-linguistically (*inter alia*, Aissen 2003; Malchukov 2008; various papers in de Hoop & de Swart 2009). Levshina (2018) shows on the basis of the large-scale AUTOTYP database that there is no statistically significant effect of the discriminatory function observable for flagging because there are only very few languages in which flagging is primarily driven by the discriminatory function. Sometimes even in these languages, the discriminatory function does not serve the purpose of discrimination between A and P alone: a function inherited from the source construction and often some ongoing conventionalization of the most frequent discrimination patterns override the discriminatory function to various extents.

Having said this, it has been repeatedly suggested that flagging might also serve the discriminatory function, especially if A and P have similarly ranked input (cf., *inter alia*, Comrie 1978; 1989; Dixon 1994; Silverstein 1976; Kibrik 1997). Bossong (1985: 117) even assumed that the emergence of DOM is primarily due to the discriminatory function. In the following section, I follow this line of thinking and provide qualitative evidence for the claim that the discriminatory function does operate across genealogically and areally diverse DOM systems and is therefore a universal according to the definition given in (1). However, it is not a typical universal in that its impact is mostly weakened by other competing processes to which it is subordinate, the effect being that there is only marginal evidence for it at the synchronic STAGE 1.

3 Evidence from DOM systems

Consider the DOM system of the rural variety of Donno Sɔ, as described in Culy (1995). The DOM suffix -*ñ* marks human and often animal-denoting pronouns and nouns if the latter are definite:

(4) Donno Sɔ (Dogon: Mali; Culy 1995: 48)
Anta-ñ   ibɛra   yaw   aa   bem.
Anta-DOM market.LOC yesterday see.PTCP AUX.1SG
'I saw Anta at the market yesterday.'

(5) Donno Sɔ (Dogon: Mali; Culy 1995: 48)
Jalɔmbe   izɔmbe-ñ   keraa   biyaa.
donkey.DEF.PL dog.DEF.PL-DOM bite.PTCP AUX.3PL
'The donkeys bit the dogs.'

In contrast, neither indefinite animates nor inanimate definites are marked. We observe that at least two referential scales are simultaneously operating here:[3]

---

[3]In this paper, I do not make any assumptions about the nature of referential scale effects: whether they stem from generalizing the most frequent patterns conditioned by the discriminatory function (cf. Aissen 2003) or from the source (i.e. from topics, cf. Dalrymple & Nikolaeva 2011), or are language-specific (Bickel et al. 2015), or whether they represent an independent phenomenon *sui generis*, is irrelevant here.

(6) Animacy scale
     human > animate > inanimate

(7) Definiteness scale
     definite >specific > indefinite

Superficially, the discriminatory function does not seem to apply in this language since scale effects from (6) and (7) predominate: all animate and definite NPs are marked regardless of whether they really need to be globally disambiguated or not. However, the animate indefinite NPs that are not (yet) affected by the scale effects do show the operation of the discriminatory function. With these NP types, the DOM marker may be employed to discriminate between A and P in a particular utterance (cf. the Disambiguation Principle in Culy 1995: 52). For example, when both the object and the subject NP are indefinite and animate and there are no other clues how to discriminate between A and P, the DOM marker may be employed "against" the force of marking definite animates only:

(8) Donno Sɔ (Dogon: Mali; Culy 1995: 53)
     Wɛzɛwɛzɛginɛ yaana po-ñ   don wo mɔ ni tɛmbɛ.
     crazy.person   woman large-DOM place 3SG PS at found
     'A crazy person found a large woman at his/her place.'

In this example, both indefinite NPs 'a crazy person' and 'a large woman' may potentially be interpreted as A (Culy 1995: 53). Therefore, the DOM marker -ñ is used here to unequivocally mark the syntactic role of 'a large woman'. The discriminatory function is the weakest among other forces here (Culy 1995: 53) because it applies in a way exceptionally by constraining only one slot on the referential scales in (6) and (7): the indefinite animate P. In accordance with Culy (1995: 51), one can thus posit the following forces and their relative weight (from the strongest to the weakest):

(9) The relative weight of the main forces on DOM in Donno Sɔ (and
     Malayalam, see below)
     animacy scale + definiteness scale > discriminatory function

Another important observation can be made here. Notice that the slot on the referential scales in (6) and (7) that is open for the application of the discriminatory function is immediately next to the slots that require rigid marking. I interpret this in the following way. In their historical developments, many DOM systems extend the DOM markers gradually from left to right on referential scales such as (6) and (7) (cf. Dalrymple & Nikolaeva 2011). For example, many languages start with a DOM system that applies only to animate nouns but then gradually extend the DOM marker onto inanimate nouns as well. Note that very often the difference in meanings between the two neighbouring slots on a referential scale is quite substantial and is certainly not graspable in terms of semantic extension. For example, the expansion of the DOM marker *-rā(y)* from mostly animates in Middle Persian (Key 2008: 244; cf. also Paul 2008: 152–153) to the inclusion of inanimates in Modern Persian is not semantically straightforward, since the two are rather antonymic in meaning. I suggest that it is precisely the discriminatory function that is responsible for the expansion of the DOM marker into the next slot on the scale because the discriminatory function is not dependent on the lexical meaning of the noun in the same way as, for example, the animacy scale. The discriminatory function then applies to the next slot until that slot also becomes conventionalized, and so on.

A constellation very similar to Donno Sɔ is found in Malayalam (Dravidian). The Accusative marker *-(y)e* is regularly used with animate specific object referents but is normally ungrammatical with inanimate referents:

(10) Malayalam (Dravidian: India; Asher & Kumari 1997: 204)
Tiiyyə kuṭil naʃippacu.
fire.NOM hut.NOM destroy.PST
'Fire destroyed the hut.'

However, in one special case, it may be used on inanimate referents as well, i.e. precisely when there is no other way to (globally) discriminate P from A (Asher & Kumari 1997: 204, cf. Stiebels 2002: 16; Subbārāo 2012: 174–176):

(11) Malayalam (Dravidian: India; Asher & Kumari 1997: 204)

  a. Kappal tiramaalakaḷ-e bheediccu.
     ship.NOM wave.PL-ACC(=DOM) split.PST
     'The ship broke through the waves.'

  b. Tiramaalakaḷ kappal-ine bheediccu.
     wave.NOM.PL ship-ACC(=DOM) split.PST
     'The waves split the ship.'

As in Donno Sɔ above, the discriminatory function becomes visible only in those slots on the referential scales that are not (yet) affected by the scale effects.

While in Donno Sɔ the indefinite animate slot became available for the discriminatory function, it is the inanimate slot (both definite and indefinite) in Malayalam. The relative weight of the discriminatory function of the DOM marker in Malayalam is lower than the effect of the referential scales, cf. (9) again.

Crucially, if one were to superficially evaluate whether or not the discriminatory function operates in Donno Sɔ or Malayalam, one would have to conclude that it does not, because of the rigid marking of animates (definite animates in Donno Sɔ) and the rigid zero with inanimates. Thus, from the perspective of the discriminatory function, utterances like (4) redundantly mark their objects; conversely, examples such as (10) are economical but equally violate the discriminatory function since same-rank A and P are not disambiguated. I summarize:

(12)   The relative weight of the main forces in DOM in Donno Sɔ and
        Malayalam
        animacy scale + definiteness scale > economy > discriminatory function

Catalan is another example of this pattern. Here, the DOM marker *a* is obligatory only for strong (non-clitic) personal, relative and reciprocal pronouns in the non-colloquial register (cf. Escandell-Vidal 2009). Thus, the DOM marker of Catalan is primarily conditioned by the parts-of-speech scale: Pronouns are marked while other NPs are unmarked:

(13)   Parts-of-speech scale
        (independent) pronouns > nouns

However, the DOM marker may exceptionally appear also with definite animate NPs in the contexts of subject–object ambiguity (Wheeler et al. 1999: 243):

(14)   Catalan (Romance: Spain; Wheeler et al. 1999: 243)
        T'estima   com a   la   seva   mare.
        2SG.OBJ=love.PRS.3SG like DOM DEF.F 3SG.F.POSS mother
        'She loves you like (she loves) her mother.'

Again, the discriminatory function is subordinate to the parts-of-speech scale (13). It may only exceptionally violate the cut-off point between pronouns and nouns on this scale that is otherwise rigid in this language. Additionally, the animacy scale (6) and definiteness scale (7) apply in that they determine the NP type for which the discriminatory function may operate: the discriminatory function can only operate on definite animates but not on inanimates or indefinites in this language. I summarize:

(15) The relative weight of the main forces in DOM in Catalan
parts-of-speech scale > animacy + definiteness scale > discriminatory function

The situation in Spanish is somewhat different but largely analogical. Animate and specific NPs must be marked while inanimate and/or non-specific NPs must remain unmarked. However, the DOM marker *a* is obligatory in certain contexts of disambiguation, even with inanimate NPs:

(16) Spanish (Romance: Spain; von Heusinger & Kaiser 2007: 89)
En esta receta, la   leche puede sustituir a=l   huevo.
in DEM recipe DET milk can   replace DOM=DET egg
'In this recipe, egg can replace the milk.'

We observe the same constellation here: the discriminatory function is subordinate to the effects of referential scales.

Another example is the DOM marker *-ăn* in Hup (Nadahup). It is obligatory with definite animates (including pronouns) as well as with the plural collective marker *=d'əh* (Epps 2008: 170–177). At the same time, the DOM marker *-ăn* may be used with indefinite animates to discriminate the P argument from A (Epps 2009: 95). Consider the following example, in which the A argument is left out because it is non-referential:

(17) Hup (Nadahup: Brazil/Columbia; Epps 2009: 95)
Húp-ăn   tə'w-ə'y, húp-ăn   dóh-óy.
person-DOM scold-DYN person-DOM curse-DYN
'(Some people) scold people, cast curses on people.'

The P argument is not referential either, let alone definite. Since it is indefinite, it should not be marked. However, in order to discriminate the P argument from a possible misinterpretation as A, the object marker is used here (Epps 2009: 95). Again, the discriminatory function is weak because it is subordinate to the referential-scale effects which primarily determine the slots in which the discriminatory function may apply (e.g. on inanimates or indefinites or non-referential NPs, etc.). The relative weight of these is the same as in Catalan in (15) above.

The subordinate discriminatory function is found in other Nahadup languages as well. For example, the object marker *-ĩ:yʔ* in Dăw accompanies topical objects but it may also be used for the discriminatory function (Martins & Martins 1999: 263–264).

Similarly, the Papuan language Awtuw obligatorily marks all pronominal and proper-name direct objects regardless of whether there is a need for discrimination or not:

(18) Awtuw (Sepik: Papua New Guinea; Feldman 1986: 109)
      *Wan rey   du-k-puy-ey.
      1SG   3M.SG FA-IPFV-hit-IPFV
      [Intended meanings] 'I'm hitting him.' / 'He's hitting me.'

In addition, overt definiteness – marked either by a demonstrative or a possessor NP – has the tendency to attract object marking regardless of the context (Feldman 1986: 109–110). By contrast, the marking of common nouns is optional. It becomes obligatory in case of ambiguity, or else the NPs will be interpreted as conjoined (Feldman 1986: 110):

(19) Awtuw (Sepik: Papua New Guinea; Feldman 1986: 109)

      a. Piyren-re yaw di-k-æl-iy.
          dog-DOM pig FA-IPFV-bite-IPFV
          'The pig is biting the dog.'

      b. Piyren yaw di-k-æl-iy.
          dog   pig FA-IPFV-bite-IPFV
          'The dog and the pig bite.' / *'The pig is biting the dog.' / *'The dog is biting the pig.'

The situation in Awtuw is slightly different from the one found in the languages above: the slot affected by the discriminatory function (common nouns) already allows for the overt marking; the discriminatory function turns the marking in a particular utterance from optional into obligatory for this particular interpretation.

The prepositional DOM marker *bǎ* of Chinese primarily occurs before animate, definite or, rarely, indefinite specific preverbal object NPs while postverbal objects are never marked with it (Li & Thompson 1981; Bisang 1992: 158–159; Yang & van Bergen 2007):

(20) Chinese (Sinitic: China; Li & Thompson 1981: 464)
      Tā bǎ fàntīng   shōushi gānjing le.
      3SG DOM dining.room tidy.up clean   PFV
      'S/He tidied up the dining room.'

The discriminatory function as defined in (3) above is not relevant in (20). In addition to the general SVO and S *bǎ* OV word orders, Chinese also allows for OSV with topical objects and prominent subjects, cf. (21):

(21)   Chinese (Sinitic: China; Bisang 1992: 158)

    a. Láng Mary chī-le.
       wolf Mary eat-PFV

       'Mary ate the wolf.'

    b. Láng bǎ   Mary chī-le.
       wolf DOM Mary eat-PFV

       'The wolf ate Mary.'

To force the interpretation of (21) with SOV, the *bǎ* marker has to be used in order to disambiguate the referentially more prominent NP (*Mary*) as P (cf. Bisang 1992: 158). Again as in the examples above, the DOM system of Chinese is primarily driven by the cut-off points on referential scales (definiteness, animacy) and some other strong rules pertaining to affectedness, aspectuality and the "disposability" of the object referent (cf. Li & Thompson 1981). Some of these functions are most probably inherited from the source, such as the requirement on disposability or the preverbal position, which may be explained as the retention of the properties of the source construction.[4] The discriminatory function is thus again limited to a particular constellation of (21) in which the source function, referential scale effects and other forces allow it to operate.

The discriminatory function in Mam (Mayan) is carried out by the obligatory cross-referencing of both A and P on the verb; no flagging is involved. By contrast, the Antipassive form of the verb does not allow for cross-referencing the P argument, which is regularly marked by the preposition / relational noun *-iʔj* 'about' or *-ee* (dative, beneficiary) (England 1983: 212):

(22)   Mam (Mayan: Guatemala; England 1983: 213)
    ma ø-tzyuu-n   Cheep *(t-iʔj)   xiinaq
    REC 3A-grab-ANTIP Jose   *(3SG-RN) man

    'Jose grabbed the man.'

However, "if there is no confusion as to which noun phrase is the agent and which is the patient" the relational noun may be omitted in order to code the meaning of an unintentional act (England 1983: 212):

---

[4]The *bǎ* marker stems from the lexical verb 'to hold' in a serial verb construction (Sun 1996: 61–62).

(23) Mam (Mayan: Guatemala; England 1983: 212–213)

    a. Ma ø-tzyuu-n   Cheep t-iʔj   ch'it.
       REC 3A-grab-ANTIP Jose   3SG-RN bird

       'Jose grabbed the bird.'

    b. Ma ø-tzyuu-n   Cheep ch'it.
       REC 3A-grab-ANTIP Jose   bird

       'Jose unintentionally grabbed the bird.'

The discriminatory function thus delimits the range of the input with which unintentional acts can be expressed (in the Antipassive). In other words, the discriminatory function of flagging is found in a very small subdomain of the language, i.e. in the unintentional use of the Antipassive.

A somewhat different constellation is found in Tamasheq (Berber). The marker *na* (*ná, nà* depending on the dialect and tone sandhi) occurs only in SOV word order – never in SVO or VSO – and only if there is no verb inflection (Perfective Indicative), i.e. when no disambiguation via indexing is possible (Heath 2007: 92, 94).[5] Moreover, both arguments must be expressed overtly. For example, the marker cannot be used in the imperative with the subject dropped (Heath 2007: 92–93). These requirements suggest that the marker is conditioned by the discriminatory function:

(24) Tamasheq (Afro-Asiatic, Berber: North Africa; Heath 2007: 91; glosses adapted)
Hàr-òó   nà háns-òò   kárú.
man-DET.SG DOM dog-DET.SG hit

'The man hit the dog.'

Without *nà*, both NPs may be misinterpreted as either a compound or as a possessor phrase 'the man's dog' (Heath 2007: 91).

Moreover, some Mande languages such as Soninke, Bambara, Wan or Songhay languages of the area also have similar markers that primarily fulfil the discriminatory function of unambiguous identification of the subject and the object in a clause (Heath 2007; Creissels & Diagne 2013; Nikitina 2018). While Tamasheq,

---

[5]It is referred to as a "bidirectional case marker" in Heath (2007) as well as in the descriptions of some Mande languages, cf. Diagana (1995), Nikitina (2018). Bidirectional case markers cannot be straightforwardly related to either A or P marking since they occur only when both are present and do not show any phonetic or syntactic fusion effects. Note that bidirectional case markers are treated under the heading of differential argument marking, cf. Nikitina (2018).

similarly to many Central Mande languages, has generalized the marker, extending it onto all SOV utterances, Wan (South-eastern Mande) employs the marker *laa* predominantly only in those input configurations which are in need of disambiguation given SOV. The marker is used with nominal A and pronominal P (62%) but not with pronominal A and nominal P (0%) (Nikitina 2018: 202). In contrast to the languages discussed above, in these languages the discriminatory function is somewhat stronger, as it applies across the board under SOV. Analogically, the DOM marker is optional in the most frequent SOV word order in Korean but becomes almost obligatorily when the object is preposed (OSV) (Ahn & Cho 2007).

At least two Loloish languages (Tibeto-Burman) also attest a strong discriminatory function that is not subordinate to some other force. The direct-object markers *tʰaʔ* in Lahu and *tʰie* in Lolo are only used if the context does not help to discriminate between A and P. That is, these markers code direct objects only where the inherent semantics of the participants (such as animacy) and the semantics of the event fail to do so:

(25) Yongren Lolo (Tibeto-Burman, Loloish: China; adapted from Gerner 2008: 299[6])

ŋo ɕɛmo tʰie ʈʂɔ ʑi.
1SG snake DOM follow go
'I will follow the snake'

(26) Yongren Lolo (Tibeto-Burman, Loloish: China; adapted from Gerner 2008: 300)

Sɨka tʰie χekʰɯ ti na.
tree DOM house smash broken
'The house smashed the tree.'

The absence of the Accusative marker would not be ungrammatical but would create ambiguity as to who is following whom in (25) or what is smashing what in (26) (Matisoff 1973: 156; Gerner 2008). However, along with the synchronically primary function of discriminating P from A (and also R from A), this marker also has the diachronically primary function of coding contrastive focus (Gerner 2008: 298–289). For example, (27a) cannot be used with the DOM marker *tʰie* because of the lack of a focal contrast. By contrast, (27b) is acceptable with it if the numeral is interpreted as bearing contrastive focus (Gerner 2008: 299):

---

[6]I simplified the transliteration and slightly adjusted the glossing of all examples from Gerner (2008).

(27) Yongren Lolo (Tibeto-Burman, Loloish: China; adapted from Gerner 2008: 299)

    a. Bɔlu mɔlu   tsɨ   ɔ.
       Bolu trousers wash PRF

       'Bolu washed trousers.'

    b. Bɔlu mɔlu   sɔ   khə tʰie tsɨ   ɔ.
       Bolu trousers NUM.3 CLF DOM wash PRF

       'Bolu washed THREE pairs of trousers [not just TWO].'

Importantly, (27b) may at first glance be interpreted as counterevidence to the discriminatory function because A and P are sufficiently disambiguated by the lexical meanings anyway. Hence, the marking is not due to the discriminatory function. I claim that this is not a piece of counterevidence for the hypothesis of a weak discriminatory function. It may only count as counterevidence for the strong hypothesis of the discriminatory function being the only force constraining DOM (which is counter-intuitive anyway). The source function of marking contrastive focus overrides the discriminatory function here. A situation where various new and inherited functions cluster on one marker is typical of many grammatical categories (cf. Hopper 1991: 22). For example, if an indefinite article does not mark plural indefinite NPs but only singular ones, this cannot be taken as counterevidence for its being an indefinite article. A more plausible account is that the restriction to the singular is just the impact of the source meaning.

Another similar DOM system is the one of Khwe. In this language, proper names must obligatorily be marked with *à/-à*; additionally, this marker encodes contrast and/or focus on the NP (Kilian-Hatz 2006: 82–83). At the same time, the marker may also be used in contexts in which the distinction between subject and object would have been impeded, for example, when both arguments are animate and topical (Kilian-Hatz 2006: 82–83):

(28) Khwe (Khoe: Southern Africa; adapted from Kilian-Hatz 2006: 83)

    a. Tcá tí à   kx'óã´.
       2SG.M 1SG DOM wait

       'You have to wait for me!'

    b. Yàá! Cáò à   tí kyá-rá-hã!
       yes 2DU.F DOM 1SG love-ACT-PST

       'That's it! I love you two (women)!'

Further examples may be added. For example, the DOM marker *-m* in Imonda (Papuan) is used obligatorily with some verbs such as *eg* 'to follow' or *hetha* 'to hit' as well as with others to denote something like resultativity ("directionality") of the action (Seiler 1985: 163). However, in addition to that, the marker may also serve to disambiguate Ps from As when both have similar-rank input (Seiler 1985: 165). Furthermore, DOM in Guaraní is primarily conditioned by animacy, definiteness and topicality but it may also marginally fulfil the discriminatory function (Shain 2009: 89–92). In Telkepe (Semitic, Aramaic), the new object marker *ta* may be employed in those situations where agreement alone does not provide for disambiguation while it is otherwise heavily constrained by its meaning of marking topics (Coghill 2014: 354). Finally, Kurumada & Jaeger (2015) show for Japanese that, in addition to animacy, disambiguation also triggers the DOM marker *-o* (see also Fedzechkina et al. 2012).

The discriminatory function may help to explain the world-wide distribution of DOM, namely, why there are more animacy-driven DOM systems than those driven by definiteness and/or specificity across languages. Thus, in a large-scale typological study by Sinnemäki (2014: 295), roughly 39% of DOM systems are conditioned by animacy, while DOM systems conditioned by definiteness/specificity are areally biased towards the Old World and occur less frequently (34% of his sample). I claim that the reason for this is that animate referents are much more strongly associated with the A role than definite/specific referents. Hence, there is a more urgent need with animate than with definite referents for the discriminatory function to apply. A number of corpus studies from various languages show that only animacy shows reversed association tendencies with A and P such that As tend to be animate while Ps tend to be inanimate; by contrast, both As and Ps – with minor differences – tend to be definite and/or specific (Dahl 2000; Hofling 2003; Everett 2009; Fauconnier & Verstraete 2014).

Finally, there is neurolinguistic evidence for the discriminatory function, suggesting that A and P are not treated symmetrically by the processor. Instead, Bornkessel-Schlesewsky & Schlesewsky (2015) claim that the effects they observe cannot be explained by simply arising from the degree of semantic associations for the A or P role. Rather, both arguments are interpreted relatively to each other (Bornkessel-Schlesewsky & Schlesewsky 2015: 336). Analogically, Kurumada & Jaeger (2015) found in their psycholinguistic study on DOM in Japanese that just the properties of the arguments are insufficient to explain the results of their experiments and that the case-marking is affected by the plausibility of role assignment given both arguments and the verb (2015: 161; cf. also Ahn & Cho 2007; Fedzechkina et al. 2012).

Above, I have argued that the global discriminatory function as defined in (3) is found to operate in many diverse languages. Moreover, I have found that it is most frequently the weakest force alongside other forces, such as referential scale effects (based on animacy, definiteness or parts of speech) or the source meaning (focus, topic, etc.). All these forces constrain the DOM systems at the same time. The weakness of the discriminatory function is not correlated, I claim, with scarce attestation across languages. On the contrary, I suspect that its impact could be found across most of the DOM systems if one took a closer look at the historical developments and if the synchronic descriptions were more detailed.

The context-dependent, global discriminatory function in (3) is relatively expensive because it requires whole-utterance planning and online decision making on the part of the speaker. It is costly for the hearer as well since ambiguous NPs (e.g. German *die Frau* 'DET.NOM=ACC woman') – if placed clause-initially – can only be interpreted by the hearer once enough context has been provided, and not incrementally (Bornkessel-Schlesewsky & Schlesewsky 2014: 107). It is perhaps for this reason that the global discriminatory function often develops into what may be called a *local discriminatory function* (cf. Aissen 2003; Zeevat & Jäger 2002; Jäger 2004; Malchukov 2008: 208, 213). By virtue of the *local discriminatory function*, the NP is disambiguated as A or P immediately and regardless of whether the whole utterance might make disambiguation redundant. The local discriminatory function is more efficient because it allows for more reliable incremental processing of the utterance. The degree of efficiency and processability, in turn, correlates with the strength of a force (Hawkins 2014: 60, 69). This is why the global discriminatory function (cf. (3)) is a weak force and its effects tend to be generalized over diachronically, for example, by conventionalizing the flagging on those NP types that tend to be disambiguated most frequently or, alternatively, by conventionalizing the marker in those constructions that require disambiguation most frequently (such as SOV in Tamasheq).

A number of languages have undergone this change towards local disambiguation. I illustrate this with the development of DOM in Russian. I base my argumentation on the philologically profound evidence from Krys'ko (1994; 1997).

Old Russian inherited from Proto-Slavic the emergent DOM system that evolved in the following way. The direct object was marked by the Accusative case in affirmative clauses and by the Genitive case in clauses with predicate negation. Already during the Proto-Slavic period, the Genitive started penetrating into affirmative transitive clauses (Klenin 1983). The reason is that, under predicate negation, the Genitive no longer carried any functional load but became just a purely syntactically conditioned rule.[7] The Genitive was thus just another way of marking direct objects (when the predicate was negated) alongside Accusative. At the same time, due to the overall loss of all word final consonants, the old Accusative and Nominative markers became phonetically indistinguishable in the singular in most of the Proto-Slavic declensions and, subsequently, turned into zero:

Table 1: Phonetically driven conflation of the old Accusative with the old Nominative in most of the declensions (cf. Arumaa 1985: 130)

	Proto-Slavic Nominative	Proto-Slavic Accusative	Resulting form Accusative = Nominative
u-declension	*-us	*-um	> *-u > -ъ > ø
i-declension	*-is	*-im	> *-i > -ь > ø
o-declension	*-os > *-us	*-om > *-um	> *-u > -ъ > ø
jo-declension	*jos > -jus	*jom > -jum	> *-ju > *-jъ > ᴶь > ᴶø

The new DOM marker – i.e. the Genitive case – replaced the old (zero) Accusative only on animate nouns and some pronouns. Importantly, only those animate nouns and pronouns were affected which belonged to the declension classes that did not differentiate between the Nominative and the Accusative anymore (cf. Table 1). Thus, the expansion of the new DOM marker (Genitive) was crucially conditioned by the local discriminatory function alongside the animacy scale (Krys'ko 1994).

The evidence for this is abundant: (i) The Genitive did not replace the old Accusative in the *a*-declension because, in this declension, the old Accusative (*-ǫ* > *-u*) had not become indistinguishable from the Nominative (*-a*) due to nasalization of the former. (ii) The first NP types affected were proper names while personal pronouns generally remained unaffected to begin with, which is atypical of DOM systems that tend to expand along the referential scales.[8] The reason for this is that personal pronouns had not undergone the phonetic conflation of the Nominative (cf. *azъ* '1SG.NOM') and the Accusative (cf. *mę* '1SG.ACC') and

---

[7]Originally it had an emphatic function similarly to double negation in, for example, French, cf. Kuryłowicz (1971).

[8]There are no unambiguous Genitive forms of pronouns in the position of a direct object in Early Slavic (Meillet 1897: 84, 97; Vondrák 1898: 327; Krys'ko 1994: 128). Following Meillet, Kuryłowicz (1962: 251) concludes that chronologically, the Accusative-from-Genitive with personal pronouns must be later than with animate masculine nouns.

hence were not in need of disambiguation. (iii) The plural of the *o*-declension – in contrast to the singular – did retain the phonetic distinction between the old Accusative (*-y*) and the old Nominative (*-i*) and thus the old Accusative was not replaced by the new DOM marker here. Only later, between the 14th and 16th c., were both the old Accusative plural and the old Nominative plural conflated into *-y*. Precisely from this period onwards, the new DOM marker (Genitive plural) started to be used instead of the Accusative in the plural (Krys'ko 1994: 144). (iv) The third person pronoun *j-* did not have a Nominative form in Early Slavic (various demonstratives were used instead here). Hence, there was no need for disambiguation; Although the form *ji* itself would have been morphologically ambiguous between the Nominative and Accusative, it was reserved for the Accusative only. This pronoun acquired the new DOM marker much later than the relative pronoun *ji-že* (both are etymologically related). Since the relative pronoun *ji-že* did have both the Nominative and the homophonous Accusative forms, it acquired DOM very early. (v) Finally, as Krys'ko (1993) shows, the conflation of the old Nominative with the old Accusative took place much later in the Old Novgorodian dialect, because the latter retained the dedicated Nominative form *-e* in the *o*-declension, as opposed to the old Accusative (*-ъ* > ø). The erstwhile retention of the dedicated Nominative affix guaranteed the distinction between A and P and hence no DOM was needed until the Nominative affix disappeared in this dialect, too.

In all instances in which either the Accusative or the Nominative was not zero or the Nominative did not exist at all, the new DOM marker was introduced much later or not at all. It was precisely the Nominative-Accusative syncretism, i.e. the indistinguishability of A and P, that triggered the introduction of the new DOM marker. This relative chronology of the expansion of the Genitive to different NP types suggests that the discriminatory function was the crucial trigger conditioning it (first in Dobrovský 1834: 39; Krys'ko 1994: 156; Tomson 1908; 1909). Although there is no direct evidence for the global discriminatory function as in (3), the consistent application of local disambiguation in different nominal and pronominal classes might suggest that there was a development from global to local disambiguation by means of conventionalization.

The domain of the discriminatory function was determined by a language-specific phonological process, namely, the loss of word-final consonants: Only those declensions were affected which had undergone the phonetic conflation of the old Nominative and Accusative. I conclude that the following forces were crucial in the development of Russian DOM (alongside some others such as analogical levelling):

(29)   The relative weight of the main forces in the development of DOM in
       Russian
       complete loss of word-final consonants > discriminatory function >
       animacy scale

It is clear that the complete loss of word-final consonants was a stronger force in
Proto-Slavic than the discriminatory function because otherwise the latter would
have blocked the former. Crucially, the resulting synchronic picture – if looked
at superficially – clearly violates the animacy scale and the global discriminatory
function as in (3). While some declensions distinguish between animate and inanimate nouns by means of the new DOM marker, other declensions do not have
this distinction and mark animate and inanimate Ps indistinguishably.

4 Discussion and conclusions

In this paper, I have taken a dynamic perspective on the development of DOM
systems. I have provided qualitative evidence from a number of areally and genealogically unrelated languages for the claim that the discriminatory function
of case keeps appearing in the diachrony of DOM systems in various subdomains
and/or leaves behind traces in the form of local disambiguation. Importantly, the
discriminatory function is not dependent on the respective historical source of
the DOM marker and its particular developmental path. It is only the range of its
application in a particular DOM system that is indeed very much constrained by
the source meaning of the marker and/or by scale effects. Even scale effects themselves are sometimes just a strong residual of the source meaning of the DOM
marker. For example, DOM markers of many languages (Persian, Romance, Kanuri, etc.) stem from topic markers (cf. Iemmolo 2010; Dalrymple & Nikolaeva
2011; see also Cristofaro 2019 [this volume]). In other instances, the scales are
epiphenomenal, as they represent conventionalizations of the most frequent patterns originally conditioned by the discriminatory function (e.g. in Russian).

Thus, the discriminatory function is frequently subordinate to other, stronger
pressures, foremost the source meaning of the relevant marker. In addition, pressures like paradigmatic levelling (cf. Jäger 2007: 102) or analogical extension play
a role in individual systems. Even those DOM systems which are primarily conditioned by the discriminatory function synchronically (such as the one of Yongren
Lolo) never have the discriminatory function as the only constraint. I conclude
that – even though recurrent from language to language in the transition – the
discriminatory function is not strong enough to resist competition with other
forces.

But what conditions the power of the discriminatory function in a particular DOM system? The degree to which the discriminatory function is found to operate synchronically in a particular DOM system or subsystem sometimes correlates positively with how recent the DOM (sub)system is in the language. Thus, the evidence for the discriminatory function is most clearly found in those DOM (sub)systems that emerged relatively recently. For example, the use of the marker *laa* in Wan (South-eastern Mande) to discriminate between A and P is a very recent phenomenon, while its original function was one of marking the focus and the focused agent in a perfect-passive-like construction (Nikitina 2018). In Wan, it is the whole system of differential marking that is recent (Nikitina 2018). In Spanish, only the subsystem of definite inanimate NPs, as in (16), has recently been affected by DOM (inanimates are not affected by DOM in Old Spanish). It is this slot where the discriminatory function is found to operate occasionally. But differential object marking as such is quite an old phenomenon in this language.

By contrast, in older DOM systems, the effects of the discriminatory function tend to conventionalize to replace context-dependent rules that are much costlier in processing. The DOM marker is generalized in those contexts that were most frequently in need of global disambiguation. The generalization may proceed (i) along particular NP types or (ii) along particular constructions / word orders. For example, (i) Catalan generalized the DOM marker with personal pronouns regardless of whether there was a need for disambiguation or not in a particular utterance. By contrast, (ii) many Mande languages, Songhay and Tamasheq (Berber) generalized the marker in the APV (SOV) word order with no auxiliaries intervening between A and P in constructions requiring both overt A and P. These were precisely those contexts in which the distinction between A and P was particularly blurred. By contrast, the imperative does fulfil the discriminatory function, albeit in a different way: The sole NP that is expressed overtly is the P argument, while A is dropped. Hence, there was no need for a distinction between A and P by means of flagging here.

There are other types of bivalent constructions, such as equative constructions or comparative constructions, which are also sometimes constrained by the discriminatory function in order for the hearer to coherently process them. Unfortunately, they have never been considered in the general discussion on the discriminatory function of flagging, probably because the conventionalization processes involved here do not proceed along the same scales as the prototypical transitive constructions. However, this effect is certainly just due to different semantic expectations, e.g., as to the standard of comparison and the comparee in the comparative construction, than in a prototypical transitive construction. Furthermore, the discriminatory function of flagging is found to apply in ditransitive constructions of some languages in order to distinguish between A and R, which have similar semantic entailments and thus often do not provide for sufficient cues for the correct interpretation themselves.

In more general terms, I have argued for the existence of weak universals – a type of universal force that applies across different languages and language families but which is not strong enough to prevail into the synchronic STAGE 1. I claim that the (global) discriminatory function of flagging is a weak universal. This claim is supported by neurolinguistic and psycholinguistic evidence which suggests that both arguments are interpreted relatively to each other and cannot be reduced to the degree of semantic association of each argument with the role it bears (Bornkessel-Schlesewsky & Schlesewsky 2015: 336; Ahn & Cho 2007; Fedzechkina et al. 2012; Kurumada & Jaeger 2015).

Its weakness is possibly motivated by a higher processing load (cf. Hawkins 2014: 60, 69) as compared to local disambiguation: it requires pre-planning of the whole clause by the speaker and hinders incremental processing by the hearer. By contrast, local disambiguation is straightforward and may be processed incrementally without "having to wait" until sufficient context is provided (cf. Bornkessel-Schlesewsky & Schlesewsky 2014: 107). This is why patterns produced by the (global) discriminatory function often become conventionalized (cf. Aissen 2003; Zeevat & Jäger 2002; Jäger 2004; Malchukov 2008: 208, 213).

The concept of STRENGTH OF UNIVERSALS, in particular, of weak universals, is relatively new to linguistics (though see Bickel 2013 for some discussion). However, it ties in with the insight that human cognition in general and language acquisition in particular are better characterized by probabilistic biases or constraints ranging from weak to strong (cf. Thompson et al. 2016). Moreover, it seems that very strong (absolute) universals have a different motivation than weak universals. The former may indeed reflect some innate properties of human beings, as suggested by nativists (cf. Chomsky 1965), though not necessarily domain-specific properties. For example, the universal that all languages must have vowels (Comrie 1989: 19) is a very strong, probably, absolute universal. It seems likely that it is caused by innate properties of the human articulatory (and auditory?) apparatus. By contrast, weak universals are rather motivated by cultural evolution, for example, by the strive towards efficient communication between individuals (Haspelmath 2019 [this volume]).

Weak universals constitute a number of challenges for typological research. While strong universals override all potentially competing pressures and can thus be detected by relatively simple techniques, weak universals enter into competition with both other functional motivations as well as language-specific factors, not least the source meaning of the relevant marker (cf. Cristofaro 2012, Cristofaro 2017, Hammarström 2015). The only way of modelling this adequately is a fine-grained competing-motivations account (cf. Haiman 1983; Du Bois 1985; Croft 2003: 59; Bickel 2014: 115; Hawkins 2014: 60, 69; *pace* Cristofaro 2019 [this volume]).[9] For the same reason, weak universals also pose a methodological problem for typological testing for universality, even on the dynamic approach that relies on the transition from STAGE 0 into STAGE 1. Dynamic methods based on transitional probabilities do take into account one of the competing motivations, namely, the impact of inheritance (transitional probabilities are measured given the original state, i.e. STATE 0). However, many other factors that may influence the probability of change towards a particular pattern are glossed over on this approach as well. Finally, weak universals raise an important question about the nature of evidence in typology. Traditionally, typologists have been interested in defining what qualifies as positive evidence. Statistically significant signals that are due to the common genealogical or areal relationships of the languages of the sample have been ruled out as not offering positive evidence for universality. Other types of signals that may not count as positive evidence, such as same-source constructions, have also been identified (cf. Cristofaro 2017; Collins 2019 [this volume]). At the same time, a definition of what really counts as negative evidence, i.e. the proof of absence, is missing. As was argued in this paper, a random distribution in the sample given coarse data mining methods without taking the dynamic and historical evidence into account, might not be sufficient. This is problematic because, intuitively, it seems probable that strong universals are only the tip of the iceberg, not being numerous, while many more universals are rather weak universals of the type investigated here.

Acknowledgements

My first thanks goes to the first editor of the volume Karsten Schmidtke-Bode, who extensively commented on and discussed with me the earlier versions of the paper. I also thank Eitan Grossman, Martin Haspelmath and Natalia Levshina. The support of the European Research Council (ERC Advanced Grant 670985, Grammatical Universals) is gratefully acknowledged.

---

[9]In contrast to optimality-theoretic approaches that also primarily assume competition among universal constraints (cf. Aissen 2003), an adequate approach to weak universals has to take language-specific forces into account as well.

Abbreviations

All examples abide by the Leipzig Glossing Rules. Additional abbreviations are:

DOM	differential object marker	PS	person
DYN	dynamic	REC	recent past
FA	factive	RN	relational noun

References

Ahn, Hee Don & Sung Eun Cho. 2007. Subject-object asymmetries of morphological case realization. *Language and Information* 11. 53–76.

Aissen, Judith. 2003. Differential object marking: Iconicity vs. economy. *Natural Language and Linguistic Theory* 21(3). 435–483. DOI:10.1023/A:1024109008573

Arumaa, Peeter. 1985. *Urslavische Grammatik. Band III*. Heidelberg: Winter.

Asher, Ronald E. & T.C. Kumari. 1997. *Malayalam*. London, New York: Routledge.

Bickel, Balthasar. 2011. Statistical modeling of language universals. *Linguistic Typology* 15. 401–413. DOI:10.1515/lity.2011.027

Bickel, Balthasar. 2013. Distributional biases in language families. In Balthasar Bickel, Lenore A. Genoble, David A. Peterson & Alan Timberlake (eds.), *Language typology and historical contingency*, 415–444. Amsterdam, Philadelphia: John Benjamins. DOI:10.5167/uzh-86870

Bickel, Balthasar. 2014. Linguistic diversity and universals. In Nick J. Enfield, Paul Kockelman & Jack Sidnell (eds.), *The Cambridge handbook of linguistic anthropology*, 101–124. Cambridge: Cambridge University Press. DOI:10.5167/uzh-98910

Bickel, Balthasar, Alena Witzlack-Makarevich, Kamal K. Choudhary, Matthias Schlesewsky & Ina Bornkessel-Schlesewsky. 2015. The neurophysiology of language processing shapes the evolution of grammar: Evidence from case marking. *PLoS ONE* 10(8). e0132819. DOI:10.1371/journal.pone.0132819

Bisang, Walter. 1992. *Das Verb im Chinesischen, Hmong, Vietnamesischen, Thai und Khmer: Vergleichende Grammatik im Rahmen der Verbserialisierung, der Grammatikalisierung und der Attraktorpositionen*. Tübingen: Narr.

Bornkessel-Schlesewsky, Ina & Matthias Schlesewsky. 2014. Competition in argument interpretation: Evidence from the neurobiology of language. In Brian MacWhnney, Andrej L. Malchukov & Edith A. Moravcsik (eds.), *Competing motivations in grammar and usage*, 107–126. Oxford: Oxford University Press. DOI:10.1093/acprof:oso/9780198709848.001.0001

Bornkessel-Schlesewsky, Ina & Matthias Schlesewsky. 2015. Scales in real-time language comprehension: A review. In Ina Bornkessel-Schlesewsky, Andrej Malchukov & Marc D. Richards (eds.), *Scales and hierarchies: A cross-disciplinary perspective*, 321–352. Berlin, New York: De Gruyter Mouton. DOI:10.1515/9783110344134.321

Bossong, Georg. 1985. Markierung von Aktantenfunktionen im Guaraní. In Frans Plank (ed.), *Relational typology*, 1–29. Berlin, New York: Mouton de Gruyter. DOI:10.1515/9783110848731.1

Chomsky, Noam A. 1965. *Aspects of the theory of syntax*. Cambridge, MASS.: MIT Press.

Coghill, Eleanor. 2014. Differential object marking in Neo-Aramaic. *Linguistics* 52(2). 335–364. DOI:10.1515/ling-2013-0065

Collins, Jeremy. 2019. Some language universals are historical accidents. In Karsten Schmidtke-Bode, Natalia Levshina, Susanne Maria Michaelis & Ilja A. Seržant (eds.), *Explanation in typology: Diachronic sources, functional motivations and the nature of the evidence*, 47–61. Berlin: Language Science Press. DOI:10.5281/zenodo.2583808

Comrie, Bernard. 1978. Ergativity. In Winfred P. Lehmann (ed.), *Syntactic typology: Studies in the phenomenology of language*, 329–394. Austin: University of Texas Press.

Comrie, Bernard. 1989. *Language universals and linguistic typology: Syntax and morphology*. 2nd edn. Chicago: University of Chicago Press.

Creissels, Denis & Anna Marie Diagne. 2013. Transitivity in Bakel Soninke. *Mandenkan* 50. 5–38. DOI:10.4000/mandenkan.211

Cristofaro, Sonia. 2012. Cognitive explanations, distributional evidence, and diachrony. *Studies in Language* 36(3). 645–670. DOI:10.1075/sl.36.3.07cri

Cristofaro, Sonia. 2017. Implicational universals and dependencies. In Nick J. Enfield (ed.), *Dependencies in language: On the causal ontology of linguistic systems*, 9–22. Berlin: Language Science Press. DOI:10.5281/zenodo.573777

Cristofaro, Sonia. 2019. Taking diachronic evidence seriously: Result-oriented vs. source-oriented explanations of typological universals. In Karsten Schmidtke-Bode, Natalia Levshina, Susanne Maria Michaelis & Ilja A. Seržant (eds.), *Explanation in typology: Diachronic sources, functional motivations and the nature of the evidence*, 25–46. Berlin: Language Science Press. DOI:10.5281/zenodo.2583806

Croft, William. 2003. *Typology and universals*. 2nd edn. Cambridge: Cambridge University Press. DOI:10.1017/CBO9780511840579

Culy, Christopher. 1995. Ambiguity and case marking in Donno Sɔ (Dogon). In Akinbiyi Akinlabi (ed.), *Theoretical approaches to African languages*, 47–58. Trento: Africa World Press.

Dahl, Östen. 2000. Egophoricity in discourse and syntax. *Functions of Language* 7. 39–77. DOI:10.1075/fol.7.1.03dah

Dalrymple, Mary & Irina Nikolaeva. 2011. *Objects and information structure*. Cambridge: Cambridge University Press. DOI:10.1017/CBO9780511993473

de Hoop, Helen & Peter de Swart (eds.). 2009. *Differential subject marking*. Dordrecht: Springer. DOI:10.1007/978-1-4020-6497-5

Diagana, Ousmane Moussa. 1995. *La langue Soninkée: Morphosyntaxe et sens*. Paris: L'Harmattan.

Dixon, R. M. W. 1994. *Ergativity*. Cambridge: Cambridge University Press. DOI:10.1017/CBO9780511611896

Dobrovský, Josef. 1834. *Grammatika jazyka slavjanskogo po drevnemu narečiju*. St.-Peterburg: Tipografija departamenta narodnogo prosvešcenija.

Dryer, Matthew S. 2013. Order of subject, object and verb. In Matthew S. Dryer & Martin Haspelmath (eds.), *The world atlas of language structures online*. Leipzig: Max Planck Institute for Evolutionary Anthropology. http://wals.info/chapter/81A, accessed 2018-5-17.

Du Bois, John W. 1985. Competing motivations. In John Haiman (ed.), *Iconicity in syntax*, 343–365. Amsterdam, Philadelphia: John Benjamins. DOI:10.1075/tsl.6

England, Nora C. 1983. *A grammar of Mam, a Mayan language*. Austin: University of Texas Press.

Epps, Patience. 2008. *A grammar of Hup*. Berlin, New York: Mouton de Gruyter. DOI:10.18130/V3FP1M

Epps, Patience. 2009. Where differential object marking and split plurality intersect: Evidence from Hup. In Patience Epps & Alexandre Arkhipov (eds.), *New challenges in typology: Transcending the borders and refining the distinctions*, 85–104. Berlin, New York: Mouton de Gruyter. DOI:10.1515/9783110219067.2.85

Escandell-Vidal, Victoria. 2009. Differential object marking and topicality. The case of Balearic Catalan. *Studies in Language* 33(4). 832–885. DOI:10.1075/sl.33.4.02esc

Everett, Caleb. 2009. A reconsideration of the motivations for preferred argument structure. *Studies in Language* 33(1). 1–24. DOI:10.1075/sl.33.1.02eve

Fauconnier, Stefanie & Jean-Christophe Verstraete. 2014. A and O as each other's mirror image? Problems with markedness reversal. *Linguistic Typology* 18(1). 3–49. DOI:10.1515/lingty-2014-0002

Fedzechkina, Maryia, T. Florian Jaeger & Elissa L. Newport. 2012. Language learners restructure their input to facilitate efficient communication. *PNAS* 109(44). 17897–17902. DOI:10.1073/pnas.1215776109

Feldman, Harry. 1986. *A grammar of Awtuw*. Canberra: Australian National University.

Gell-Mann, Murray & Merritt Ruhlen. 2011. The origin and evolution of word order. *PNAS* 108(42). 17290–17295. DOI:10.1073/pnas.1113716108

Gerner, Matthias. 2008. Ambiguity-driven differential object marking in Yongren Lolo. *Lingua* 118. 296–331. DOI:10.1016/j.lingua.2007.06.002

Greenberg, Joseph H. 1963. Some universals of grammar with particular reference to the order of meaningful elements. In Joseph H. Greenberg (ed.), *Universals of language*, 58–90. Cambridge, MA: MIT Press.

Greenberg, Joseph H. 1969. Some methods of dynamic comparison in linguistics. In Jan Puhvel (ed.), *Substance and structure of language*, 147–203. Berkeley: University of California Press.

Greenberg, Joseph H. 1978. Diachrony, synchrony and language universals. In Joseph H. Greenberg, Charles A. Ferguson & Edith A. Moravcsik (eds.), *Universals of human language I: Method and theory*, 61–92. Stanford: Stanford University Press.

Haiman, John. 1983. Iconic and economic motivation. *Language* 59(4). 781–819. DOI:10.2307/413373

Hammarström, Harald. 2015. The basic word order typology: An exhaustive study. http : / / www . eva . mpg . de / fileadmin / content _ files / linguistics / conferences/2015-diversity-linguistics/Hammarstroem_slides.pdf, accessed 2017-11-24. Paper given at the closing conference of the Department of Linguistics at the Max Planck Institute for Evolutionary Anthropology Leipzig.

Handschuh, Corinna. 2014. *A typology of marked-S languages*. Berlin: Language Science Press. DOI:10.17169/langsci.b18.10

Haspelmath, Martin. 2019. Can cross-linguistic regularities be explained by constraints on change? In Karsten Schmidtke-Bode, Natalia Levshina, Susanne Maria Michaelis & Ilja A. Seržant (eds.), *Explanation in typology: Diachronic sources, functional motivations and the nature of the evidence*, 1–23. Berlin: Language Science Press. DOI:10.5281/zenodo.2583804

Hawkins, John A. 2014. Patterns in competing motivations and the interaction of principles. In Brian MacWhinney, Andrej L. Malchukov & Edith A. Moravcsik (eds.), *Competing motivations in grammar and usage*, 54–69. Oxford: Oxford University Press. DOI:10.1093/acprof:oso/9780198709848.003.0004

Heath, Jeffrey. 2007. Bidirectional case-marking and linear adjacency. *Natural Language & Linguistic Theory* 25. 83–101. DOI:10.1007/s11049-006-9000-y

Hofling, Charles. 2003. Tracking the deer: Nominal reference, parallelism and Preferred Argument Structure in Itzaj Maya narrative genres. In John Du Bois & Kumpf & Ashby (eds.), *Preferred argument structure: Grammar as architecture for function*, 353–384. Amsterdam, Philadelphia: John Benjamins. DOI:10.1075/sidag.14

Hopper, Paul J. 1991. On some principles of grammaticization. In Elizabeth C. Traugott & Bernd Heine (eds.), *Approaches to grammaticalization. Vol. I: Focus on theoretical and methodological issues*, 17–35. Amsterdam, Philadelphia: John Benjamins. DOI:10.1075/tsl.19.1.04hop

Iemmolo, Giorgio. 2010. Topicality and differential object marking: Evidence from Romance and beyond. *Studies in Language* 34(2). 239–272. DOI:10.1075/sl.34.2.01iem

Jäger, Gerhard. 2004. Learning constraint subhierarchies: The bidirectional gradual learning algorithm. In Reinhard Blutner & Henk Zeevat (eds.), *Optimality theory and pragmatics*, 251–287. Basingstoke; New York: Palgrave MacMillan. DOI:10.1057/9780230501409_11

Jäger, Gerhard. 2007. Evolutionary game theory and typology: A case study. *Language* 83(1). 74–109. DOI:10.1353/lan.2007.0020

Key, Gregory. 2008. Differential object marking in a medieval Persian text. In Simin Karimi, Vida Samiian & Don Stilo (eds.), *Aspects of Iranian linguistics*, 227–247. Newcastle-upon-Tyne: Cambridge Scholars Publishing. DOI:10.3765/bls.v38i0.3333

Kibrik, Aleksandr E. 1997. Beyond subject and object: Toward a comprehensive relational typology. *Linguistic Typology* 1(3). 279–346. DOI:10.1515/lity.1997.1.3.279

Kilian-Hatz, Christa. 2006. Topic and focus in Khwe. In Sonia Ermisch (ed.), *Focus and topic in African languages*, 69–90. Cologne: Rüdiger Köppe.

Kiparsky, Paul. 2008. Universals constrain change; change results in typological generalizations. In Jeff Good (ed.), *Linguistic universals and language change*, 23–53. Oxford: Oxford University Press. DOI:10.1093/acprof:oso/9780199298495.003.0002

Klenin, Emily. 1983. *Animacy in Russian: A new interpretation*. Columbus, OH: Slavica Publishers.

Krys'ko, Vadim B. 1993. Novye materialy k istorii drevnenovgorodskogo nomi-nativa na-*e*. *Voprosy jazykoznanija* 6. 78–88.

Krys'ko, Vadim B. 1994. *Razvitie kategorii oduševlennosti v istorii russkogo jazyka.* Moscow: Lyceum.

Krys'ko, Vadim B. 1997. *Istoričeskij sintaksis russkogo jazyka: Ob" ekt i perechod-nost'.* Moscow: Indrik.

Kurumada, Chigusa & T. Florian Jaeger. 2015. Communicative efficiency in lan-guage production: Optional case-marking in Japanese. *Journal of Memory and Language* 83. 152–178. DOI:10.1016/j.jml.2015.03.003

Kuryłowicz, Jerzy. 1962. Personal and animate genders in Slavic. *Lingua* 11. 249–255. DOI:10.1016/0024-3841(62)90032-3

Kuryłowicz, Jerzy. 1971. Słowiański genetivus po negacij. *Sesja naukowa między-narodowej komisji budowy gramatycznej języków słowiańskich.* 11–14.

Levshina, Natalia. 2018. *Towards a theory of communicative efficiency in human languages.* Leipzig: Leipzig University (Habilitation thesis). DOI:10.5281/zen-odo.1542857

Li, Charles N. & Sandra A. Thompson. 1981. *Mandarin Chinese: A functional ref-erence grammar.* Berkeley: University of California Press.

Malchukov, Andrej L. 2008. Animacy and asymmetries in differential case mark-ing. *Lingua* 118(2). 203–221. DOI:10.1016/j.lingua.2007.02.005

Martins, Silvana A. & Valteir Martins. 1999. Makú. In R. M. W. Dixon & A. Y. Aikhenvald (eds.), *The Amazonian languages*, 251–268. Cambridge: Cambridge University Press.

Matisoff, James. 1973. *The grammar of Lahu.* Berkeley: University of California Press.

Maurits, Luke & Thomas L. Griffiths. 2014. Tracing the roots of syntax with Bayesian phylogenetics. *PNAS* 111(37). 13576–13581. DOI:10.1073/pnas.1319042111

Meillet, Antoine. 1897. *Recherches sur l'emploi du génitif-accusatif en vieux-slave.* Paris: É. Bouillon.

Moravcsik, Edith A. 1993. Government. In Joachim Jacobs, Armin von Stechow, Wolfgang Sternefeld & Theo Vennemann (eds.), *Syntax: Ein internationales Handbuch zeitgenössischer Forschung. Vol. 1.* 707–721. Berlin: De Gruyter. DOI:10.1515/9783110095869.1.11.705

Nikitina, Tatiana. 2018. Focus marking and differential argument marking: The emergent bidirectional case marker in Wan. In Adamou Evangelia, Katharina Haude & Martine Vanhove (eds.), *Information structure in lesser-described lan-*

guages: Studies in prosody and syntax. Amsterdam, Philadelphia: John Benjamins. DOI:10.1075/slcs.199.07nik

Paul, Ludwig. 2008. Some remarks on the Persian suffix *-rā* as a general and historical linguistic issue. In Simin Karimi, Vida Samiian & Don Stilo (eds.), *Aspects of Iranian linguistics*, 329–337. Newcastle-upon-Tyne: Cambridge Scholars Publishing.

Plank, Frans, Thomas Meyer, Tatsiana Mayorava & Elena Filimonova. 2002ff. *The Universals Archive.* http://typo.uni-konstanz.de/archive/.

Seiler, Walter. 1985. *Imonda, a Papuan language.* Canberra: Australian National University. DOI:10.21256/zhaw-4756

Shain, Cory Adam. 2009. *The distribution of differential object marking in Paraguayan Guaraní.* Ms., Ohio State University. https://etd.ohiolink.edu/!etd.send_file?accession=osu1243450139, accessed 2017-8-15.

Silverstein, Michael. 1976. Hierarchy of features and ergativity. In R. M. W. Dixon (ed.), *Grammatical categories in Australian languages*, 112–171. Canberra: Australian Institute of Aboriginal Studies.

Sinnemäki, Kaius. 2014. A typological perspective on differential object marking. *Linguistics* 52(2). 281–313. DOI:10.1515/ling-2013-0063

Stiebels, Barbara. 2002. *Typologie des Argumentlinkings: Ökonomie und Expressivität.* Berlin: Akademie Verlag. DOI:10.1515/9783050080178

Subbārāo, Kārumūri V. 2012. *South Asian languages: A syntactic typology.* Cambridge: Cambridge University Press. DOI:10.1017/CBO9781139003575

Sun, Chaofen. 1996. *Word-order change and grammaticalization in the history of Chinese.* Stanford: Stanford University Press.

Thompson, Bill, Simon Kirby & Kenny Smith. 2016. Culture shapes the evolution of cognition. *PNAS* 113(16). 4530–4535. DOI:10.1073/pnas.1523631113

Tomson, A. I. 1908. Roditel'nyj-vinitel'nyj padez pri nazvanijax zivyx susc estv v slavjanskix jazykax. *Izvestija Otdelenija russkago jazyka i slovesnosti Imperatorskoj akademii nauk* 13(1–2). 232–264.

Tomson, A. I. 1909. K voprosu o vozniknovenii rod.-vin. p. v slavjanskix jazykax: priglagol'nyj rod. p. v praslav. jazyke. *Izvestija ORJaS* 13(3). 281–302.

von Heusinger, Klaus & Georg A. Kaiser. 2007. Differential object marking and the lexical semantics of verbs in Spanish. In Georg A. Kaiser & Manuel Leonetti (eds.), *Proceedings of the Workshop Definiteness, Specificity and Animacy in Ibero-Romance Languages*, 85–110. Konstanz: Fachbereich Sprachwissenschaft der Universität Konstanz.

Vondrák, Wenzel. 1898. Einige Bemerkungen anlässlich Meillet's 'Recherches sur l'emploi du génitif-accusatif en vieux-slave'. *Archiv für slavische Philologie* 20. 325–342.

Wheeler, Max W., Alan Yates & Nicolau Dols. 1999. *Catalan: A comprehensive grammar*. London: Routledge.

Yang, Ning & Geertje van Bergen. 2007. Scrambled objects and case marking in Mandarin Chinese. *Lingua* 117(9). 1617–1635. DOI:10.1016/j.lingua.2006.06.009

Zeevat, Henk & Gerhard Jäger. 2002. A reinterpretation of syntactic alignment. In Dick de Jongh, Marie Nilsenovai & Henk Zeevat (eds.), *Proceedings of the Fourth International Tbilisi Symposium on Language, Logic and Computation*. Amsterdam: University of Amsterdam. http://www.blutner.de/signalling/zeevat_jaeger.pdf, accessed 2016-12-15.

Chapter 8

Support from creole languages for functional adaptation in grammar: Dependent and independent possessive person-forms

Susanne Maria Michaelis

Leipzig University & Max Planck Institute for the Science of Human History (Jena)

It seems to be a robust empirical observation that independent possessive person-forms (such as English *mine, yours, hers*) are always longer than (or as long as) the corresponding adnominal possessive person-forms (such as English *my, your, her*). Since adnominal forms are also much more frequent in discourse than independent forms, this universal coding asymmetry can be subsumed under the grammatical form-frequency correspondence hypothesis (Haspelmath et al. 2014). In other words, the fact that independent possessive forms are longer can be seen as a functional response to the need to highlight rarer, less predicatable forms.

In this paper, I present evidence from creole languages and show that irrespectively of their young age and extremely accelerated grammaticalization processes, these high-contact languages confirm the coding asymmetry. Moreover, creole languages, just as non-creole languages, show a diverse array of diachronic pathways all leading eventually to longer independent possessive person-forms. Such a case of multi-convergence of structures through very different diachronic processes strongly suggests that the current patterns cannot be explained exclusively on the basis of the sources and the kinds of changes that commonly give rise to independent (and adnominal) possessive forms, but that there is an overarching functional efficiency principle underlying these coding asymmetries.

Susanne Maria Michaelis. 2019. Support from creole languages for functional adaptation in grammar: Dependent and independent possessive person-forms. In Karsten Schmidtke-Bode, Natalia Levshina, Susanne Maria Michaelis & Ilja A. Seržant (eds.), *Explanation in typology: Diachronic sources, functional motivations and the nature of the evidence*, 179–201. Berlin: Language Science Press. DOI:10.5281/zenodo.2583818

1 Introduction

Languages are functionally adapted to their users' needs in a variety of ways. This can be seen in a range of different domains, such as (i) text genres, (ii) social structure and (iii) the ecological environment. The genre of informal, spontaneous face-to-face communication is reflected in grammatical features of loosely connected discourse with mainly coordinated or juxtaposed sentences, many hesitation phenomena, overlapping utterances, and piecemeal structuring of information in accordance with online processing needs, whereas text genres intended for formal, planned, out-of-context, written communication show densely integrated information, multiple syntactic embedding strategies and therefore longer sentences, and greater syntagmatic variation (Koch & Oesterreicher 2012[1985] [1985]). Secondly, languages are adapted to the social structuring of their users, for instance to the percentage of second language speakers in a speech community: In a well-known study, Lupyan & Dale (2010) analyzed data from the *World atlas of language structures* (Haspelmath et al. 2005) and found that the greater the number of second language speakers in a speech community, the simpler are aspects of the morphology of the languages spoken by these communities. In a similar vein, Bentz & Winter (2013) found that languages with many second language speakers tend to have fewer morphological cases. And third, it has been shown that speakers adapt their languages to their ecological environments, for example by using whistled speech in distant communication to overcome the background noise of rural environments (Meyer 2005; 2008).

In the present chapter, I will look at yet another instance of functionally adapted linguistic structures: efficiency-based universal coding asymmetries in grammar, also called form-frequency correspondences (see Haspelmath 2019 [this volume]). More specifically, I will discuss one specific universal coding asymmetry resulting from asymmetric frequency of use patterns in discourse: the difference between dependent and independent possessive person-forms. Independent person-forms such as *mine, yours, hers*, and *ours* are coded with forms that are longer than or equally long as dependent possessive person-forms such as *my, your, her,* and *our*. I claim that the reason for this is a general efficiency principle: Less frequent and therefore more surprising meanings need more costly coding than more frequent and therefore more predicatable meanings.

Such functional-adaptive explanations have a diachronic component (Bybee 1988): Since the current system is often rigidly conventional, the adaptive forces must have been active in earlier diachronic change. But how can we understand such a development? Functionally adapted coding asymmetries, as seen in depen-

dent/independent possessive person-forms, are the outcome of hundreds, sometimes thousands of years of language change processes. These processes reflect
countless speech acts between interlocutors adding up incrementally and resulting in the crystallization of functionally adapted grammatical structures over
time. As grammatical change progresses at an extremely slow pace compared
to other cultural evolutionary processes, the step-by-step changes which bring
about functionally adapted grammatical structures are often opaque or difficult
to trace, even in languages with a well-documented written history (see Seržant
2019 [this volume]). To circumnavigate this difficulty, I will focus on creole languages, which are born out of extremely accelerated change processes in the
context of the European colonial expansion, roughly during the 16th to 20th cen-
turies. These high-contact languages have evolved their complex grammatical
structures within only a few hundred years. In this way they are a good test case
for functional-adaptive change processes because creoles demonstrate in a kind
of fast motion what happens to grammatical structures under functional pressures, which in less contact-influenced languages would have taken hundreds
(or thousands) of years to evolve. In this way, creoles open a unique window on
grammatical change processes which in these languages can be traced gradually
from their transparent source constructions to various further grammaticalized
stages, processes which are supposed to be operative in all languages at all times,
but which take much more time to proceed in languages less heavily influenced
by contact.

I make two main points in this paper:

(i) Evidence from creole languages indeed confirms the coding asymmetry:
Independent person-forms are coded with forms that are always longer than, or
as long as, the dependent person-forms, but never shorter.

(ii) Creole languages, just as non-creole languages, show a diverse array of
diachronic pathways all leading eventually to longer independent possessive
person-forms. Such a case of multi-convergence of structures through very different diachronic processes strongly suggests that there is an overarching functional efficiency principle underlying these coding asymmetries (see Haspelmath
2019 [this volume]).

After introducing the coding asymmetry in possessive person-forms in §2,
in §3 I discuss various types of source constructions and diachronic pathways
which lead to longer independent possessive person-forms. Then in §4, I present
a range of cases from creole languages and their various diachronic pathways.
In §5, I consider but ultimately reject some alternative explanations against the
background of the functional efficiency-based explanation adopted in this article.

2 Coding asymmetry: Dependent vs. independent possessive person-forms

Dependent possessive person-forms always occur together with an overt noun within a nominal phrase, as in *your house*, whereas independent possessive person-forms occur without an overt noun, as in *mine*. In the latter case, the referent of the noun is understood from the context because of an anaphoric relationship, as in (1a) and (1b), or because of a predicative use, as in (1c).

(1) English

    a. Your house is bigger than mine. (= 'than my house')

    b. Their dog is in a kennel, but ours sleeps under my bed. (= 'our dog')

    c. Is this bike yours? (= 'your bike')

In a recent study, Ye (2017)[1] has found that in the world's languages independent possessive person-forms like English *mine*, French *le mien* 'mine', and Mandarin Chinese *wo de* 'mine' are coded with forms that are longer than or equally long as the corresponding dependent possessive person-forms, such as English *my*, French *mon* 'my', or at least not shorter, as illustrated by Mandarin Chinese *wo de* 'my'. Coding length here refers to the number of segments in the signal, or possibly to the amount of biomechanical effort (see Napoli et al. 2014 with regard to sign languages). Most importantly, examples of counter-asymmetric coding are not attested, i.e. there are no languages where the dependent possessive person-forms are longer than independent possessive person-forms, e.g. *mine house vs. *my* 'mine'. Note that (in)dependent possessive person-form can be manifested through a range of language-specific structures, also embracing complex forms, such as combinations of articles or adpositions with pronouns, as in French *le mien* and Mandarin Chinese *wo de* [I GEN].

Table 1 shows a number of different types of correspondences between dependent and independent person-forms in the world's languages: Firstly, many languages code the two types of person-forms identically and thus with equally long forms, as for instance in Mandarin Chinese. In other languages, the independent person-form has an additional marker compared to the dependent form. This can be a substantivizer, as in Lezgian (*-di*), or an additional stem, as in Kanuri (*kaá-*). In some languages the definite article is used to form the independent person-form, such as in Italian *la mia* (with kinship terms like *sorella* 'sister').[2]

---

[1]Ye (2017) analyzes a sample of 69 genealogically and areally unrelated languages.

[2]If nouns like *casa* 'house' or *libro* 'book' were considered, Italian would be classified just like Chinese (identical pattern) because there would be no coding difference: *la mia casa* 'my house' vs. *la mia* 'mine', *il mio libro* 'my book' vs. *il mio* 'mine'.

Yet another synchronic pattern in independent person-forms consists in having extra material on the dependent form, as in Coptic *p-ô-k* [ART-INDEP-2SG] 'yours' (vs. *p-ek-ran* [ART-2SG-name] 'your name').

Table 1: Some types of correspondences of dependent and independent person-forms

Pattern type	Language	Dependent person-form	Independent person-form	Source
identical	Mandarin Chinese	*wo de shu* I GEN book 'my book'	*wo de* I GEN 'mine'	
additional marker	Lezgian	*zi ktab* I.GEN book 'my book'	*zi-di* I.GEN-SUBST 'mine'	Haspelmath (1993: 110)
additional stem	Kanuri	*fewá-ndé* COW-1PL.POSS 'our cows'	*kaá-nde* INDEP-1PL 'ours'	Cyffer (1998: 31f.)
additional article	Italian	*mia sorella* 'my sister'	*la mia* 'mine'	Schwarze (1988: 44,286f.)
longer form	Coptic	*p-ek-ran* ART-2SG-name 'your name'	*p-ô-k* ART-INDEP-2SG 'yours'	Haspelmath (2015: 277)

Apparently the only possible generalization which can be drawn from the typological variation is that the independent person-form is always longer than, or as long as, the dependent person-form, but never shorter[3].

Now the claim is that these coding asymmetries reflect asymmetries of frequency of use. More frequent meanings (here: dependent possessives) are more predicatable and therefore speakers or signers can reduce the amount of the linguistic signal in taking into account how much of the signal hearers and receivers (in sign languages) need in order to successfully reconstruct the intended meaning. By contrast, less frequent meanings (here: independent possessives) are in

---

[3]See also Croft (1991), who very similarly predicts "function-indicating morphosyntax" in all the atypical combinations of lexical semantic class and pragmatic functions, whereas typical combinations lack function-indicating markers (Croft 1991: 51)), e.g. marked predicative nominals vs. unmarked nouns, or marked predicative adjectives vs. unmarked attributive adjectives.

need of a greater amount of signal coding for the hearer to be able to infer the meaning.

Indeed, frequency counts of three large text corpora of three different languages (English, Korean, and Mandarin Chinese[4]) confirm the hypothesis that dependent and independent person-forms are unequally spread over discourse in such a way that dependent possessive person-forms are generally more frequent than their independent counterparts. Table 2 shows data from British English.

Table 2: (In)dependent possessive person-forms in the British National Corpus

Dependent	Token frequency	Independent	Token frequency
my	145,250	*mine*	6,067
your	132,598	*yours*	4,059
our	92,314	*ours*	1,658
their	251,410	*theirs*	976

Interestingly, frequency counts from Mandarin Chinese, a language without a coding asymmetry in possessive person-forms, give the same results as counts for English and Korean, which have the coding asymmetry in possessive person-forms (see Ye 2017). Therefore, the prediction is that we find similar frequency distributions of dependent and independent possessive person-forms in all languages, independently of whether the universal coding asymmetry is grammaticalized or not.

3 Types of source constructions and diachronic pathways

As noted earlier, synchronic universal coding asymmetries have a diachronic correlate because the adaptive forces must have been active in earlier stages of the language and have kept shaping grammatical structures according to the functionally motivated efficiency principle: less predicatable meanings need more coding and more predicatable meanings need less coding.

There is a wide variety of sources and diachronic pathways by which independent possessive person-forms come to be longer than the dependent forms. Generally, one can distinguish two scenarios: either the more frequent member of the grammatical opposition is shortened (Bybee 2007), or the rarer member of

---

[4]For frequency counts in Korean and Mandarin Chinese, see Ye 2017.

the grammatical opposition is lengthened[5] (Haspelmath 2008). In the shortening scenario, speakers assess what hearers can predict and adjust their articulations accordingly, resulting in shortening of the signal of the more frequent form of a grammatical opposition. In this way, Old English *min* 'my' was eventually short-enend to Modern English *my*, likewise Old Spanish *mío* was shortened to Modern Spanish *mi*. The Coptic contrast between *pôk* 'yours' and *pek* 'your' that we saw in Table 1 is likewise attributable to shortening of the earlier full person-form *pôk* to *pek-*. The shortened form became a dependent person-form whereas the old from *pôk* became restricted to the independent function (Eitan Grossman p.c.).

The lengthening scenario can be described as follows: When hearers are in danger of making wrong predictions, speakers tend to help them by using forms which – compared to the rarer member of the opposition – have been lengthened with some extra material. One example comes from German, where the independent form *der mein-ig-e* [DEF 1SG.POSS-INDEP-MASC.SG.NOM] 'mine' is based on the dependent form *mein* 'my' plus an additional suffx *-ig*, which occurs in other derived adjectives (like *selb-ig* 'same', *bärt-ig* 'bearded', *ehrgeiz-ig* 'ambitious'). As we see in Tables 3 and 4, the array of source constructions and diachronic pathways which give rise to longer independent possessive person-forms is very diverse.

Table 3: Shortened dependent form

Language	Strategy	Dependent form	Independent form
English	phonological reduction of dependent form	*my*	*mine*

The different strategies range from the use of a dummy noun ('my thing', 'my property'), intensified person forms ('my own'), the use of adpositions ('of my') and definite articles ('the my') to general nominalizer ('my one'). One special strategy to arrive at longer independent possessive person-forms consists in re-cruiting already existing pronominal (lengthened) forms which have been used for other grammatical functions. One example comes from Middle English va-rieties, where the independent possessive forms *her-n, our-n, their-n* (still sur-viving in English dialects today, see Kortmann & Lunkenheimer 2013) go back

---

[5]Here, the term 'lengthening' mainly refers to processes by which a given linguistic form is expanded or augmented by new lexical or morphosyntactic material. But – in principle – lengthening may also pertain to phonological/phonetic processes, such as vowel lengthening or gemination.

Susanne Maria Michaelis

Table 4: Lengthened independent form

Language	Strategy	Dependent form	Independent form
German	affixal lengthening	*mein* [1SG.POSS]	*der mein-ige* [DEF 1SG.POSS-INDEP]
Arabic	dummy noun: 'property'	*-ii* [1SG.POSS]	*milk-ii* [property-1SG.POSS]
Greek	intensified person form 'own'	*mu* [1SG.POSS]	*dhikó mu* [INTENS 1SG.POSS]
Diu Indo-Portuguese	use of adposition 'of, for'	*mi* [1SG.POSS]	*də mi* [of 1SG.POSS]
Albanian	use of definite article	*im* [1SG.POSS]	*im-i* [1SG.POSS-DEF]
Berbice Dutch	general nominalizer	*ɛkɛ* [1SG.POSS], [1SG]	*ɛkɛ-jɛ* [1SG.POSS-NMLZ]
English (dialectal)	exaptation	*her* [3SG.F.POSS]	*her-n* [3SG.POSS-INDEP]

to erstwhile feminine dative case-marked pronominal forms with the suffix *-n* (*hire-n* [3SG.FEM.DAT] 'to her'). In Middle English, such dative forms got re-used, or "exapted", to function as independent possessive forms, also under the additional analogical pressure from the *my/mine* and *thy/thine* oppositions (see Allen 2002, and for the notion of exaptation, see Lass 1990; 2017; Norde & Van de Velde 2016 and the discussion below).

Irrespectively of the shortening or the lengthening scenario, ALL these developments result in coding asymmetries which work in the SAME direction: The less frequent member (here the independent possessive person-form) is coded with a form that is always coded as least as long as the more frequent member of the pair, but never shorter.

186

Now how do creole languages fit into this picture? In the next section, I will consider possessive person-forms in various creole languages from around the world (based on the *Atlas of pidgin and creole language structures*, Michaelis et al. 2013, apics-online.info) to check whether the universal trend identified by typological work can be supported by these high-contact languages.

4 Diverse pathways in creoles

Before looking at possessive person-forms in creole languages, I would like to highlight one characteristic feature of these languages which is crucial for the argument put forward in this paper: Creole languages show an unusual amount of freshly grammaticalized material due to an accelerated pace of grammatical change processes (Haspelmath & Michaelis 2017; Michaelis & Haspelmath forthcoming). Examples come from tense-aspect-mood markers, such as the Negerhollands future tense marker *lo* < *loo* 'go' < Dutch *lopen* 'run', or the Jamaican anterior marker *wehn* < English *been*. Creoles also show newly grammaticalized case markers, such as the dative marker *pe* in Diu Indo-Portuguese (< Portuguese *para*), the accusative marker *ku* in Papiá Kristang (< Portuguese *com* 'with'), or voice markers, such as the reciprocal marker *kanmarad* in Seychelles Creole (< French *camarade*). The explanation for these widespread newly grammaticalized markers appears to be as follows: Speakers communicating in high-contact situations which involve many second language speakers tend to rely on extra transparency of their utterances in order to successfully get their messages across.[6] These instances of extra transparency give rise to newly grammaticalized structures by refunctionalizing erstwhile content words or otherwise less grammaticalized constructions, as seen in the examples cited above.

Turning to possessive forms, let us now consider the following three guiding questions:

- Do creoles confirm the universal coding asymmetry discussed in this paper?

- Does the need for extra transparency translate into freshly grammaticalized constructions also in the domain of possessive person-forms?

- Which kinds of source constructions give rise to the various possessive person-forms?

---

[6]See already Seuren & Wekker (1986) for the notion of transparency in the creolization process.

Susanne Maria Michaelis

The answer to the first question is a straightforward yes: The creole evidence, which comes from 59 creoles world-wide with different lexifier and substrate languages (see Haspelmath & APiCS Consortium 2013 and Figure 1 in the Appendix), confirm the universal coding asymmetry: Independent possessive person-forms are coded with forms that are longer than or equally long as dependent possessive person-forms. Some examples are given in Table 5.

Table 5: Dependent and independent possessive person-forms in some creole languages

Creole language	Dependent form	Independent form
Bislama (Meyerhoff 2013)	*blong yu* [POSS 2SG] 'your'	*blong yu* [POSS 2SG] 'yours'
Kinubi (Luffin 2013)	*tá-i* [POSS-1SG] 'my'	*tá-i* [POSS-1SG] 'mine'
Batavia Creole (Maurer 2013)	*minya* [1SG.POSS] 'my'	*minya sua* [1SG.POSS POSS] 'mine'
Martinican Creole (Colot & Ludwig 2013)	*-mwen* [1SG.POSS] 'my'	*ta mwen* [POSS 1SG.POSS] 'mine'
Pichi (Yakpo 2013)	*yù* [2SG.POSS], [2sg] 'you'	*yù yon* [2SG.POSS own] 'yours'
Palenquero (Schwegler 2013)	*mi* [1SG.POSS] 'my'	*ri mi* [of 1SG.POSS] 'mine'

The following Table 6 presents a quantitative overview of the different construction types found in creole languages of *APiCS*. Here, only languages with an exclusive value assignment are considered (48 out of 59 creole languages).

Likewise, the answer to the second question raised above is positive: The majority of the possessive person-forms are indeed freshly grammaticalized and therefore still transparent enough to be traced quite closely with respect to the different diachronic processes that have brought about their coding asymmetry.

188

Table 6: Distribution of different construction types over 48 creoles in independent possessive person-forms (*APiCS* Feature 39)

Coding pattern	Feature value	Number of creole languages in *APiCS*
Symmetry	Identical to dependent pronominal possessor	20
Asymmetry	Special adposition plus pronoun	9
	Other word plus dependent pronominal possessor	13
	Special form for independent pronominal possessor	6
	Total	48

Coding asymmetries explicitly allow for the two forms of an opposition to be equally long (either overtly or zero-coded)[7], as is the case in Mandarin Chinese *wo de* 'my', 'mine' cited above. As Table 6 shows, there are quite a number of creole languages which show this coding pattern, i.e. no length difference in the coding of both forms, as for instance in Tok Pisin *bilong mi* [POSS 1SG] 'my', 'mine' or the related language Bislama (see Table 5). These languages do not contradict the universal coding asymmetry, as they do not show the opposite coding pattern, i.e. longer dependent forms against shorter independent forms.

Let us now turn to creole languages for which we can attest a coding asymmetry in possessive forms. As for the source constructions, I will first look at cases of shortening that parallel the English development from *mine to my*. One example comes from Juba Arabic , where the original form *bita-i* [POSS-1SG] 'my/mine' gets shortened and at some point reanalyzed as the dependent possessive *tá-i* 'my', as in *ída tái* [hand 1SG.POSS] 'my hand' (Manfredi & Petrollino 2013), whereas the older non-shortened form *bita-i* continues to be used as the independent possessive form meaning 'mine'.

However, the vast majority of asymmetric correspondence types in creole languages – as in non-creole languages – follow the second scenario described in §3: the coding asymmetry comes about by some process of expanding the less

---

[7]See also Croft (1991: 58f.), who calls such cases NEUTRAL evidence.

frequent member of the grammatical opposition. One widespread source is the use of an adposition going back to 'of' or 'for' in one of the European lexifier languages French, Portuguese, English etc. An example comes from Portuguese-based Santome (Hagemeijer 2013), where the dependent possessive person-form *mu* 'my', which is expanded by the genitive preposition *ji* (< Portuguese *de* 'of'), gives rise to the independent possessive form *ji mu* 'mine'. Jamaican *fi-mi* 'mine' is another instance of the lengthening of the dependent form *mi* '1SG.POSS' (and also 1SG 'I') by the preposition *fi* 'for' (< English *for*).

A second source construction for independent possessive person-forms in creole languages involves the use of a dummy noun, such as 'part' or 'thing' (as mentioned above), as in Haitian Creole *pa m nan* [part 1SG.POSS DEF] 'mine' (lit. 'my part', *pa* < French *part* 'part') as opposed to dependent forms, such as -*m* (*nan*) [1SG.POSS (DEF)] 'my' in *se m* [sister POSS.1SG] 'my sister'. The polysemous morpheme *pa*, which in some contexts still has the original lexical meaning 'part', has grammaticalized into a possessive form which can also be used in contexts where the possessor is stressed, as in (2).

(2) Haitian Creole (Fattier 2013)
     Liv pa m   nan bèl.
     book POSS POSS.1SG DEF beautiful
     'MY book is beautiful.'

However, the non-stressed noun phrase would be *liv m* [book POSS.1SG] 'my book' (Fattier 2013). Here, we clearly see that the postposed morpheme *pa* in *pa m* does not denote a part of something, but has grammaticalized into a possessive marker, as the literal meaning 'book my part' is not available for this construction. The same holds for the independent possessive form *pa m nan* 'mine': the meaning is not 'my this part', but *pa* has become part of the newly grammaticalized independent possessive form 'mine'.

A third source construction for independent possessive forms features an intensifier which is added to the dependent possessive, as in Krio *mi yon* [1SG.POSS INTENS.OWN] 'mine' (the dependent possessive form being *mi* 'my') (Finney 2013).

There is a fourth source of independent forms involving a general (adjectival) nominalizer, such as 'one'. In Berbice Dutch, there is a general nominalizer -*jɛ* which is added to the personal pronoun *ɛkɛ* [1SG.POSS]/[1SG] 'my' ('I'), resulting in *ɛkɛ-jɛ* [1SG.POSS-NMLZ] 'mine' (see Table 4). This nominalizer goes back to Eastern Ijo, the substrate language of Berbice Dutch, where it has singular nonhuman reference, whereas in Berbice Dutch it has grammaticalized into a generic nominalizer (Kouwenberg 2013).

8 Support from creole languages for functional adaptation in grammar

A fifth source can be illustrated with an example from Reunion Creole, where the determiner/demonstrative *sa* is one of the lengthening elements (besides the genitive preposition *d*) in the independent possessive person-form *sa d mwen* [DEM of 1SG] 'mine', compared to the dependent form *mon* [1SG.POSS] 'my'.

In some creole languages the source construction is not known, as in Louisiana Creole. Here, the marker *kenn* is used as a morpheme to code the independent possessive person-forms, as in *mo-kenn* [1SG.POSS-POSS] 'mine'. This morpheme could perhaps be traced back to a 2SG.FEM independent person-form in French *tienne* 'yours', which has developed into /kien/, which would then have analogically spread to the whole paradigm, as in *mo-kenn* [1SG.POSS-POSS] 'mine', *to-kenn* [2SG.POSS-POSS] 'yours', *li-kenn* [1SG.POSS-POSS] 'his' (Neumann-Holzschuh & Klingler 2013, Neumann-Holzschuh p.c.). The unusual feature in this scenario is the idea that it is the second-person form which analogically spreads to all other persons, and not the more frequent 1SG or 3SG forms. Whether this is the right reconstruction of the origin of *kenn* is not clear.

Generalizing over all instances of newly grammaticalized independent possessive forms in creole languages, we can state that irrespectively of the diverse source constructions, it is the independent possessive person-form that, in ALL instances, is longer than, or as long as, the dependent person-form, but never shorter.

5 Possible alternative explanations

We have seen that the cross-creole data support the universal coding asymmetry in possessive person-forms, and that this synchronic asymmetry can be explained by a functional-adaptive constraint of coding efficiency: More frequently expressed meanings (dependent possessives) need less costly signal encoding because they are highly predicable, whereas less frequently expressed meanings need more robust signal encoding because they are less predicable (Haspelmath 2019 [this volume]; see Norcliffe & Jaeger 2016 and Jaeger & Buz 2018 for supporting psycholinguistic evidence in other domains of morphosyntax). Before concluding this paper, I will consider several alternative explanations, but reject them all as less convincing.

5.1 Semantics, iconicity, and syntax

Some functional linguists might argue for an alternative, semantically based or iconicity-based explanation here, namely that the independent possessive form is semantically more complex in that it combines possession and referentiality, and so additional material has to be adduced in order to express this more complex concept, or to compensate for the absence of an overt nominal.

But I would reject such a proposal because it is not obvious that independent possessors are semantically more complex. Rather, we can think of the situation as follows: Possessors refer to objects and persons, but at the same time, when used in possessive constructions, they also express properties, like adjectives. In the most frequent use, possessive forms (again like adjectives) have a modification function, as in *my house* (the "unmarked" use in terms of Croft 1991). But when possessive forms are used in the less frequent referential function, as in *mine*, specific marking is needed to highlight this unusual noun-like usage. Semantically, there is not really any difference in complexity of both kinds of person-forms: dependent possessive forms combine person and property with regard to possession in a MODIFICATION function, whereas independent person-forms combine person and property with regard to possession in a REFERENCE function. There is thus only a difference in the propositional function in which the semantic concepts are expressed (modification vs. reference), but there is no ADDITIONAL semantic complexity in independent possessive person-forms.

Likewise, some linguists might argue that the motivation for the coding asymmetry is purely syntactic, as the two possessive forms occupy different syntactic slots. As the modifier, such as French *mon*, cannot occur as the head of a NP, it has to be transformed into a noun by what Croft (1991: 58f.) calls "function-indicating markers", thus yielding *le mien* 'mine' in French. The use of the definite article represents one of the lengthening processes in independent possessive person-forms that I described above. But I would interpret the mere use of function-indicating markers as the frozen grammaticalized results of hundreds or thousands of years of speakers performing communicatively efficient speech acts by marking the less predicatable meanings with more elaborate linguistic matter. In this respect, there is no contradiction between today's syntax and yesterday's (and earlier) speakers' preferences to highlight less predicatable meanings by more morphosyntactic material, which accumulated over generations and eventually contributes to the shaping of syntactic categories (see Norcliffe & Jaeger 2016: 171[8]).

---

[8]"Communicative efficiency therefore holds explanatory potential not just for patterns of real-time language use, but also for the shape of grammars" (Norcliffe & Jaeger 2016: 171.

5.2 Diachronic change as a possible explanatory factor

Yet a different type of explanatory account might propose that the diachronic origins of the relevant patterns give rise to the observed cross-linguistic distributions (see Cristofaro 2017, and Cristofaro 2019 [this volume]). The claim would be that the kinds of sources and diachronic pathways that bring about the observed patterns are tightly constrained (mutational constraints, see Haspelmath 2019 [this volume]) and, crucially, that the coding asymmetry is a direct but incidental result of how independent possessive person-forms emerge from their respective sources.

The strongest argument against such a possible claim, and for an interpretation of the data in terms of a functional-adaptive, result-oriented approach, is the fact that we see convergence of multiple sources and pathways toward a UNIFORM outcome. In particular, the asymmetric coding can come about through shortening or through lengthening. If there were no overarching functional constraint, we would expect many more counter-examples in the data, i.e. cases where the dependent possessive person-forms are longer than the independent ones, such as dependent *mine book* vs. independent *my* 'mine', or German dependent *mein-iges Buch* 'my book' vs. independent *mein* 'mine', or Jamaican dependent *fi-mi buk* 'my book' vs. independent *mi* 'mine'. But this is not what we find.

The creole data make clear that there is a surprisingly large array of source constructions which enter the pool of possible dependent and independent possessives. Many of these source constructions had different communicative functions when they were first grammaticalized. The use of a dummy noun 'part', for instance, which is the source of current Haitian Creole independent possessive *pa m nan* 'mine', may have started out as a predicative focus construction, such as 'this is MY part'. This focussing function is still present in constructions like in example (2). But at some point, the morpheme *pa* got refunctionalized into the phrase *pa m nan*, which eventually got grammaticalized into the independent possessive person-form 'mine'. How did this happen? I assume that speakers must have somehow felt that they needed a more elaborate, more fully marked form to convey to hearers that a less predicatable meaning (independent possessive) was expressed. Therefore they chose (elements of) an already existing construction, here the focus construction, and through a kind of inflationary overuse grammaticalized it into the independent possessive form *pa m nan*, where the morpheme *pa* does not have the meaning 'part' anymore. It is only at this moment that speakers created a grammatical opposition between a dependent and an independent possessive form.

Another source of a longer independent possessive person-form is the use of a preposition 'of/for' together with a possessive person form 'my/I', yielding complex forms, such as 'of my' or 'for me', as seen in the Jamaican independent possessive form *fi-mi* 'mine' (vs. dependent possessive *mi* [1SG.POSS] 'my'/[1SG] 'I', already cited above). Forms like *fi-mi* may go back to a kind of predicative construction, such as 'this is for me/this is of my'. But here again, at some point in time, the creators of Jamaican refunctionalized the chunk *fi-mi* to fit the need to highlight the more unusual, less predicatable independent possessive meaning 'mine'.

In this context, another fact makes a source-oriented account less convincing. Quite a few creole languages show lengthened forms, such as *fi-mi*, not only in the independent, but also in the dependent possessive person-form, as for instance in Zamboanga Chabacano *dimíyo* ('of.1SG') 'my/mine' or in Tok Pisin *bilong mi* (of.1SG) 'my/mine'. This is the situation where there is no length difference in both forms, as illustrated for Mandarin Chinese in §2 (identical pattern in Table 1). If a hypothesized predicative construction were the source of the independent possessive person-forms, it certainly cannot be the source for the dependent form. Therefore, here we must allow for some kind of analogical extension to the dependent forms. Interestingly, it is only in the dependent possessive function that *dimíyo* can be shortened to *mí* (Steinkrüger 2013), thus again giving rise to a new coding asymmetry in the predicted direction: the independent possessive form *dimíyo* 'mine' is longer than the dependent possessive form *mí* (similar to English *mine/my* and Juba Arabic *bitai/tái*).

Coming back to both lengthening scenarios of independent possessive forms described above: The crucial point here is the fact that the change process from a focus or predicative construction to an independent possessive form should not be seen as a self-propelling grammaticalization process, but as a result of speakers' unconscious choices to communicate efficiently by highlighting the less predicatable meaning, thus ultimately bringing about functionally adapted linguistic structures. In other words: If speakers did not sense the communicative need to mark independent possessives with more linguistic material, they would not drag parts of a focus or predicative construction into an emergent independent possessive person-form in the first place.

Therefore, speaking of SYNCHRONIC "lengthening" strategies in independent possessive forms, as I have done in the previous sections, could be misinterpreted. What generations of speakers really do while communicating is recruiting ALREADY EXISTING structures (lexical or grammatical) to fit new grammatical functions (parts of old focus constructions and old predicative constructions are used to express new independent possessive forms). Linguists subscribing to the source-oriented approach would probably completely agree with this statement. But, as I laid out in the preceding paragraph, there is a second part to this story, where mere persistence accounts fail to explain the data: While recruiting existing structures for new grammatical functions, speakers unconsciously comply with the efficiency principle. As a result of the cumulative individual speech acts, we observe ever changing functionally adapted structures, which overwhelmingly point into the SAME direction: rarer, less predicatable meanings tend to be coded with longer forms than, or equally long forms as, the more predicatable meaning, but never with shorter forms.

Moreover, the examples of Haitian Creole *pa* and Jamaican *fi-mi* make clear that a functional-adaptive approach in terms of coding efficiency has no problem with the fact that the function or motivation of the source construction, here a focus or predicative construction, is different from the function at the synchronic level, here the independent possessive meaning. However, what is important is the fact that speakers always refunctionalize existing lexical or grammatical material in a predicatable way. In many cases, the newer grammatical functions that are expressed with already grammaticalized material follow quite narrow grammaticalization paths. In other more extreme cases, speakers exapt existing grammatical material to make it fit to their communicative needs, i.e. highlighting less predicatable meanings. This is the case with the erstwhile Middle English dative case form *hern* that was exapted into the independent possessive form (see §3). The mere existence of such exaptations in grammatical change supports the idea that the source constructions can be irrelevant for the synchronic grammatical patterns. But what is indeed effective in every utterance and gives rise to universal coding asymmetries is the overarching functional efficiency principle in signal coding: Spend as little energy as necessary to reach the intended goals, from which it follows that less frequent and therefore less predicatable meanings come to be coded with more material than more frequent and therefore more predicatable meanings.

Thus, creole languages help sharpen our understanding of functional-adaptive forces unfolding in situations of unusually accelerated language change.

Acknowledgments

I am grateful to Martin Haspelmath, to the co-editors of the present volume and to Eitan Grossman and Mark Dingemanse for their comments on an earlier draft of this paper. Furthermore, the support of the European Research Council (ERC

Advanced Grant 670985, Grammatical Universals) is gratefully acknowledged. This paper is closely related to a joint workshop talk with Martin Haspelmath at the SLE meeting in Naples, September 2016.

Appendix

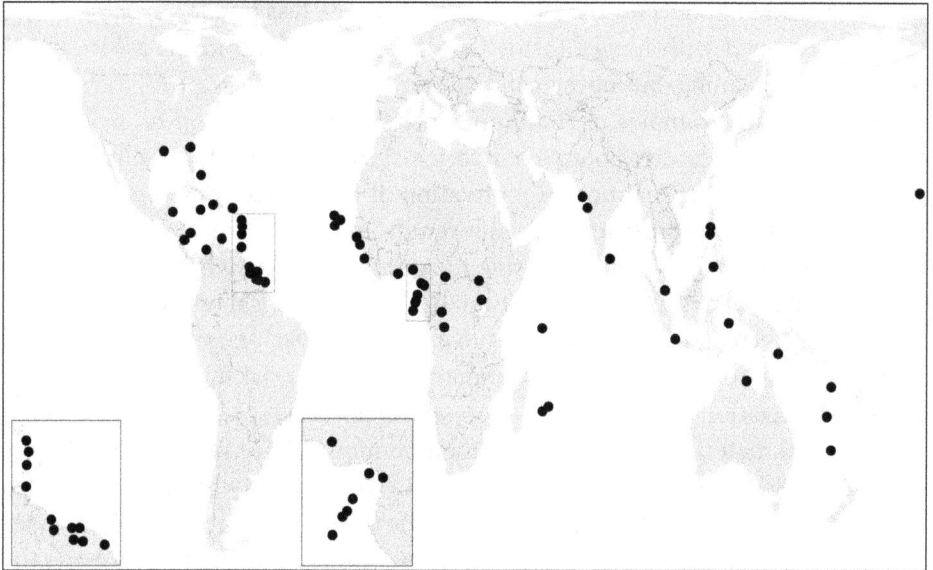

Figure 1: Distribution of the 59 creole languages in *APiCS* (for more information see apics-online.info) (CC BY-SA 4.0, Hans-Jörg Bibiko, MPI-SHH Jena)

References

Allen, Cynthia L. 2002. The development of 'strengthened' possessive pronouns in English. *Language Sciences* 24(3). 189–211. DOI:10.1016/S0388-0001(01)00028-6

Bentz, Christian & Bodo Winter. 2013. Languages with more second language learners tend to lose nominal case. *Language Dynamics and Change* 3(1). 1–27. DOI:10.1163/22105832-13030105

Bybee, Joan L. 1988. The diachronic dimension in explanation. In John A. Hawkins (ed.), *Explaining language universals*, 350–379. Oxford: Blackwell.

Bybee, Joan L. 2007. Introduction. In Joan L. Bybee (ed.), *Frequency of use and the organization of language*, 5–22. Oxford: Oxford University Press. DOI:10.1093/acprof:oso/9780195301571.001.0001

Colot, Serge & Ralph Ludwig. 2013. Martinican creole structure dataset. In Susanne Maria Michaelis, Philippe Maurer, Martin Haspelmath & Magnus Huber (eds.), *Atlas of pidgin and creole language structures online*. Leipzig: Max Planck Institute for Evolutionary Anthropology. http://apics-online.info/contributions/49, accessed 2017-7-2.

Cristofaro, Sonia. 2017. Implicational universals and dependencies. In Nick J. Enfield (ed.), *Dependencies in language: On the causal ontology of linguistic systems*, 9–22. Berlin: Language Science Press. DOI:10.5281/zenodo.573777

Cristofaro, Sonia. 2019. Taking diachronic evidence seriously: Result-oriented vs. source-oriented explanations of typological universals. In Karsten Schmidtke-Bode, Natalia Levshina, Susanne Maria Michaelis & Ilja A. Seržant (eds.), *Explanation in typology: Diachronic sources, functional motivations and the nature of the evidence*, 25–46. Berlin: Language Science Press. DOI:10.5281/zenodo.2583806

Croft, William. 1991. *Syntactic categories and grammatical relations: The cognitive organization of information*. Chicago: University of Chicago Press.

Cyffer, Norbert. 1998. *A sketch of Kanuri*. Cologne: Rüdiger Köppe.

Fattier, Dominique. 2013. Haitian structure data set. In Susanne Maria Michaelis, Philippe Maurer, Martin Haspelmath & Magnus Huber (eds.), *Atlas of pidgin and creole language structures online*. Leipzig: Max Planck Institute for Evolutionary Anthropology. http://apics-online.info/contributions/49, accessed 2017-7-2.

Finney, Malcolm Awadajin. 2013. Krio structure data set. In Susanne Maria Michaelis, Philippe Maurer, Martin Haspelmath & Magnus Huber (eds.), *Atlas of pidgin and creole language structures online*. Leipzig: Max Planck Institute for Evolutionary Anthropology. http://apics-online.info/contributions/15, accessed 2017-7-1.

Hagemeijer, Tjerk. 2013. Santome structure data set. In Susanne Maria Michaelis, Philippe Maurer, Martin Haspelmath & Magnus Huber (eds.), *Atlas of pidgin and creole language structures online*. Leipzig: Max Planck Institute for Evolutionary Anthropology. http://apics-online.info/contributions/35, accessed 2017-7-1.

Haspelmath, Martin. 1993. *A grammar of Lezgian*. Berlin, New York: Mouton de Gruyter. DOI:10.1515/9783110884210

Haspelmath, Martin. 2008. Creating economical morphosyntactic patterns in language change. In Jeff Good (ed.), *Language universals and language change*, 185–214. Oxford: Oxford University Press. DOI:10.1093/acprof:oso/9780199298495.003.0008

Haspelmath, Martin. 2015. A grammatical overview of Egyptian and Coptic. In Eitan Grossman, Martin Haspelmath & Tonio Sebastian Richter (eds.), *Egyptian-Coptic linguistics in typological perspective*, 103–143. Berlin, New York: De Gruyter Mouton. DOI:10.1515/9783110346510.103

Haspelmath, Martin. 2019. Can cross-linguistic regularities be explained by constraints on change? In Karsten Schmidtke-Bode, Natalia Levshina, Susanne Maria Michaelis & Ilja A. Seržant (eds.), *Explanation in typology: Diachronic sources, functional motivations and the nature of the evidence*, 1–23. Berlin: Language Science Press. DOI:10.5281/zenodo.2583804

Haspelmath, Martin & APiCS Consortium. 2013. Alignment of case marking of personal pronouns. In Susanne Maria Michaelis, Philippe Maurer, Martin Haspelmath & Magnus Huber (eds.), *The atlas of pidgin and creole language structures*, 232–235. Oxford: Oxford University Press.

Haspelmath, Martin, Andreea Calude, Michael Spagnol, Heiko Narrog & Elif Bamyacı. 2014. Coding causal–noncausal verb alternations: A form–frequency correspondence explanation. *Journal of Linguistics* 50(3). 587–625. DOI:10.1017/S0022226714000255

Haspelmath, Martin, Matthew S. Dryer, David Gil & Bernard Comrie (eds.). 2005. *The world atlas of language structures*. Oxford: Oxford University Press.

Haspelmath, Martin & Susanne Maria Michaelis. 2017. Analytic and synthetic: Typological change in varieties of European languages. In Isabelle Buchstaller & Beat Siebenhaar (eds.), *Language variation – European perspectives VI: Selected papers from the 8th International Conference on Language Variation in Europe (ICLaVE 8), Leipzig 2015*, 3–22. Amsterdam, Philadelphia: John Benjamins. DOI:10.1075/silv.19.01has

Jaeger, T. Florian & Esteban Buz. 2018. Signal reduction and linguistic encoding. In Eva M. Fernández & Helen Smith Cairns (eds.), *The handbook of psycholinguistics*, 38–81. Oxford: Wiley-Blackwell. DOI:10.1002/9781118829516.ch3

Koch, Peter & Wulf Oesterreicher. 2012[1985]. Language of immediacy – language of distance: Orality and literacy from the perspective of language theory and linguistic history. In Claudia Lange, Beatrix Weber Weber & Göran Wolf (eds.), *Communicative spaces: Variation, contact, and change. Papers in honour of Ursula Schaefer*, 441–473. Frankfurt/Main: Peter Lang. DOI:10.15496/publikation-20415

Kortmann, Bernd & Kerstin Lunkenheimer (eds.). 2013. *The electronic world atlas of varieties of English.* Leipzig: Max Planck Institute for Evolutionary Anthropology. https://ewave-atlas.org/.

Kouwenberg, Silvia. 2013. Berbice Dutch. In Susanne Maria Michaelis, Philippe Maurer, Martin Haspelmath & Magnus Huber (eds.), *The survey of pidgin and creole languages. Volume 1: English-based and Dutch-based languages,* 275–284. Oxford: Oxford University Press.

Lass, Roger. 1990. How to do things with junk: Exaptation in language evolution. *Journal of Linguistics* 26(1). 79–102. DOI:10.1017/S0022226700014432

Lass, Roger. 2017. Review of *Exaptation and language change,* eds. Muriel Norde & Freek Van de Velde, Amsterdam: John Benjamins, 2016. *Diachronica* 34(1). 117–126. DOI:10.1075/dia.34.1.06las

Luffin, Xavier. 2013. Kinubi structure dataset. In Susanne Maria Michaelis, Philippe Maurer, Martin Haspelmath & Magnus Huber (eds.), *Atlas of pidgin and creole language structures online.* Leipzig: Max Planck Institute for Evolutionary Anthropology. http://apics-online.info/contributions/63, accessed 2017-7-2.

Lupyan, Gary & Rick Dale. 2010. Language structure is partly determined by social structure. *PloS ONE* 5(1). e8559. DOI:10.1371/journal.pone.0008559

Manfredi, Stefano & Sara Petrollino. 2013. Juba Arabic structure data set. In Susanne Maria Michaelis, Philippe Maurer, Martin Haspelmath & Magnus Huber (eds.), *Atlas of pidgin and creole language structures online.* Leipzig: Max Planck Institute for Evolutionary Anthropology. http://apics-online.info/contributions/64, accessed 2017-7-2.

Maurer, Philippe. 2013. Angolar structure dataset. In Susanne Maria Michaelis, Philippe Maurer, Martin Haspelmath & Magnus Huber (eds.), *Atlas of pidgin and creole language structures online.* Leipzig: Max Planck Institute for Evolutionary Anthropology. http://apics-online.info/contributions/36, accessed 2017-7-2.

Meyer, Julien. 2005. *Description typologique et intelligibilité des langues sifflées, approche linguistique et bioacoustique.* Lyon: Université Lumière Lyon 2 (Doctoral dissertation).

Meyer, Julien. 2008. Typology and acoustic strategies of whistled languages: Phonetic comparison and perceptual cues of whistled vowels. *Journal of the International Phonetic Association* 38(1). 69–94. DOI:10.1017/S0025100308003277

Meyerhoff, Miriam. 2013. Bislama structure dataset. In Susanne Maria Michaelis, Philippe Maurer, Martin Haspelmath & Magnus Huber (eds.), *Atlas of pidgin and creole language structures online.* Leipzig: Max Planck Institute for Evolutionary Anthropology. http://apics-online.info/contributions/23, accessed 2017-7-2.

Michaelis, Susanne Maria & Martin Haspelmath. Forthcoming. Grammaticalization in creole languages: Accelerated functionalization and semantic imitation. In Andreij L. Malchukov & Walter Bisang (eds.), *Handbook of areal patterns of grammaticalization and cross-linguistic variation in grammaticalization scenarios*. Berlin: De Gruyter Mouton.

Michaelis, Susanne Maria, Philippe Maurer, Martin Haspelmath & Magnus Huber (eds.). 2013. *The atlas of pidgin and creole language structures*. Oxford: Oxford University Press.

Napoli, Donna Jo, Nathan Sanders & Rebecca Wright. 2014. On the linguistic effects of articulatory ease, with a focus on sign languages. *Language* 90(2). 424–456. DOI:10.1353/lan.2014.0043

Neumann-Holzschuh, Ingrid & Thomas A. Klingler. 2013. Louisiana Creole structure data set. In Susanne Maria Michaelis, Philippe Maurer, Martin Haspelmath & Magnus Huber (eds.), *Atlas of pidgin and creole language structures online*. Leipzig: Max Planck Institute for Evolutionary Anthropology. http://apics-online.info/contributions/53, accessed 2017-7-2.

Norcliffe, Elizabeth & T. Florian Jaeger. 2016. Predicting head-marking variability in Yucatec Maya relative clause production. *Language and Cognition* 8. 167–205. DOI:10.1017/langcog.2014.39

Norde, Muriel & Freek Van de Velde (eds.). 2016. *Exaptation and language change*. Amsterdam, Philadelphia: John Benjamins. DOI:10.1075/cilt.336

Schwarze, Christoph. 1988. *Grammatik der italienischen Sprache*. Tübingen: Niemeyer.

Schwegler, Armin. 2013. Palenquero structure dataset. In Susanne Maria Michaelis, Philippe Maurer, Martin Haspelmath & Magnus Huber (eds.), *Atlas of pidgin and creole language structures online*. Leipzig: Max Planck Institute for Evolutionary Anthropology. http://apics-online.info/contributions/48, accessed 2017-7-2.

Seržant, Ilja A. 2019. Weak universal forces: The discriminatory function of case in differential object marking systems. In Karsten Schmidtke-Bode, Natalia Levshina, Susanne Maria Michaelis & Ilja A. Seržant (eds.), *Explanation in typology: Diachronic sources, functional motivations and the nature of the evidence*, 149–178. Berlin: Language Science Press. DOI:10.5281/zenodo.2583816

Seuren, Pieter A. M. & Herman Wekker. 1986. Semantic transparency as a factor in creole genesis. In Pieter Muysken & Norval Smith (eds.), *Substrata versus universals in creole genesis*, 57–70. Amsterdam, Philadelphia: John Benjamins. DOI:10.1075/cll.1.05seu

Steinkrüger, Patrick O. 2013. Zamboanga Chabacano. In Susanne Maria Michaelis, Philippe Maurer, Martin Haspelmath & Magnus Huber (eds.), *The survey of pidgin and creole languages. Volume 2: Portuguese-based, Spanish-based and French-based languages*, 156–162. Oxford: Oxford University Press.

Yakpo, Kofi. 2013. Pichi structure dataset. In Susanne Maria Michaelis, Philippe Maurer, Martin Haspelmath & Magnus Huber (eds.), *Atlas of pidgin and creole language structures online*. Leipzig: Max Planck Institute for Evolutionary Anthropology. http://apics-online.info/contributions/19, accessed 2017-7-2.

Ye, Jingting. 2017. *Independent and dependent possessive person forms: A cross-linguistic study*. Paper presented at the Diversity linguistics seminar, Leipzig University.

Chapter 9

Linguistic Frankenstein, or How to test universal constraints without real languages

Natalia Levshina

Leipzig University

The scarcity of diachronic data represents a serious problem when linguists try to explain a typological universal. To overcome this empirical bottleneck, one can simulate the process of language evolution in artificial language learning experiments. After a brief discussion of the main principles and findings of such experiments, this paper presents a case study of causative constructions showing that language users have a bias towards the efficient organisation of communication. They regularise their linguistic input such that more frequent causative situations are expressed by shorter forms, and less frequent situations are expressed by longer forms. This supports the economy-based explanation of the universal form-meaning mapping found in causative constructions of different languages.

1 Problems with testing functional explanations

Functional linguists have formulated many universal principles that are meant to explain the structure and use of human languages, such as the principles of economy, iconicity, cognitive complexity, minimization of domains, avoidance of identity, and so on (e.g. Haiman 1983; Rohdenburg 1996; 2003; Hawkins 2004; Haspelmath 2008). How can one decide which explanation is relevant for a certain cross-linguistic pattern and how does one make sure that the latter is not a result of a historical coincidence in the sense of Collins (2019 [this volume])? Ideally, we would need data from genealogically and geographically diverse languages over a large time span. Needless to say, this is unrealistic: as a rule, such

Natalia Levshina. 2019. Linguistic Frankenstein, or How to test universal constraints without real languages. In Karsten Schmidtke-Bode, Natalia Levshina, Susanne Maria Michaelis & Ilja A. Seržant (eds.), *Explanation in typology: Diachronic sources, functional motivations and the nature of the evidence*, 203–221. Berlin: Language Science Press. DOI:10.5281/zenodo.2583820 data are not available. The time depth and typological breadth of available diachronic data are very limited. Moreover, even in an ideal world where any kind of linguistic data is obtainable at the click of a button, this might still be insufficient. First, real language data are observational, which makes a causal interpretation of the correlational results rather difficult (this does not mean there are no successful attempts, e.g. Moscoso del Prado 2014). Second, real language is a battleground of various forces, many of which can be mutually exclusive, e.g. over- and underspecification, iconicity and economy-driven arbitrariness, and so on. Disentangling these factors in real 'messy' language data is not a trivial task. Moreover, as pointed out by Smith et al. (2017) in their discussion of the universal bias against free variation, transmission of language in populations can mask the biases of learners: the language in a population might retain variability even though every learner is biased against acquiring such variation. Unless the data contain meta-information about the speakers, these effects may go undetected.

These problems can be solved with the help of the artificial language learning paradigm, which has gained popularity recently. One can observe in real time how linguistic systems undergo change, revealing the cognitive and communicative biases of language users. One can control for some factors while testing those of interest, and study the behaviour of each individual speaker within a population. Similar to the protagonist of Mary Shelley's gothic novel, Victor Frankenstein, who created a sentient living creature in his laboratory, a linguist can design a new language and watch it develop.

Moreover, there have been quite a few experiments that put to test typological universals, such as Greenberg's Universal 18 about harmonic word order within the NP (Culbertson et al. 2012), the suffixing preference (St. Clair et al. 2009), definiteness hierarchy (Culbertson & Legendre 2011) or the bias towards consistency in head-dependent order (Christiansen 2000). In the present paper, however, I will focus on the experiments that demonstrate more abstract functional and learning biases, which, in their turn, can be used to explain language universals and language-specific phenomena. An overview of the main principles and discoveries of artificial language learning with human subjects is provided in §2. To illustrate the approach, I will also present the results of a recent study, which tests the principle of economy on artificial causative constructions (see §3). A brief summary and outlook are provided in §4.

2 The artificial language learning paradigm

2.1 Main types of artificial language learning experiments

There are several popular types of artificial language learning experiments (see Figure 1). First of all, learning can be iterated and non-iterated. In non-iterated learning, one can only study the individual process of acquisition. There is no further language transmission. In iterated learning, a subject learns a certain linguistic behaviour by observing the behaviour of one or more subjects who learnt it the same way, i.e. in the process of implicit induction and production (Kirby et al. 2014). The output of one generation of speakers serves as the input for the next one, similar to the transmission of real language and culture in general.

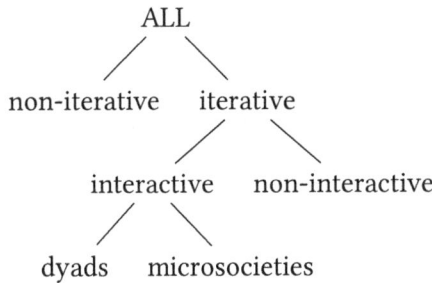

```
                    ALL
                   /   \
          non-iterative   iterative
                         /   \
                 interactive   non-interactive
                /   \
          dyads    microsocieties
```

Figure 1: Main types of artificial language learning experiments.

Some communicative and learning biases may be strong enough to be detected in non-iterated learning. Sometimes even one generation is enough to radically change the language (Hudson Kam & Newport 2009). Weaker biases may require several generations in order to manifest themselves (e.g. Reali & Griffiths 2009; Smith & Wonnacott 2010).

Iterated learning can be further subdivided into interactive and non-interactive (cf. Tamariz 2017). In non-interactive designs, one creates transmission chains where one subject's output is another subject's input. There is no actual interaction between the subjects. No common ground is created, and no feedback is given. Interactive experiments involve dyads of interacting users or even microsocieties, where everyone interacts with everyone else (Tamariz 2017). Language is transferred from one dyad to the following one, or from old members of a microsociety to the new ones. By using this approach, one can preserve common ground and feedback, which are crucial in everyday communication (Caldwell & Smith 2012).

The artificial language learning paradigm is very flexible, allowing for investigation of diverse forms: non-existent words, whistles, graphical scribbles. A language can also be fully artificial or semi-artificial. For instance, Smith & Wonnacott (2010) use some lexical items (nouns) from English, but novel verbs and plural noun markers. Usually, it is assumed that the results based on various media are comparable, although some recent studies suggest that the role of universal constraints (e.g. iconicity and compositionality) varies across different media (e.g. manual signs vs. sounds in Little et al. 2017).

Crucially, the studies based on artificial language learning share one fundamental assumption. Namely, those linguistic features that are easier to learn and use in communication will spread at the expense of less "fit" alternatives (Smith et al. 2017). By adjusting the linguistic input in a similar way, language users reveal their communicative and learning biases, which are so strikingly similar that one can speak about universal preferences.

2.2 Evidence of universal constraints from artificial language learning

The main results of recent studies can be concisely and non-exhaustively presented in a list of the following universal biases:

1. A bias towards **arbitrariness** (as opposed to iconicity), conventionalization and simplification of signs in interaction (e.g. Caldwell & Smith 2012). Simplified arbitrary signs are easier to select, produce and replicate than more complex iconic signs. At the same time, symbolic signs are more difficult to learn at first encounter, while iconicity seems to enhance the learnability of signs for new group members, as shown by Fay & Ellison (2013). They also found that the semiotic systems of larger populations reach a kind of a compromise: they favour simple iconic signs, i.e. those that are minimally complex and maximally informativeinformativity.

2. A bias towards **combinatorial structure**, when meaningless elements (which serve as basic building blocks) are combined in higher-order units. This is also known as duality of patterning (Verhoef 2012).

3. A bias towards **compositional structure** of syntax (Kirby et al. 2008). During the process of iterative learning, language becomes more structured.

4. A bias towards **discrete structure** as opposed to holistic signals. For example, in an iterated language learning experiment with a language based on whistles, participants come up with categorical distinctions, rather than

paying attention to the precise acoustic realizations, e.g. in terms of pitch (Verhoef 2012).

5. A bias towards **regularity**. Languages exhibiting free variation become increasingly regular, revealing a strong bias towards regularity in adult learners (Smith & Wonnacott 2010). This bias may be obscured by so-called probability matching: in a language in which two forms are in free variation, adult learners have also been found to produce each variant in accordance with its relative frequency in the input (Hudson Kam & Newport 2009; Wonnacott & Newport 2005). The interplay between regularization and probability matching depends on the frequency distribution. The more forms with lower frequencies are used as free variants of the main form, the more scattered the pattern and the stronger the bias towards production of the main form (Hudson Kam & Newport 2009);

6. A bias towards **economy and communicative efficiency**, when more predictable information gets less formal coding, and less predictable information gets more formal coding. This bias has been observed in a study of differential case marking (Fedzechkina et al. 2012). The hypothesis is that a referential expression should be more likely to receive overt case marking when its intended grammatical function is less expected. The experiment shows that learners deviate from the initial input to make the language more communicatively efficient;

7. A bias towards **underspecification** of irrelevant conceptual dimensions. Silvey et al. (2015) have found that their artificial language, which was originally fully specified in the sense that it had a unique label for each object, became underspecified by losing contrasts across irrelevant dimensions, i.e. those that are not important for discriminating between the stimuli. In contrast, Tinits et al. (2017) found a bias towards overspecification and redundancy in the contexts when the relevant dimensions were difficult to discern.

A key question is whether these biases are due to higher learnability or communicative advantages of the preferred features, or both. Using the terms from Haspelmath (2019 [this volume]), are we dealing with acquisitional or functional-adaptive constraints?

It is clear from the existing evidence that more learnable systems are not necessarily the ones that are also more usable, and the other way round. As was shown above, arbitrary signs, which are more usable in interaction, are less learnable than more iconic ones. One can find a similar clash between learnability and usability with regard to regularization and underspecification. As found by Kirby et al. (2008), Verhoef (2012) and others, languages that are more regular and compositional are easier to learn and are more successfully passed from one generation to another. Their studies demonstrate that the learning errors decrease with time (number of generations), as compositionality and regularity increase. At the same time, such emerging systems also exhibit greater ambiguity because the number of lexical items drops. As a result, the languages become increasingly underspecified, which would reduce their usability.

Interestingly, it has been claimed that children tend to regularize, or systematize more strongly than adults (Hudson Kam & Newport 2009). This finding has been attributed to children having less cognitive resources than adults – in particular, memory limitations. However, Smith et al. (2017) do not find this argument very convincing because, as they claim, memory limitations do not always lead to regularization. Alternatively, one may suppose that adult learners may be better at conforming to social expectations and norms. In general, there are important differences in the emergent languages depending on the social circumstances of communication. For instance, Perfors (2016) observes that adults regularize strongly when they believe that the variation is unpredictable (i.e. they are told that the previous person was under time pressure and might have made a few errors), than when they are asked to match an imaginary output of another person, who is believed to be performing the same naming task at the same time. When the participants believe that the variation is predictable (even if they do not know what it actually depends on), and their goal is to learn the language as closely as possible, they do probability matching more and regularize less. There is also evidence that speakers produce more regular language when they believe they are addressing a person, even though they are in fact communicating with a computer (Fehér et al. 2016). Apparently, speakers believe that producing a more regular language will facilitate communication with their human partner. Similarly, Little (2011) discovered that morphosyntactic complexity decreases when expert participants, who have been trained in an artificial language, interact with naïve ones who have little knowledge of the same language. This effect, however, was not observed when the experts interacted with other experts. Thus, the emergent language system depends on the social circumstances and pragmatic goals of the subjects. This relationship, which seems to be present already at the learning stage, makes a neat separation of acquisitional and functional-adaptive constraints a very challenging task.

In the remaining part of the paper, I will focus on the bias towards communicatively efficient, economical form-meaning mapping, using a non-iterative online experiment.

3 Case study: Frequency effects in causative constructions

3.1 Hypothesis: Economy and formal length

As was shown above, there is ample evidence that language learners are generally sensitive to frequency information. In this case study, I focus on the claim that more frequent situations are expressed by means of less coding material than less frequent ones. Such differences are predicted by the principle of economy and – broadly speaking – the principle of communicative efficiency. According to these principles, more predictable information needs less coding material than more predictable information. The experiment in Fedzechkina et al. (2012), which was mentioned above, demonstrated the effect of predictability based on semantic categories. In my own study, I want to focus on predictability based on frequency information. To the best of my knowledge, these effects have not been tested previously in artificial language learning experiments.

Causatives serve as convenient and well-studied material for testing the bias in question. There is a cross-linguistic correlation between form and meaning: more formally integrated causatives, such as lexical causatives *kill* or *break*$_{TR}$, tend to denote more integrated causing and caused events than less integrated forms, such as *cause to die* or *make break*$_{INTR}$. As Comrie (1981: 165) puts it, "the kind of formal distinction found across languages is identical: the continuum from analytic via morphological to lexical causative correlates with the continuum from less direct to more direct causation". Consider the example in (1):

(1)   English (personal knowledge)

    a.   John killed Bill in his mansion on Tuesday...

        i.   ...?? by shooting him in the forest on Monday.

        ii.   ... ?? by tampering with his gun.

    b.   John caused Bill to die in his mansion on Tuesday...

        i.   ... by shooting him in the forest on Monday.

        ii.   ... by tampering with his gun.

In this example, the lexical causative *kill* expresses direct causation with high spatiotemporal integration of the causing and caused events (John's killing and Bill's

dying, respectively) and with direct impact of the Causer (*John*) on the Causee
(*Bill*), whereas the analytic causative (*cause to die*) expresses indirect causation
without spatiotemporal integration of the events and without direct impact of the
Causer. This correlation between conceptual and formal integration of events has
also been found in a large typologically diverse sample of languages (Levshina
2018a).

Haspelmath (2008) suggests an alternative account of this correlation based on
the principle of economy: more frequent forms are usually shorter, whereas less
frequent ones tend to be longer. As my current corpus-based work shows (Levshina 2018b: Ch. 3), the frequencies of direct causation and related properties (e.g.
lack of autonomy on the part of the Causee, implicative causation, factitive causation, etc.) are substantially higher than those of indirect causation. Thus, these
parameters (conceptual integration, formal compactness and relative frequency)
are intercorrelated: more compact causatives represent both more frequent situations and more integrated events, whereas less compact causatives represent
less frequent situations and also less integrated events. This creates a situation
in which it is very difficult to decide based on observational data alone which
of the functional principles actually explains the cross-linguistic correlation between formal and conceptual integration, i.e. iconicity or economy. The purpose
of the present study is to test whether the economy effect is still observed when
the iconic correspondence is not present.

3.2 Design and procedure

The participants of the experiment were asked to learn an alien language. At the
beginning, they read an introduction:

> In this experiment you will learn the lingua franca of a highly developed
> civilization that exists on a planet in a galaxy far, far away... The planet is
> called Atruur. Its only vegetation form is called 'grok'. It is similar to a cactus
> and is used by the Atruurians for food, as fuel for their flying vehicles and
> for entertainment. Because the Atruurians traditionally detest any form of
> physical activity, they have developed a technology for teleportation and
> telekinesis.

The introduction also mentioned that the word order is SV (for intransitives) or
SOV (for transitives). To explain that to non-linguists, examples were provided,
which are shown below for illustration:

(2) Grok babum.
    cactus grow
    'A grok (cactus) grows.'

(3) Sia   grok   hum.
    Atruurian cactus see
    'An Atruurian sees a grok (cactus).'

The subjects were first asked to learn the language by copying the sentences in Atruurian that describe situations shown in video clips. At first, they saw four situations: a cactus-like plant appears, disappears, grows and shrinks in size. The goal of that task was to introduce the basic vocabulary.

Next, the participants saw 32 causal situations, which represented a causal version of the same situations. In each of these causal situations, there was a flying saucer (sometimes with an alien inside) which hovered above the plant and flashed a yellow or blue light three times in a row. As a result, the plant either appeared, disappeared, grew or shrunk. Varying types of saucers were shown.

Crucially, the subjects saw two types of causing events. The first of them involved the saucer flashing a yellow light above the plant. The other one was when the saucer flashed a blue light from the left of the plant. The yellow-light causing event was three times as frequent as the blue-light causing event (i.e. 75% vs. 25%). The distribution of the four caused events was the same for each of the causing events. There were no reasons to assume that one type of causation is more or less direct than the other. The colour and the position of the Causer with regard to the Causee are not mentioned in the semantic parameters that are distinctive of different causative constructions in the languages of the world (Levshina 2018b: Ch. 3).

As for the artificial language, the most important thing is that each causing event is represented by two allomorphs. One of the causing events was associated with the forms *tere-* or *te-*, as in (4), and the other one was described by using the forms *gara-/ga-*.

(4) a. Sia   grok te-babum.
       Atruurian plant CAUS-grow
       'The Atruurian caused the plant to grow (by flashing with yellow light from above).'

 b. Sia   grok tere-babum.
   Atruurian plant CAUS-grow

   'The Atruurian caused the plant to grow (by flashing with yellow light from above).'

Note that the form-meaning mapping varied across the subjects. That is, for some of them, *te-/tere-* denoted the causing event with yellow light flashed from above, whereas the *ga-/gara-* forms were used for the causing event with blue light flashed from the left of the plant. For the others, this was the other way round. The prefixes were evenly distributed among the stimuli, so that there was truly free variation. There was no condition in the experimental design that could explain the preference for the longer or the shorter form.

One should mention here that free variation is less exotic than it seems. It occurs in the language of late learners of a second language, e.g. hearing parents of a deaf child who learn to sign, or during the emergence of a new language, e.g. Tok Pisin and other pidgins and creoles (see an overview in Hudson Kam & Newport 2009). This is why the input language is not completely outlandish from a functional point of view. However, since language users have a bias towards regularization and against free variation, I expected that the subjects would regularize the free variation in the input, preferring the short allomorphs to convey the frequent causing events, and using the long allomorph to express the rare causing events.

After the training session, the subjects were asked to describe in Atruurian what is going on in video clips. The stimuli represented a selection from the previous stimuli: each of the caused events was presented with causing event A and causing event B. In total, there were eight test situations.

The experiment was performed online, using *Google Forms* with built-in *YouTube* videos. The latter were created with the help of *Adobe Animate CC* software by myself. Figure 2 demonstrates four fragments from one of the video clips, with the causing event A and the caused event of disappearance.

3.3 Participants

The participants were recruited via my personal network and LinguistList. Most of them had a background in linguistics or languages. After the experiment, they were asked about the aims of the experiment. None of them guessed the true purpose. Overall, I obtained responses from 84 participants. Some of the responses were removed. This was the case if the participants did not follow the training procedure instructions (e.g. a participant did not type in the training sentences),

1.   2.

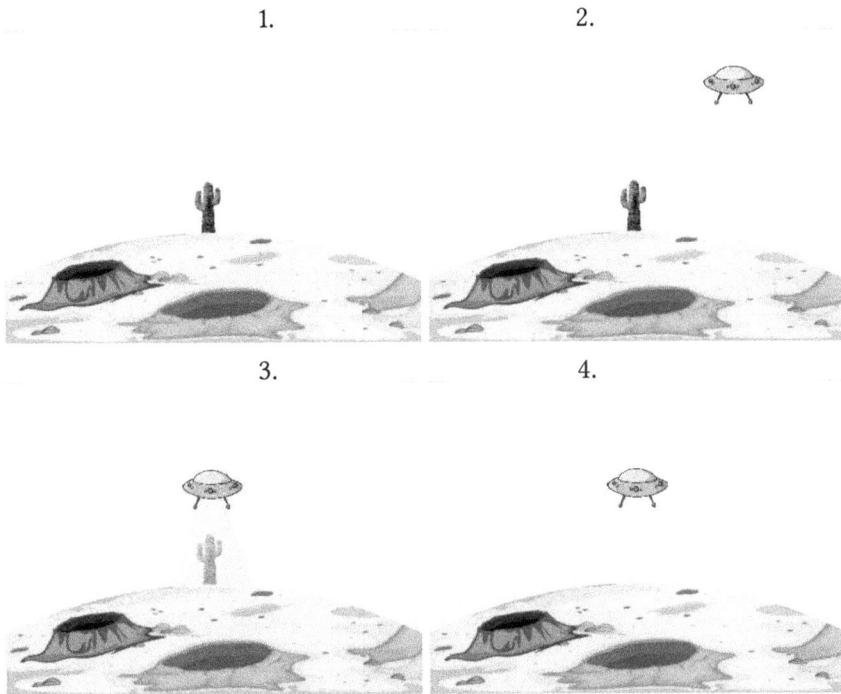

3.   4.

Figure 2: Fragments from one of the video clips.

or if the output was unanalysable. As a result, I had 554 valid data points from 70 participants.

The participants with valid responses had different L1s, but mostly had a Slavic and Germanic linguistic background. There were 40 native Czech speakers, 12 native German speakers, 7 native English speakers, 2 Dutch speakers, 2 Italian speakers, as well as native speakers of Brazilian Portuguese, Croatian, Danish, Polish, Russian, Slovak and Turkish. None of these languages has productive causative prefixes.

3.4 Results of the artificial language learning experiment

The counts aggregated across all participants are presented in Table 1. Lexical and spelling errors were ignored. Figure 3, which visualizes these counts, shows that there is a difference between the proportions of short and long forms expressing the frequent and rare causing events. The short forms are overall more preferred than the long ones, but the situations with the more frequent causing event are more frequently expressed by the short forms in comparison with the situations that involve the rare causing event, where the proportions of the short and long forms are almost equal.

Table 1: The number of forms selected and their marginal sums.

	Frequent	Rare	Total
Short	168	137	305
Long	109	140	249
Total	277	277	554

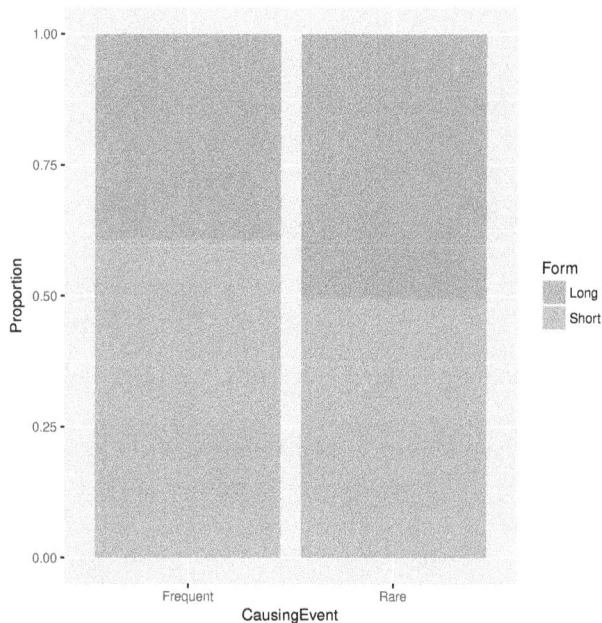

Figure 3: Proportions of short and long forms.

A closer look at the individual subjects' preferences reveals that most of them use both long and short forms. Seven subjects produced only the short forms. There were no subjects who always preferred the long forms. The distribution is shown in Figure 4.

The main question, however, is whether the choice of forms is influenced by the type of causing event. In order to test this, I fit a generalized linear mixed-effects model with logit as the link function (R package *lme4*, function *glmer*,

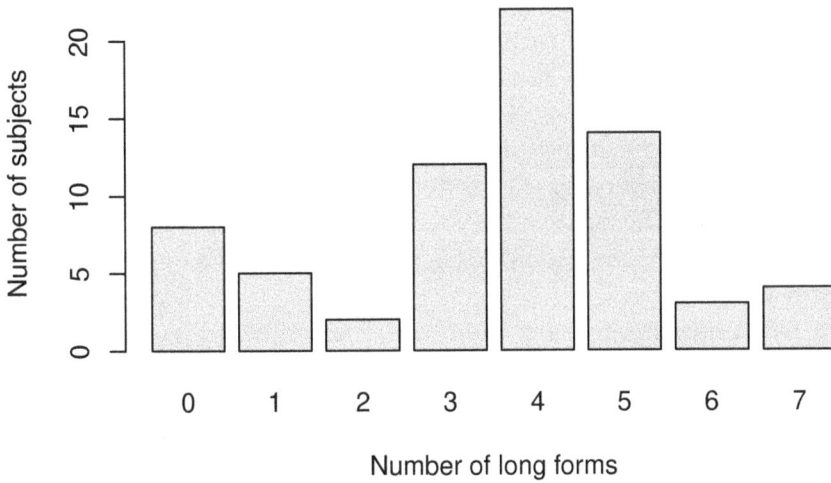

Figure 4: Individual preferences for the long and short forms

Bates et al. 2015). The type of prefix – long or short – was the response variable. The individual participants were treated as random effects (intercepts). There is a significant effect of the type of causing event: if the event is rare, the odds of the longer form to be chosen are 1.66 times greater than when the event is frequent (log-odds ratio $b = 0.501$, $p = 0.006$). This result supports the hypothesis that speakers have a bias towards the use of shorter forms to represent more frequent situations, and longer forms to represent less frequent situations. Random slopes, which represented individual differences in the effect of the predictor on the response, were tested as well, but they did not improve the explanatory power of the model.

The likelihood ratio test, a standard tool for variable selection and model comparison in regression analysis, demonstrates that the caused event does not have a significant effect on the choice of form ($p = 0.84$), and does not interact with the type of causing event ($p = 0.6$). This means that lexical conditioning can be excluded (cf. Smith & Wonnacott 2010).

4 Discussion

This paper has provided an overview of the applications of the artificial language learning paradigm in testing universal biases suggested by functional and cognitive linguists. One of them, known as the principle of economy, was tested in an online experiment. The results demonstrate that frequent causative situations are more commonly expressed by shorter forms, whereas the subjects are more tolerant of longer forms when expressing rarer causative situations. Therefore, the results of previous corpus-based studies, typological evidence and experimental approaches converge. The fact that the effect was detected in a non-iterative experiment with only one "generation" of language learners, suggests that the bias is very strong.

An important question remains about the nature of this bias and its place in Haspelmath's (2019 [this volume]) classification. Can it be characterized as a functional-adaptive, acquisitional, mutational or maybe even representational constraint? The mutational type can be discarded because we do not have any qualitative changes in the constructions (e.g. possessed nouns becoming adpositions). As for representational constraints, they reflect the properties of the innate language faculty. Even if we accept that economy is an innate principle, since humans and other species are genetically programmed to gain maximal benefits from their behaviour at minimum costs (cf. Parker & Smith 1990), it represents a domain-general bias that is not restricted to human language only. There is evidence that the evolution of sense organs and brains is driven by the need to minimize the energy spent for each bit of information received from the environment (Stone 2015: 3). This is why linguistic economy is not a part of Universal Grammar in the generativist sense.

Thus, we are left with the functional-adaptive and acquisitional types. It is true that Haspelmath (2019 [this volume]) defines the latter as related to L1 by children only, but the overview presented in §2 demonstrates that learnability constraints can also be detected in artificial language learning by children and adults. §2 also showed that a clear distinction between communicative efficiency and learnability is often problematic within the artificial language learning paradigm. Similar to Slobin's (1996) famous "thinking for speaking", we can also speak about "learning for using". This makes the task of distinguishing between these types very difficult. My preliminary answer is that we are dealing with a functional-adaptive constraint because it helps to optimize communication, even though there is no immediate interaction in the experiment. Obviously, more research with a clearer separation between the learning and communication stages is needed. The most pertinent question at this stage is the following: Is it easier to learn a more communicatively efficient language, in which frequent meanings are expressed by shorter forms, and rare functions are expressed by longer forms, than a less efficient one, in which frequent meanings are expressed by longer forms and rare ones by shorter forms?

The artificial language learning paradigm, as I tried to demonstrate in this paper, represents a valuable addition to the toolkit of typologists and functional linguists. However, there are a few caveats that need to be mentioned. First, the experiments involve very limited interaction, if any, in an artificial context. Second, the populations are extremely small. Third, even when a fully artificial language is used, one cannot exclude transfer effects from real language. For example, Goldberg (2013), in her critical evaluation of Culbertson et al.'s (2012) study of Greenberg's Universal 18, argues that the word orders Adj + N and N + Adj can be transferred either from English (e.g. *a blue bird* vs. *something red, all things nice*) or from the Spanish-type languages. Note, however, that Culbertson et al. studied a specific formal pattern. As we move to more abstract properties of language or communicative behaviour, such as compositionality or economy, it becomes more difficult to explain these properties by transfer from real languages, although one cannot exclude a possibility that these biases represent very abstract generalizations from the users' experience with language, and their intuitive expectations about what a "normal" human language should be like. This uncertainty will probably always loom until we find a real alien and have it learn an artificial language.

Acknowledgements

This project has received funding from the European Research Council (ERC) under the European Union's Horizon 2020 research and innovation programme (grant agreement n° 670985). I'm extremely grateful to all colleagues who patiently participated in the experiment, helped to improve the design and to recruit the participants, especially to my good friends from Olomouc university, Michaela Martinkova and Marketa Janebova. All usual disclaimers apply.

References

Bates, Douglas, Martin Maechler, Ben Bolker & Steven Walker. 2015. Fitting linear mixed-effects models using lme4. *Journal of Statistical Software* 67(1). 1–48. DOI:10.18637/jss.v067.i01

Caldwell, Christine A. & Kenny Smith. 2012. Cultural evolution and perpetuation of arbitrary communicative conventions in experimental microsocieties. *PLoS ONE* 7(8). e43807. DOI:10.1371/journal.pone.0043807

Christiansen, Morten H. 2000. Using artificial language learning to study language evolution: Exploring the emergence of word order universals. In Jean-Louis Dessalles & Laleh Ghadakpour (eds.), *The evolution of language: 3rd international conference*, 45–48. Paris: École Nationale Supérieure des Télécommunications.

Collins, Jeremy. 2019. Some language universals are historical accidents. In Karsten Schmidtke-Bode, Natalia Levshina, Susanne Maria Michaelis & Ilja A. Seržant (eds.), *Explanation in typology: Diachronic sources, functional motivations and the nature of the evidence*, 47–61. Berlin: Language Science Press. DOI:10.5281/zenodo.2583808

Comrie, Bernard. 1981. *Language universals and linguistic typology: Syntax and morphology*. Chicago: University of Chicago Press.

Culbertson, Jennifer & Géraldine Legendre. 2011. Investigating the evolution of agreement systems using an artificial language learning paradigm. In Dina Bailey & Victoria Teliga (eds.), *Proceedings of the 2010 Western Conference on Linguistics. Vol. 1*, 46–58. Fresno: Department of Linguistics, California State University.

Culbertson, Jennifer, Paul Smolensky & Géraldine Legendre. 2012. Learning biases predict a word order universal. *Cognition* 122(3). 306–329. DOI:10.1016/j.cognition.2011.10.017

Fay, Nicolas & T. Mark Ellison. 2013. The cultural evolution of human communication systems in different sized populations: Usability trumps learnability. *PloS ONE* 8(8). e71781. DOI:10.1371/journal.pone.0071781

Fedzechkina, Maryia, T. Florian Jaeger & Elissa L. Newport. 2012. Language learners restructure their input to facilitate efficient communication. *PNAS* 109(44). 17897–17902. DOI:10.1073/pnas.1215776109

Fehér, Olga, Elizabeth Wonnacott & Kenny Smith. 2016. Structural priming in artificial languages and the regularisation of unpredictable variation. *Journal of Memory and Language* 91. 158–180. DOI:10.1016/j.jml.2016.06.002

Goldberg, Adele E. 2013. Substantive learning bias or an effect of familiarity? Comment on Culbertson, Smolensky, and Legendre (2012). *Cognition* 127(3). 420–426. DOI:10.1016/j.cognition.2013.02.017

Haiman, John. 1983. Iconic and economic motivation. *Language* 59(4). 781–819. DOI:10.2307/413373

Haspelmath, Martin. 2008. Frequency vs. iconicity in explaining grammatical asymmetries. *Cognitive Linguistics* 19(1). 1–33. DOI:10.1515/COG.2008.001

Haspelmath, Martin. 2019. Can cross-linguistic regularities be explained by constraints on change? In Karsten Schmidtke-Bode, Natalia Levshina, Susanne Maria Michaelis & Ilja A. Seržant (eds.), *Explanation in typology: Diachronic sources, functional motivations and the nature of the evidence*, 1–23. Berlin: Language Science Press. DOI:10.5281/zenodo.2583804

Hawkins, John A. 2004. *Efficiency and complexity in grammars*. Oxford: Oxford University Press. DOI:10.1093/acprof:oso/9780199252695.001.0001

Hudson Kam, Carla L. & Elissa L. Newport. 2009. Getting it right by getting it wrong: When learners change languages. *Cognitive Psychology* 59(1). 30–66. DOI:10.1016/j.cogpsych.2009.01.001

Kirby, Simon, Hannah Cornish & Kenny Smith. 2008. Cumulative cultural evolution in the laboratory: An experimental approach to the origins of structure in human language. *PNAS* 105(31). 10681–10686. DOI:10.1073/pnas.0707835105

Kirby, Simon, Tom Griffiths & Kenny Smith. 2014. Iterated learning and the evolution of language. *Current Opinion in Neurobiology* 28. 108–114. DOI:10.1016/j.conb.2014.07.014

Levshina, Natalia. 2018a. Finding the best fit for direct and indirect causation: A typological study. *Lingua Posnaniensis* 58(2). 65–83. DOI:10.1515/linpo-2016-0010

Levshina, Natalia. 2018b. *Towards a theory of communicative efficiency in human languages*. Leipzig: Leipzig University (Habilitation thesis). DOI:10.5281/zenodo.1542857

Little, Hannah. 2011. *Foreigner directed speech: Its role in the cultural transmission of language and the resulting effects on language typology*. Edinburgh: University of Edinburgh (MSc thesis).

Little, Hannah, Kerem Eryılmaz & Bart De Boer. 2017. Signal dimensionality and the emergence of combinatorial structure. *Cognition* 168. 1–15. DOI:10.1016/j.cognition.2017.06.011

Moscoso del Prado, Fermin. 2014. Grammatical change begins within the word: Causal modeling of the co-evolution of Icelandic morphology and syntax. In *Proceedings of the Cognitive Science Society*, vol. 36, 2657–2662.

Parker, Geoffrey A. & J. Maynard Smith. 1990. Optimality theory in evolutionary biology. *Nature* 348(6296). 27–33. DOI:10.1038/348027a0

Perfors, Amy. 2016. Adult regularization of inconsistent input depends on pragmatic factors. *Language Learning and Development* 12(2). 138–155. DOI:10.1080/15475441.2015.1052449

Reali, Florencia & Thomas L. Griffiths. 2009. The evolution of frequency distributions: Relating regularization to inductive biases through iterated learning. *Cognition* 111(3). 317–328. DOI:10.1016/j.cognition.2009.02.012

Rohdenburg, Günter. 1996. Cognitive complexity and increased grammatical explicitness in English. *Cognitive Linguistics* 7(2). 149–182. DOI:10.1515/cogl.1996.7.2.149

Rohdenburg, Günter. 2003. Cognitive complexity and horror aequi as factors determining the use of interrogative clause linkers in english. In Günter Rohdenburg & Britta Mondorf (eds.), *Determinants of grammatical variation in English*, 205–250. Berlin, New York: Mouton de Gruyter. DOI:10.1515/9783110900019.205

Silvey, Catriona, Simon Kirby & Kenny Smith. 2015. Word meanings evolve to selectively preserve distinctions on salient dimensions. *Cognitive Science* 39(1). 212–226. DOI:10.1111/cogs.12150

Slobin, Dan I. 1996. From "thought and language" to "thinking for speaking". In John J. Gumperz & Stephen C. Levinson (eds.), *Rethinking linguistic relativity*, 70–96. Cambridge: Cambridge University Press.

Smith, Kenny, Amy Perfors, Olga Fehér, Anna Samara, Kate Swoboda & Elizabeth Wonnacott. 2017. Language learning, language use and the evolution of linguistic variation. *Philosophical Transactions of the Royal Society* B 372(1711). 20160051. DOI:10.1098/rstb.2016.0051

Smith, Kenny & Elizabeth Wonnacott. 2010. Eliminating unpredictable variation through iterated learning. *Cognition* 116(3). 444–449. DOI:10.1016/j.cognition.2010.06.004

St. Clair, Michelle C., Padraic Monaghan & Michael Ramscar. 2009. Relationships between language structure and language learning: The suffixing preference and grammatical categorization. *Cognitive Science* 33(7). 1317–1329. DOI:10.1111/j.1551-6709.2009.01065.x

Stone, James V. 2015. *Information theory. A tutorial introduction.* Wrocław: Septel Press. DOI:10.13140/2.1.1633.8240

Tamariz, Monica. 2017. Experimental studies on the cultural evolution of language. *Annual Review of Linguistics* 3. 389–407. DOI:10.1146/annurev-linguistics-011516-033807

Tinits, Peeter, Jonas Nölle & Stefan Hartmann. 2017. Usage context influences the evolution of overspecification in iterated learning. *Journal of Language Evolution* 2(2). 147–159. DOI:10.1093/jole/lzx011

Verhoef, Tessa. 2012. The origins of duality of patterning in artificial whistled languages. *Language and Cognition* 4(4). 357–380. DOI:10.1515/langcog-2012-0019

Wonnacott, Elizabeth & Elissa L. Newport. 2005. Novelty and regularization: The effect of novel instances on rule formation. In *BUCLD 29*, 663–673.

Chapter 10

Diachronic sources, functional motivations and the nature of the evidence: A synthesis

Karsten Schmidtke-Bode

Leipzig University and Friedrich Schiller University Jena

Eitan Grossman

Hebrew University of Jerusalem

In this epilogue, we summarize and reflect on the major threads and arguments from the individual contributions to this volume (§1), and we also briefly outline some challenges and directions for future work on the topic (§2).

1 The voices of the present volume

Above all, this volume has been concerned with the theoretical status of the historical processes that lead to statistical universals of grammatical structure. In the typological research programme initiated by Greenberg, it was recognized from early on that a "dynamic" perspective on universals is vital (e.g. Greenberg 1969), and it was also occasionally suggested that the diachronic origins of the structures in question may themselves be able to *explain* current universal patterns (e.g. Givón 1975; Greenberg 1978).

In the last decade or so, this position appears to have become more popular and to be pursued more systematically, and it is now often explicitly contrasted with the widespread view that universal grammatical patterns reflect adaptations to language users' needs, such as a preference for iconic or efficient grammatical

Karsten Schmidtke-Bode & Eitan Grossman. 2019. Diachronic sources, functional motivations and the nature of the evidence: A synthesis. In Karsten Schmidtke-Bode, Natalia Levshina, Susanne Maria Michaelis & Ilja A. Seržant (eds.), *Explanation in typology: Diachronic sources, functional motivations and the nature of the evidence*, 223–241. Berlin: Language Science Press.
DOI:10.5281/zenodo.2583822

structures. As argued in the lead article to the present volume, this latter position can be characterized as "result-oriented": Languages develop similar traits by virtue of their users selecting and propagating more adaptive variants over less adaptive ones.[1] Accordingly, there is an important diachronic element in this line of explanation, but the individual diachronic processes that bring the synchronic results about "merely serve to realize the adaptation" (Haspelmath, p. 9; see also Hawkins (2004: 266) for a similar formulation). This is the crucial difference from the "source-oriented" approach, in which synchronic typological patterns are explained directly in terms of their source constructions: They are seen as long-term reflections of the particular ways in which each structure originally emerged, and it is argued not only that these "birth processes" do not provide evidence for an overarching functional-adaptive force being at work (e.g. Cristofaro's paper), but that there is simply no need to appeal to such forces because the diachronic development produces the synchronic pattern as a natural by-product that persists into the present time (e.g. Cristofaro's, Collins's and partly also Dryer's and Diessel's contributions).

The general thrust of source-oriented typology is thus that it can provide an immediate, or "first-level" (Creissels 2008: 1), explanation for synchronic distributions, and Haspelmath proposes in his lead article that whenever immediate explanations in terms of source constructions are feasible, they should actually be preferred to functional-adaptive ones, following a logic similar to Occam's Razor: Immediate explanations are less "costly", in that no independent evidence for alleged functional principles, and their interaction with possibly overriding forces, has to be adduced. Cristofaro (2014), for example, suggests that a language without any case markers for core arguments may come to develop a specific A-marker by processes of grammaticalization (e.g. instrumental to ergative reanalysis); the direct result of this development is a case system that retains zero marking for S and P. Typologically, such a system thus patterns with others in which one core argument of transitive clauses, as well the S argument of intransitive clauses, remains unmarked. But since the diachronic facts give us this constellation "for free", in Bybee's (2010: 111) words, it would be costlier to summon additional functional-adaptive forces to explain the pattern: If one assumes that the above scenario is representative of how ergative case systems arise in general, there is no need to appeal to overarching discourse-pragmatic similarities

---

[1]For many readers, the term "result-oriented" will conjure up the notion of teleology. But as, for example, Keller (1994) and Croft (2000: 64–71) show, there are many functional-adaptive changes that can be interpreted non-teleologically: They are made in pursuit of individual communicative goals rather than with the intention of changing the distribution of grammatical marking in the language at large.

between S and P (Du Bois 1987) or to a general drive for economical alignment systems (Comrie 1989). The same logic applies to P-marking systems and, at least in some cases, even to split-intransitive systems (Creissels 2008).[2]

Source-based accounts, then, are simultaneously more and less elegant than many functional-adaptive motivations: They are composed of individual, partly heterogeneous strands of explanation (Cristofaro, p. 41), which makes them arguably less elegant than highly general principles like "harmonic alignment" (Aissen 2003) or "early immediate constituents" (Hawkins 1994), but also perhaps less susceptible to postulating motivations that, in fact, may not apply.[3] At the same time, their immediate and hence uncostly way of accounting for universals makes them more economical than functional-adaptive explanations.

But there is a critical issue with accepting such low-cost explanations, which is epistemological in nature: While we have robust evidence for synchronic states – and typological research has produced a number of sophisticated tools for isolating truly universal tendencies in those states from contingencies like geographical and genealogical relatedness (e.g. Bickel 2013; forthcoming; Jaeger et al. 2011) – we do not have comparable world-wide evidence for diachronic trajectories and diachronic sources. It is thus inevitable that the data provided by source-oriented typologists are highly biased (to certain well-documented or convincingly reconstructed families), sketchy and, as Creissels (2008: 3) readily admits, often "largely speculative". As long as we have no way of knowing whether the historical scenarios postulated for a particular domain are typical of that domain or, indeed, exhaust the possibilities by which a given synchronic pattern can arise in that domain, we cannot be sure that the sources provide the best explanation for the synchronic patterns.[4]

---

[2]Note that Creissels uses the terms "direct" and "indirect" explanation for what is here called result-oriented and source-oriented, respectively. For Creissels, source-oriented accounts are less direct than the functional motivations commonly invoked in typology, but according to Haspelmath's "cost scale" of explanation, it makes sense to say that source-based accounts are actually more direct than result-oriented approaches, as the former lead us directly from the source construction to the present distributions. This is why we called them "immediate" explanations above.

[3]An example from the present volume is Diessel's critique of (specific aspects of) Hawkins's processing account of the position of subordinating morphemes. Diessel argues that there is a plausible source-based explanation for these patterns that simply does not need to appeal to overarching processing principles.

[4]In Dryer's contribution, this point is made with regard to nominalizations being the (alleged) major origin of the V–O & N–Gen correlation: He argues (against Collins) that the diachronic evidence for this scenario is currently too scanty and speculative to be accepted as a valid explanation, and that there are "many [other] ways" (Dryer, p. 83) in which this correlation can come about diachronically.

This epistemological problem is the basis for Haspelmath's distinction between "recurrent patterns of change" and the much stronger "mutational constraints"; crucially, he claims that it is only the latter that can constitute a genuine explanation for language universals. The word-order correlations described in Collins's (and in the main part of Dryer's) paper may well be due to such mutational constraints: Even in the absence of more balanced historical evidence, the pieces of the diachronic puzzle that we do have suggest that there are very strong restrictions on the possible sources of auxiliaries and adpositions. The fact that the position of these categories correlates with that of their sources may thus be sufficiently explained by diachronic persistence effects.[5] But in many other cases, especially those involving coding contrasts rather than pairs of linear order, things are not as clear-cut: The pathways we know of are usually more diverse, so the many cases for which we do not have historical data may just as well result from yet other sources and trajectories. And yet the synchronic states they yield are strikingly more uniform than expected by chance, and it is precisely for such situations that Haspelmath finds the costlier functional-adaptive motivations appropriate.

While the distinction between "recurrent patterns of change" and "mutational constraints" may be very difficult to maintain in practice, it highlights that alternative terms like "diachronic approach" or "diachronic explanation" are actually misleading: Both source- and result-oriented approaches in typology rely fundamentally on diachronic processes, as even result-oriented motivations must somehow be implemented in the developments that produce the synchronic pattern (Haspelmath 1999). Haspelmath's terminological proposal thus helps to clarify the essence of the contrast, which lies precisely in the theoretical status attributed to diachronic processes in the two approaches.

At the same time, the opposition of "mutational" and "functional-adaptive" constraints makes one wonder whether the former are not also ultimately driven by functional motivations. We will return to this question in more detail in §2 again, but let us still ask at this point how supporters of source-oriented explanations *motivate* the kinds of diachronic developments they discuss: They clearly argue against functional-adaptive, i.e. result-oriented, motivations in Haspelmath's sense, but they neither claim that diachronic processes are entirely accidental,[6]

---

[5]Though see, e.g., Harris & Campbell (1995: 210–215) for important qualifications of this view: It is not always the case that the ordering pattern from the source construction is actually retained in the target construction and, conversely, correlating orders may come about by processes other than reanalysis. We will return to this latter point below.

[6]This even holds for Collins's contribution, who claims that "some universals are historical *accidents*" (p. 47): He uses the term "accidental" as an antonym of "functional-adaptive", but not as a synonym of "random" or "chaotic".

nor that they are triggered by innate "representational constraints" (in Haspelmath's terms).[7] It seems to us that source-oriented explanations chiefly make reference to online processes of categorization and inferencing (Bybee 2010), which can lead to the reanalysis of the form-function mappings in a given surface string (Croft 2000; De Smet 2009). It is in this way that new grammatical markers (e.g. case or number morphemes) as well as new syntactic structures (e.g. Aux–V constructions) "naturally" emerge from pre-existing material, in all languages. To be sure, these diachronic processes work by applying domain-general cognitive mechanisms to communicative interactions, so they are *ultimately* motivated in terms of these mechanisms. Crucially, however, the reanalysis itself is not adaptive in nature: It does not happen in order to produce a more efficient coding strategy for, say, number or case, or to disambiguate the core arguments of transitive clauses. This is one of Cristofaro's major arguments for rejecting functional-adaptive motivations for case and number marking (and similar grammatical categories). If anything, then, the major mechanism of grammatical innovation in source-based accounts, i.e. reanalysis, is itself motivated by whatever perceptual, cognitive or communicative factors invite a reanalysis in the first place.[8]

But a critical question is whether reanalysis is really the only way in which existing morphemes and constructions can give rise to grammatical innovations. Result-oriented approaches allow for the possibility that the agents of such innovations are not exclusively listeners (as in reanalysis), but also speakers. In particular, speakers may re-functionalize existing material in precisely those contexts where additional marking is felt to be beneficial for information processing. Some of the diachronic scenarios proposed in Michaelis' paper appear to rely on this mechanism: She argues that when possessive person forms (e.g. *your*) are employed to express a relatively unusual function, namely reference (*yours*) instead of attribution, speakers summon additional marking to signal this deviation (see also Croft 1991; 2001 for a similar proposal). Zeevat & Jäger (2002) refer to this functional-adaptive recruitment of marking as "annexation" or "semantic epenthesis", and they use this mechanism to explain, for example, the rise of

---

[7]Because of the latter, the debate in the present book – in contrast to earlier volumes on the topic (e.g. Hawkins 1988; Good 2008) – takes place entirely within the non-generative, i.e. usage-based, camp.

[8]There are a number of interesting proposals as to the kinds of context that facilitate or even induce reanalysis (e.g. Detges & Waltereit 2002; Hansen & Waltereit 2006; Rosemeyer & Grossman 2017; Schwenter & Waltereit 2009; Traugott & Dasher 2002). To take but one recent example, Eckardt (2009) argues that listeners typically reanalyze utterances in situations of "pragmatic overload", e.g. utterances whose presuppositions are not easily accommodated. In addition, it has also been suggested that reanalysis is sanctioned by the cognitive mechanism of analogy, in that reanalysis is often contingent on a model, or supporting construction, in the language in question (see Fischer 2011; De Smet & Fischer 2017).

differential argument marking (e.g. the flagging of objects with statistically un-expected referential properties). Whether or not one finds these particular examples convincing, one could – in principle – imagine that some of the diachronic sources of plural marking that Cristofaro discusses are not due to reanalysis either, but go back further, namely to a speaker's insertion of a lexical marker like 'all', 'people', etc. in contexts where plurality is relatively unexpected or in need of disambiguation (as in Present-Day English *you all, you guys,* etc.); it is only afterwards that such markers get reanalyzed and grammaticalized as plural morphemes, but their ultimate origin may have been a pattern of functional-adaptive "annexation".[9] Therefore, although we will never be able to replay the innovation of highly grammaticalized markers, we should not exclude a priori the possibility that it is driven by processes other than reanalysis.

An immediately related issue is that source-based typologies also tend to be too narrow on another plane: When Cristofaro pleads to "take diachronic evidence seriously" (p. 25), one wonders why her arguments against particular functional motivations revolve entirely around the innovation stage of grammatical change, to the exclusion of further developments. The contributions by Schmidtke-Bode and by Seržant highlight the importance of diffusion processes, i.e. the gradual extension of innovations to new environments, and particularly also stages at which the use of a grammatical marker is (still) variable. There is ample evidence from corpus data, grammatical descriptions, psycholinguistic experimentation and, as Levshina's paper shows, from artificial language learning, that a significant part of such variability is driven by functional-adaptive motivations. Therefore, we believe that a more appropriate way of taking diachronic evidence seriously would be to return to Bybee's (1988) original formulation: Bybee argues that, for functional-adaptive explanations to be valid, "it must be shown that the factor appealed to as explanation actually contributes to the creation of the particular grammatical convention" (Bybee 1988: 357). As the creation of a grammatical convention goes well beyond the processes and motivations by which a pattern first arose, the absence of evidence for functional-adaptive moti-

---

[9] In Croft's (2000) systematization of grammatical innovations, a mechanism very similar to annexation is actually described as a particular kind of reanalysis: In his so-called "cryptanalysis", speakers feel that a conventionalized construction does not code an intended meaning component sufficiently and thus add appropriate material (e.g. double plurals like English *feet-s* or Uzbek *bi-z-lar* 'we-PL-PL', see also Koch 1995 for further examples from different grammatical domains). However, all of Croft's examples differ from the above cases in that they already contain an overt grammatical marker that is analyzed as not being present (typically, it seems, as a result of chunking and entrenchment (Bybee 2015: 102ff.)). The notion of annexation, by contrast, is intended to capture the *first* kind of grammatical marking that arises (e.g. an accusative case marker on formerly bare object NPs). It is thus not a kind of contextual reanalysis of previously existing material, but the recruitment of a marker from another domain.

vations at the innovation stage does not provide evidence for the absence of such motivations in the development of the grammatical pattern in question.

This leads us (back) to the nature of the evidence that is brought to bear on the present discussion. Haspelmath adopts the strong position that "diachronic evidence is not strictly speaking necessary" (p. 16) to explain a typological regularity in functional-adaptive terms. This radical position appears to stem, at least in part, from the observation that where we do have pieces of diachronic stories, it often seems to be the case that "all diachronic roads lead to the same synchronic Rome" (Kiparsky 2008: 38). In other words, one and the same typological state can arise in manifold ways, which Haspelmath (just like Kiparsky) takes as evidence for convergent evolution towards a common attractor state. This is perhaps one of the most interesting aspects of the present debate, as exactly the same type of evidence (i.e. the available or reconstructed historical data) is interpreted in opposite ways. Michaelis' contribution endorses the Haspelmath–Kiparsky stance: the coding asymmetry between attributive and referential possessive forms is sometimes due to phonetic reduction processes in the more predictable (i.e. the attributive) function, and often due to the annexation and grammaticalization of more coding material in the less predictable (i.e. the referential) function, and again from a variety of different sources. Cristofaro, by contrast, argues (for number marking) that the phonetic erosion of overt singulars may have various language-internal motivations, and that the sheer variety of different sources for the grammaticalization of new plural markers simply does not point towards a single, unifying force. There is no obvious way to settle this issue, given the above-mentioned quantity and depth of resolution of actual diachronic data. This is exactly why proponents of functional-adaptive motivations have long sought to triangulate typological data with behavioural evidence from other sources.

Within the confines of the present volume, we have not been able to represent most of these other data sources, but the contributions by Seržant and by Levshina do highlight the potential of analyzing performance data from historical transition phases and from artificial language learning, respectively. The latter is a relatively novel experimental paradigm that, despite certain drawbacks (e.g. potential L1 influence), provides a useful addition to classic psycholinguistic, neurolinguistic and simulative experimentation on typologically relevant phenomena (see, e.g. Kurumada & Jaeger 2015; Bickel et al. 2015; Lestrade 2018 for these different types of data on typological preferences in case marking). All of these performance data point to the existence of functional-adaptive forces in grammar and hence cannot be neglected in the study of typological patterns. In fact, the recent movement in usage-based linguistics to view language as an instance of a "complex *adaptive* system" (e.g. Gell-Mann 1992; Beckner et al. 2009) suggests that grammatical structure is shaped over time to adapt to interlocutors' (partially conflicting) needs.

At the same time, another important property of such complex adaptive systems is that their developmental trajectories crucially depend on the system's initial conditions – i.e. precisely on the nature of each "source construction". This ties in nicely with Cristofaro's (p. 41) argument that a source-based approach to universals is not only able to capture the cross-linguistic commonalities (because there are, after all, strong preferences in the kinds of grammaticalization processes that happen across languages) but also the exceptions: The latter, she argues, also fall out directly from the initial conditions, in that the languages with exceptional patterns may have different source constructions, or even no sources of the relevant type.[10]

While this is an attractive (again: "low-cost") proposal, we feel that it needs to be made more rigorous. At present, source-oriented accounts are often selective in their interpretation of the data. For example, when Cristofaro (p. 28) claims that ergatives do not apply to first- and second-person pronouns because their instrumental source tended not to do so either (for obvious semantic reasons), one wonders why the same kind of restriction does not carry over to similar cases. For instance, Kiparsky (2008: 36) mentions, among quite a few other examples, that when ablatives develop from a source with separative meaning ('away from X'), these sources are often limited to animates and physical objects, "and yet we don't find ablatives with zero allomorphs on abstract nouns". In other words, purely source-based accounts are sometimes too general, as they predict all kinds of restrictions that get levelled as diachrony unfolds. Conversely, they can also be too limited because, as noted by Kiparsky (2008) as well, some synchronic patterns of differential marking are rather difficult to derive from their sources (e.g. animacy restrictions on the Genitive in Yukaghir). While Kiparsky's critique was directed chiefly against Garrett (1990), it seems to us that the same argument applies to more recent incarnations of source-oriented explanations.

This observation rounds off our survey of the arguments laid out in the volume, and we now proceed to some implications from and possible future directions for the debate as a whole.

---

[10]This argument is also supported by Diessel's contribution: He shows (p. 115) that instances of postposed adverbial clauses with final subordinators ('his going-to-the-movies because') are unexpected from a processing perspective, but receive a natural explanation in diachronic terms if one realizes that these structures exist in OV languages which place the source construction, i.e. oblique PPs, in postverbal rather than preverbal position.

2 Lessons, challenges and future directions

One important general lesson from Haspelmath's lead article is that the very notion of "diachronic explanation" in typology is too vague, as both source- and result-oriented explanations crucially involve diachronic processes, but in different ways (see §1 above). Furthermore, it is necessary to specify the requirements, as Haspelmath does, on when a so-called source-oriented account of universals is considered a genuine explanation, which is precisely what a terminological proposal like "mutational explanation" is meant to capture. But it is less clear to us whether such a mutational explanation is best described as a "constraint" on language, and whether it is as such felicitously juxtaposed with "functional-adaptive", "acquisitional" and "representational" constraints (Haspelmath, p. 7). The primary reason for this uncertainty is that "mutational constraints", unlike the others proposed by Haspelmath, do not have a clear locus, as it were. The changes they are intended to capture are themselves rooted in forces operating on language users (and thus ultimately on language systems) and these could, in principle, be functional-adaptive constraints, constraints on learning or constraints on change from innate linguistic representations, and possibly others. In other words, "mutational constraints" are always due to something else, something that really constrains the mutations (as Haspelmath notes himself (p. 9, fn. 7)), and so they do not, strictly speaking, form a paradigmatic opposition with these other constraints.

To give just one example, Haspelmath argues that the universal generalization that all languages with nasal vowels also have nasal consonants can be accounted for directly by the restricted ways in which nasal vowels come about, i.e. most typically by regressive assimilation to a following nasal consonant. But this mutational constraint is motivated, at least in part, by processes that one may well describe as "functional", viz. the anticipation and consequent retiming of articulatory gestures that come with repeated exposure and practice of the VC sequences in question (Bybee 2015: 38; but cf. Ohala 1989; 2003 for alternative explanations). Is this "functional" in the sense of "functional-adaptive" (because it *results in* easier or more economical articulation for the speaker) or in the sense of being a natural consequence of frequency-based memory representations and our predictions based on those frequencies? In the latter case, could this possibly count as a "representational constraint"? According to Haspelmath, it cannot, because the representational constraints he envisages are innate linguistic representations (= "costly" stipulations of structure that cannot be explained in more direct terms). But then it is unclear how to classify the frequency effects from exemplar representations that are not straightforwardly adaptive in nature, such as some of the "conserving effects of token frequency" discussed in many places by Bybee and others (e.g. Bybee & Thompson 1997; Pierrehumbert 2001; Bybee 2001; see also Cristofaro 2015 for discussion): Well-entrenched representations are more resistant to change, but that does not necessarily mean that they make speaker-hearer interactions (or a linguistic system) more efficient or otherwise better adapted.[11] Similar remarks apply to the pragmatic processes that constrain reanalysis (see fn. 8 above): These are quite systematic and thus principled constraints on the development of languages, yet they are not adaptive according to Haspelmath's definition and, therefore, defy classification according to his schema.

A related difficulty pertains to the separation of representational and acquisitional constraints (see also Levshina's paper). In generative approaches, innate representations are invoked precisely in order to solve learnability problems, making it hard to draw the line between acquisition and representation. In non-generative approaches, by contrast, a constraint on acquisition only makes sense if it can be disentangled from functional-adaptive constraints (cf. "What is functional is learnt best"). And crucially, in both approaches it would have to be shown that processes of language learning are causally involved in the diachronic development of languages. While much scepticism has been voiced that (monolingual) L1 acquisition should be causally related to language change (see e.g., Croft 2000; Heine & Kuteva 2007; Diessel 2011 for recent surveys), it is very likely that certain forms of bilingualism and L2 acquisition play such a causal role, namely in situations of language contact (Matras 2009; Meisel et al. 2013; Gast 2017 and many others). But then again, the difficulty remains of separating the acquisition processes from either representational or functional-adaptive forces involved in them.[12]

---

[11]Incidentally, Diessel's contribution also distinguishes between "functional" and "cognitive" motivations for the development of preposed adverbial clauses (p. 115). The former relate, for example, to information structure and iconicity, and are adaptive in Haspelmath's sense. The latter refer to the cognitive processes involved in the grammaticalization of adverbial clauses, notably "automatization, semantic bleaching and formal reduction" (p. 112). Apparently, then, these specific effects of cognitive representation are to be kept distinct from "functional" factors, which shows that they do not fit easily into Haspelmath's typology of constraints.

[12]More generally, the issue of language contact has received rather little attention in this volume (apart from Michaelis' contribution on contact languages, of course). Needless to say, we do not wish to marginalize the role of contact for diachronic development. But for one thing, the entire discussion revolves around the notion of universals, which are usually seen as "distilled" properties of linguistic structure after contact-induced similarities are controlled for (Bickel 2011). Secondly, as argued above, what happens in contact situations deserves its own detailed investigation in order to clearly disentangle different types of forces on diachronic development in these contexts. This may reveal similar pressures on development as in non-contact

It is beyond the scope of this short epilogue to elaborate on these important issues. The critical point is simply that Haspelmath's constraint typology must be interpreted carefully for what it is, namely a typology of different types of explanation: If we neglect the more elusive acquisitional constraints for now, the three remaining "mutational", "functional-adaptive" and "(UG-)representational" approaches indeed constitute three very different practices of explaining how universals in language develop. And as such, they can plausibly be ranked on a cost scale which characterizes the number of explanatory principles beyond those that are necessary to explain the origin of each individual construction in one's sample (mutational > functional-adaptive > UG-representational). But this does not exhaust what we may wish to call constraints on language, i.e. the sum of all pressures or forces that "cause languages to change in preferred or 'natural' ways" (Bickel et al. 2015: 29). The different types of explanation rather highlight that either there is or there is not more to the motivation of language universals than the persisting properties of individual source constructions.[13]

Our own view is that persistence effects from source constructions are one of many forces which constrain the development of linguistic structure and thus have a role to play in the explanation of universals pertaining to these structures. But as laid out in §1 above, they are rarely ever the whole story. Seržant's contribution to the present volume is particularly insightful in this regard, as he shows that the respective sources of individual differential object markers exert a strong influence on the current use of these markers, but that functional-adaptive considerations of efficient information processing (particularly ambiguity avoidance) interact with the source meaning at particular historical stages, and can even pave the way for the further development of the marker in question. So, just as we argued above, each synchronic state of a complex adaptive system depends to some extent on its initial conditions; but it is adaptive nevertheless. As

---

languages (as argued by Michaelis) or else point to the overriding importance of other, more contact-specific, factors (e.g. patterns of L2 learning, constraints on borrowing, etc.). See also Matras (2009) for a book-length survey of these issues, and Hickey (2017) for a state-of-the-art collection on areal linguistics.

[13]Ultimately, such a typology of constraints on language would have to accommodate, for example, environmental factors (humidity, altitude), socio-cultural factors (population size, socio-cultural practices, social goals in communication), communicative/pragmatic factors (biases in inference making and the resulting utterance interpretation) and cognitive factors, with the latter to be worked out more specifically in terms of whether or not they are domain-general abilities or domain-specific biases and to what extent they are innate or learned acquisition. Some recent systematizations include Christiansen & Chater (2008), Evans & Levinson (2009) and Bybee (2010), but none of them addresses all of the above dimensions (or claims to be exhaustive).

Shibatani (2006: 263) puts it, a language should be seen "as a historically-evolving functional organism sustaining constant pressure for adaptation".

Therefore, while the present volume sought to encourage a lively debate between, and hence often a rigid juxtaposition of, source- and result-oriented explanations, it seems likely that most typological phenomena will need a nuanced mixture of both (see also Dryer's and Diessel's contributions to this volume). In fact, this echoes an assessment given by Nichols (2008: 287–288):

> Rather than synchronic patterns always being the goal and driving force of language change, various synchronic patterns are the predictable consequences of diachronic processes which have their own logic independent of the synchrony they produce. Thus, to a greater extent than [one might presume], synchronic structural patterns are epiphenomenal. But they are not entirely so. Economies of various kinds appear to be targets of change [...], and there appear to be [...] structural patterns that may be goals of change but are not its accidental results.

The methodological challenge ahead is thus to calibrate more precisely, for each grammatical domain and typological generalization at a time, how much room for functional-adaptive motivations is left once one controls for persistence effects in the data as much as possible. As Collins (p. 47) reminds us, constraints inherited from the source add yet another kind of dependency (on top of areal and genealogical relations) to typological samples. It then becomes an empirical question whether the sources are so clearly circumscribed that they, indeed, suggest a mutational explanation and give us the synchronic distributions for free, or whether it is necessary to resort to costlier explanations along functional-adaptive lines that go beyond the individual sources.

Another avenue for conceptual work on universals and diachrony would be to expand and flesh out a framework developed by Greenberg (1978), Nichols (1992; 2003) and Bickel (2013). This framework lays the conceptual foundations for modelling probabilities of cross-linguistic unity and diversity in diachronic terms. For example, according to Greenberg (1978: 76), a particular linguistic phenomenon should be universal or near-universal "if it can arise very frequently and is highly stable once it occurs. [...] If a particular property rarely arises but is highly stable when it occurs, it should be fairly frequent on a global basis but be largely confined to a few linguistic stocks." Nichols (2008: 287–288) further develops such predictions by bringing contact-induced phenomena (borrowing and substrate influence) and functional-adaptive factors ("harmony", "unmarkedness") into the equation. Elaborating on these lines of thinking, one may look at some of the themes of the present volume in the following way (see Grossman 2016 and Grossman et al. 2018 for more details):

(1) Types of diachronic influence on language universals

    a. SOURCE: frequency of the source construction (Cristofaro 2019 [this volume])

    b. TYPE: frequency of type of change (e.g. assimilatory changes are more common than dissimilatory ones). This has rarely been studied on the basis of large samples and for a wider range of phenomena (largely due to the epistemological problems discussed in §1 above), thus constituting a desideratum in typological research.

    c. PATH: number of pathways that lead to a particular item type (e.g. Bybee et al. 1994 on tense-aspect-mood constructions)

    d. STAGE: number of stages necessary to yield a certain outcome (e.g. Harris 2008)

    e. STABILITY: inherent stability of item type (Greenberg 1978, Nichols 2003)

    f. DIFFUSABILITY: likelihood to diffuse through contact (borrowing, calquing, contact-induced grammaticalization)

Note that (a), (b), (e) and (f) may themselves be causally related to functional-adaptive forces. For example, a given phenomenon may be faithfully inherited and hence be diachronically stable precisely because it is adaptive in Haspelmath's sense; and it may easily diffuse in language contact for the same reason (see also Bickel 2013; 2017 for the same observations). Just as in Greenberg (1978), then, the basic idea is that the more these factors converge, the stronger the cross-linguistic preponderance of the structure in question. In other words, if a property develops from cross-linguistically frequent sources, as a result of common types of change that involve few stages, if there are multiple pathways that lead to it, it is stable once present, and it is likely to diffuse through borrowing, this property is predicted to be (nearly) universal. Conversely, a property that involves rare source constructions, rare changes, and so on, is predicted to be cross-linguistically rare or limited areally and/or phylogenetically. Of course, these factors might have varying strengths, and it is a goal of typological research to determine their relative ranking for each case in question. For example, it may be that a property develops often, from multiple and common sources, but if it is inherently unstable – say, due to a strong functional-adaptive pressure to eliminate it – then it is predicted to be sporadically attested areally and genealogically. If it is diffusable, then it has a good chance to take root in particular areas. In phonology, for example, this seems to be the case for aspirated fricatives (Jacques 2011) and for affricate-rich systems (Nikolaev & Grossman 2018), the latter of which are diachronically unstable unless supported areally. As far as we are aware, Bickel's (2011; 2013) Family Bias Method has offered the first principled way of incorporating some of these considerations into actual typological methodology (see Schmidtke-Bode's paper for an application). It is to be hoped that such methods, alongside more classic sampling methods with built-in controls for source-related dependencies (as suggested above), will become de rigeur in future typological research.

Above all, we hope that the present volume has offered an insight into current ways of thinking about the role of diachronic processes in explaining universal generalizations, and that it has contributed to specifying the arguments, strengths and weaknesses of different positions in that debate.

References

Aissen, Judith. 2003. Differential object marking: Iconicity vs. economy. *Natural Language and Linguistic Theory* 21(3). 435–483. DOI:10.1023/A:1024109008573

Beckner, Clay, Richard Blythe, Joan L. Bybee, Morten H. Christiansen, William Croft, Nick C. Ellis, John Holland, Jinyun Ke, Diane Larsen-Freeman & Tom Schoenemann. 2009. Language is a complex adaptive system: Position paper. *Language Learning* 59(s1). 1–26. DOI:10.1111/j.1467-9922.2009.00533.x

Bickel, Balthasar. Forthcoming. Large and ancient linguistic areas. In Mily Crevels, Jean-Marie Hombert & Pieter Muysken (eds.), *Language dispersal, diversification, and contact: A global perspective*. Oxford: Oxford University Press.

Bickel, Balthasar. 2011. Statistical modeling of language universals. *Linguistic Typology* 15. 401–413. DOI:10.1515/lity.2011.027

Bickel, Balthasar. 2013. Distributional biases in language families. In Balthasar Bickel, Lenore A. Genoble, David A. Peterson & Alan Timberlake (eds.), *Language typology and historical contingency*, 415–444. Amsterdam, Philadelphia: John Benjamins. DOI:10.5167/uzh-86870

Bickel, Balthasar. 2017. Areas and universals. In Raymond Hickey (ed.), *The Cambridge handbook of areal linguistics*, 40–54. Cambridge: Cambridge University Press. DOI:10.1017/9781107279872.004

Bickel, Balthasar, Alena Witzlack-Makarevich, Kamal K. Choudhary, Matthias Schlesewsky & Ina Bornkessel-Schlesewsky. 2015. The neurophysiology of language processing shapes the evolution of grammar: Evidence from case marking. *PLoS ONE* 10(8). e0132819. DOI:10.1371/journal.pone.0132819

Bybee, Joan L. 1988. The diachronic dimension in explanation. In John A. Hawkins (ed.), *Explaining language universals*, 350–379. Oxford: Blackwell.

Bybee, Joan L. 2001. *Phonology and language use.* Cambridge: Cambridge University Press. DOI:10.1017/CBO9780511612886

Bybee, Joan L. 2010. *Language, usage and cognition.* Cambridge: Cambridge University Press. DOI:10.1017/CBO9780511750526.011

Bybee, Joan L. 2015. *Language change.* Cambridge: Cambridge University Press. DOI:10.1017/CBO9781139096768

Bybee, Joan L., Revere D. Perkins & William Pagliuca. 1994. *The evolution of grammar: Tense, aspect and modality in the languages of the world.* Chicago: University of Chicago Press.

Bybee, Joan L. & Sandra A. Thompson. 1997. Three frequency effects in syntax. *Berkeley Linguistics Society* 23. 378–388. DOI:10.3765/bls.v23i1.1293

Christiansen, Morten H. & Nick Chater. 2008. Language as shaped by the brain. *Behavioral and Brain Sciences* 31(5). 489–509. DOI:10.1017/S0140525X08004998

Comrie, Bernard. 1989. *Language universals and linguistic typology: Syntax and morphology.* 2nd edn. Chicago: University of Chicago Press.

Creissels, Denis. 2008. Direct and indirect explanations of typological regularities: The case of alignment variations. *Folia Linguistica* 42(1). 1–38. DOI:10.1515/FLIN.2008.1

Cristofaro, Sonia. 2014. Competing motivation models and diachrony: What evidence for what motivations? In Brian MacWhinney, Andrej L. Malchukov & Edith A. Moravcsik (eds.), *Competing motivations in grammar and usage*, 282–298. Oxford: Oxford University Press. DOI:10.1093/acprof:oso/9780198709848.001.0001

Cristofaro, Sonia. 2015. *Synchronic vs. diachronic explanations of typological universals: Redefining the role of frequency.* Paper presented at the Diversity Linguistics Conference, MPI Leipzig. https://www.eva.mpg.de/fileadmin/content_files/linguistics/conferences/2015-diversity-linguistics/Cristoforo_handout.pdf, accessed 2018-2-19.

Cristofaro, Sonia. 2019. Taking diachronic evidence seriously: Result-oriented vs. source-oriented explanations of typological universals. In Karsten Schmidtke-Bode, Natalia Levshina, Susanne Maria Michaelis & Ilja A. Seržant (eds.), *Explanation in typology: Diachronic sources, functional motivations and the nature of the evidence*, 25–46. Berlin: Language Science Press. DOI:10.5281/zenodo.2583806

Croft, William. 1991. *Syntactic categories and grammatical relations: The cognitive organization of information*. Chicago: University of Chicago Press.

Croft, William. 2000. *Explaining language change: An evolutionary approach*. London: Harlow. DOI:10.1075/jhp.6.1.09rau

Croft, William. 2001. *Radical Construction Grammar: Syntactic theory in typological perspective*. Oxford: Oxford University Press. DOI:10.1093/acprof:oso/9780198299554.001.0001

De Smet, Hendrik. 2009. Analysing reanalysis. *Lingua* 119. 1728–1755. DOI:10.1016/j.lingua.2009.03.001

De Smet, Hendrik & Olga Fischer. 2017. The role of analogy in language change: Supporting constructions. In Marianne Hundt, Sandra Mollin & Simone Pfenninger (eds.), *The changing English language: Psycholinguistic perspectives*, 240–268. Cambridge: Cambridge University Press. DOI:10.1017/9781316091746.011

Detges, Ulrich & Richard Waltereit. 2002. Grammaticalization vs. reanalysis: A semantic-pragmatic account of functional change in grammar. *Zeitschrift für Sprachwissenschaft* 21(2). 151–195. DOI:10.1515/zfsw.2002.21.2.151

Diessel, Holger. 2011. Grammaticalization and language acquisition. In Bernd Heine & Heiko Narrog (eds.), *Handbook of grammaticalization*, 130–141. Oxford: Oxford University Press. DOI:10.1093/oxfordhb/9780199586783.013.0011

Du Bois, John W. 1987. The discourse basis of ergativity. *Language* 63(4). 805–855. DOI:10.2307/415719

Eckardt, Regine. 2009. APO: avoid pragmatic overload. In Maj-Britt Mosegaard Hansen & Jacqueline Visconti (eds.), *Current trends in diachronic semantics and pragmatics*, 21–41. Bingley: Emerald. DOI:10.1163/9789004253216_003

Evans, Nicholas & Stephen C. Levinson. 2009. The myth of language universals: Language diversity and its importance for cognitive science. *Behavioral and Brain Sciences* 32(5). 429–448. DOI:10.1017/S0140525X0999094X

Fischer, Olga. 2011. Grammaticalization as analogically driven change? In Bernd Heine & Heiko Narrog (eds.), *Handbook of grammaticalization*, 31–42. Oxford: Oxford University Press. DOI:10.1093/oxfordhb/9780199586783.013.0003

Garrett, Andrew. 1990. The origin of NP split ergativity. *Language* 66(2). 261–296. DOI:10.2307/414887

Gast, Volker. 2017. Paradigm change and language contact: A framework of analysis and some speculation about the underlying cognitive processes. *JournaLIPP* 5. 49–70.

Gell-Mann, Murray. 1992. Complexity and complex adaptive systems. In John A. Hawkins & Murray Gell-Mann (eds.), *The evolution of human languages*, 3–18. Redwood City, CA: Addison-Wesley.

Givón, Talmy. 1975. Serial verbs and syntactic change: Niger-Congo. In Charles N. Li (ed.), *Word order and word order change*, 47–112. Austin: University of Texas Press.

Good, Jeff (ed.). 2008. *Linguistic universals and language change.* Oxford: Oxford University Press. DOI:10.1093/acprof:oso/9780199298495.001.0001

Greenberg, Joseph H. 1969. Some methods of dynamic comparison in linguistics. In Jan Puhvel (ed.), *Substance and structure of language*, 147–203. Berkeley: University of California Press.

Greenberg, Joseph H. 1978. Diachrony, synchrony and language universals. In Joseph H. Greenberg, Charles A. Ferguson & Edith A. Moravcsik (eds.), *Universals of human language I: Method and theory*, 61–92. Stanford: Stanford University Press.

Grossman, Eitan. 2016. From rarum to rarissimum: An unexpected zero person marker. *Linguistic Typology* 20(1). 1–23. DOI:10.1515/lingty-2016-0001

Grossman, Eitan, Guillaume Jacques & Anton Antonov. 2018. A cross-linguistic rarity in synchrony and diachrony: Adverbial subordinator prefixes exist. *STUF – Language Typology and Universals* 71(4). 513–538. DOI:10.1515/stuf-2018-0020

Hansen, Maj-Britt Mosegaard & Richard Waltereit. 2006. GCI theory and language change. *Acta Linguistica Hafniensia* 38(1). 235–268. DOI:10.1080/03740463.2006.10412210

Harris, Alice C. 2008. On the explanation of typologically unusual structures. In Jeff Good (ed.), *Linguistic universals and language change*, 59–76. Oxford: Oxford University Press. DOI:10.1093/acprof:oso/9780199298495.003.0003

Harris, Alice C. & Lyle Campbell. 1995. *Historical syntax in cross-linguistic perspective.* Cambridge: Cambridge University Press. DOI:10.1017/CBO9780511620553

Haspelmath, Martin. 1999. Optimality and diachronic adaptation. *Zeitschrift für Sprachwissenschaft* 18(2). 180–205. DOI:10.1515/zfsw.1999.18.2.180

Hawkins, John A. (ed.). 1988. *Explaining language universals.* Oxford: Blackwell.

Hawkins, John A. 1994. *A performance theory of order and constituency.* Cambridge: Cambridge University Press. DOI:10.1017/CBO9780511554285

Hawkins, John A. 2004. *Efficiency and complexity in grammars.* Oxford: Oxford University Press. DOI:10.1093/acprof:oso/9780199252695.001.0001

Heine, Bernd & Tania Kuteva. 2007. *The genesis of grammar: A reconstruction.* Oxford: Oxford University Press.

Hickey, Raymond (ed.). 2017. *The Cambridge handbook of areal linguistics.* Cambridge: Cambridge University Press. DOI:10.1017/9781107279872

Jacques, Guillaume. 2011. A panchronic study of aspirated fricatives, with new evidence from Pumi. *Lingua* 121(9). 1518–1538. DOI:10.1016/j.lingua.2011.04.003

Jaeger, T. Florian, Peter Graff, William Croft & Daniel Pontillo. 2011. Mixed effect models for genetic and areal dependencies in linguistic typology. *Linguistic Typology* 15(2). 281–320. DOI:10.1515/lity.2011.021

Keller, Rudi. 1994. *Language change: The invisible hand in language.* London: Routledge.

Kiparsky, Paul. 2008. Universals constrain change; change results in typological generalizations. In Jeff Good (ed.), *Linguistic universals and language change*, 23–53. Oxford: Oxford University Press. DOI:10.1093/acprof:oso/9780199298495.003.0002

Koch, Harold. 1995. The creation of morphological zeroes. In Geert Booij & Jaap van Marle (eds.), *Yearbook of morphology 1994*, 31–71. Dordrecht: Springer. DOI:10.1007/978-94-017-3714-2_2

Kurumada, Chigusa & T. Florian Jaeger. 2015. Communicative efficiency in language production: Optional case-marking in Japanese. *Journal of Memory and Language* 83. 152–178. DOI:10.1016/j.jml.2015.03.003

Lestrade, Sander. 2018. The emergence of differential case marking. In Ilja A. Seržant & Alena Witzlack-Makarevich (eds.), *Diachrony of differential argument marking*, 481–508. Berlin: Language Science Press. DOI:10.5281/zenodo.1228275

Matras, Yaron. 2009. *Language contact.* Cambridge: Cambridge University Press. DOI:10.1017/CBO9780511809873

Meisel, Jürgen M., Martin Elsig & Esther Rinke. 2013. *Language acquisition and change: A morphosyntactic perspective.* Edinburgh: Edinburgh University Press. DOI:10.3366/edinburgh/9780748642250.001.0001

Nichols, Johanna. 1992. *Linguistic diversity in space and time.* Chicago: University of Chicago Press. DOI:10.7208/chicago/9780226580593.001.0001

Nichols, Johanna. 2003. Diversity and stability in language. In Brian D. Joseph & Richard D. Janda (eds.), *Handbook of historical linguistics*, 283–310. Oxford: Blackwell. DOI:10.1002/9780470756393.ch5

Nichols, Johanna. 2008. Universals and diachrony: Some observations. In Jeff Good (ed.), *Linguistic universals and language change*, 287–294. Oxford: Oxford University Press. DOI:10.1093/acprof:oso/9780199298495.003.0012

Nikolaev, Dmitry & Eitan Grossman. 2018. Areal sound change and the distributional typology of affricate richness in Eurasia. *Studies in Language* 42(3). 562–599. DOI:10.1075/sl.17043.nik

Ohala, John J. 1989. Sound change is drawn from a pool of synchronic variation. In Leiv Egil Breivik & Ernst Håkon Jahr (eds.), *Language change: Contributions to the study of its causes*, 173–198. Berlin, New York: Mouton de Gruyter. DOI:10.1515/9783110853063.173

Ohala, John J. 2003. Phonetics and historical phonology. In Brian D. Joseph & Richard D. Janda (eds.), *Handbook of historical linguistics*, 669–686. Oxford: Blackwell. DOI:10.1002/9780470756393.ch22

Pierrehumbert, Janet B. 2001. Exemplar dynamics: Word frequency, lenition and contrast. In Joan L. Bybee & Paul J. Hopper (eds.), *Frequency and the emergence of linguistic structure*, 137–157. Amsterdam, Philadelphia: John Benjamins. DOI:10.1075/tsl.45.08pie

Rosemeyer, Malte & Eitan Grossman. 2017. The road to auxiliariness revisited: The grammaticalization of finish anteriors in spanish. *Diachronica* 34(4). 516–558. DOI:10.1075/dia.16024.ros

Schwenter, Scott A. & Richard Waltereit. 2009. Presupposition accommodation and language change. In Kristin Davidse, Lieven Vandelanotte & Hubert Cuyckens (eds.), *Subjectification, intersubjectification and grammaticalization*, 75–102. Berlin, New York: Mouton de Gruyter. DOI:10.1515/9783110226102.2.75

Shibatani, Masayoshi. 2006. On the conceptual framework for voice phenomena. *Linguistics* 44(2). 217–269. DOI:10.1515/LING.2006.009

Traugott, Elizabeth Closs & Richard B. Dasher. 2002. *Regularity in semantic change*. Cambridge: Cambridge University Press. DOI:10.1017/CBO9780511486500

Zeevat, Henk & Gerhard Jäger. 2002. A reinterpretation of syntactic alignment. In Dick de Jongh, Marie Nilsenovai & Henk Zeevat (eds.), *Proceedings of the Fourth International Tbilisi Symposium on Language, Logic and Computation*. Amsterdam: University of Amsterdam. http://www.blutner.de/signalling/zeevat_jaeger.pdf, accessed 2016-12-15.

Name index

Language index

Subject index

www.ingramcontent.com/pod-product-compliance
Lightning Source LLC
Chambersburg PA
CBHW082147150426
42812CB00076B/2288